T0271190

This book is concerned with the issue of wage rigidities in macroeconomic theory, and their implications for public policy. It offers an analysis of the microeconomic foundations of rigid wages, considering their consequences for normative economics, and their role in explaining involuntary unemployment. The initial chapters examine short-run macroeconomic equilibrium with nominal rigidities within the framework of fix-price temporary equilibria. This is followed by an overview and assessment of the main microeconomic mechanisms likely to account for real wage rigidity, including implicit contract theory, union behaviour and efficiency wage models. The effect of efficiency wages on macroeconomic fluctuations and public policy is also considered.

Pierre Picard is Professor of Economics at the University of Paris X—Nanterre and Research Fellow at the Centre d'Etudes Prospectives d'Economie Mathématique Appliquées à la Planification.

Wages and unemployment

Wages and unemployment

A study in non-Walrasian macroeconomics

PIERRE PICARD

CAMBRIDGE
UNIVERSITY PRESS

Published by the Press Syndicate of the University of Cambridge
The Pitt Building, Trumpington Street, Cambridge CB2 1RP
40 West 20th Street, New York, NY 10011-4211, USA
10 Stamford Road, Oakleigh, Victoria 3166, Australia

First published 1993

A catalogue record for this book is available from the British Library

Library of Congress cataloguing in publication data
Picard, Pierre.
Wages and unemployment: a study in non-Walrasian macroeconomics / Pierre
Picard.
    p.   cm.
Includes bibliographical references and index.
ISBN 0 521 35057 3
1. Wages – Government policy. 2. Unemployment. 3. Equilibrium (Economics).
4. Macroeconomics. I. Title.
HD4906.P53 1993
339.5–dc20   92-19475   CIP
ISBN 0 521 35057 3 hardback

Transferred to digital printing 2003

VN

Contents

Acknowledgements

This book takes its origin in my doctoral thesis to which the late Professor Claude Fourgeaud extensively contributed. I owe him a debt of thanks for his outstanding counselling and his friendly support.

I would like to thank Jean-Pascal Bénassy, Jean-Michel Grandmont, Bruno Jullien and Guy Laroque for commenting upon various parts of this book and for helpful discussions on many issues.

The Centre d'Etudes Prospectives d'Economie Mathématique Appliquées à la Planification (CEPREMAP) provided a stimulating environment without which the project of writing this book would not have succeeded. I had the opportunity to put the final touches to several chapters during a brief but productive stay at the University of Montréal, arranged by Lise and Camille Bronsard to whom I am grateful.

Finally, I am indebted to Sonia Ben Ouagrham who gave freely of her time and her best to translate this book, and to Josselyne Bitan for her outstanding secretarial assistance.

Introduction

When either addressing the issue of fluctuations in output and employment, or explaining long-term inefficiencies of market economies, macro-economic theory frequently places the determination of wages at the heart of the matter. Indeed, new classical and neo-Keynesian approaches to economic fluctuations basically differ in the sense that the first, true to the Walrasian tradition, assumes the perfect flexibility of prices and wages, while the second hypothesizes nominal rigidities. On the labour market, nominal wage rigidity, which the Keynesian approach assumes, may for instance result from long-term contracts providing for wages that are insensitive to monetary and real shocks, because frequent negotiations or wage-setting are costly and detailed contingent contracts are unfeasible. When applied to all markets, the Keynesian approach leads to contemplating nominal rigidities which affect all money prices and wages, and are likely to account for the kind of disequilibria an economy might encounter in the short run. However, the mere existence of high and long-lasting unemployment, especially in European economies since the early 1970s, has shown that labour market disequilibrium, revealed through job queues, layoffs, dual labour markets or discrimination among workers, must also be contemplated in the long run, with constraints affecting real rather than nominal wages.

Whether rigidities are nominal or real, assuming that wages are not determined by supply equalling demand on the labour market, leads to the substitution of other equilibrium concepts for the usual definition of the Walrasian general equilibrium model. It is to that non-Walrasian approach to macroeconomics that the present book is to be related. It provides a general approach to wage rigidities and involuntary unemployment in macroeconomic theory. Our study of short-run macroeconomic equilibrium with nominal rigidities will be based mainly on fix-price equilibrium theory. The latter comes down to assuming that money prices are sticky and allows for clear difference between nominal rigidities, valid in the short

1

run, and real rigidities which are the only ones that can be viewed in the long run. We shall also contemplate appropriate models to explain real wage rigidities, the main objective being to understand why long-lasting involuntary unemployment can appear to be an equilibrium, in a non-Walrasian sense of course.

Although this book does not clearly divide into two distinct parts, chapters 1 to 4 mainly focus on short-run equilibria, especially within the context of the fix-price approach, while chapters 5 to 8 address real wage rigidities, their microeconomic justifications, and their consequences for normative economics.

Chapter 1 presents a conceptual framework for the following chapters: the temporary equilibrium approach and, more specifically, fix-price equilibrium theory. We consider an abstract exchange economy where agents live for several periods and make transactions taking into account the current and expected prices and quantity constraints. For given expectations schemes (that may result from a learning procedure and include data from past history), a Walrasian temporary equilibrium is defined by supply equalling demand on all markets in the current period. After a real or monetary shock, prices do not immediately adjust to the new Walrasian temporary equilibrium: they are supposed to be sticky during the current period (this is the nominal rigidity hypothesis) and market equilibrium is obtained through quantity rationing. We define what a fix-price equilibrium is and we also show that fix-price equilibria correspond to a strong inefficiency property which is the basis of Keynes' multiplier mechanism. Finally, we provide a justification for the nominal rigidity hypothesis through near-rationality and bargaining cost arguments, when fix-price allocations are transitory deviations in the neighbourhood of the Walrasian temporary equilibrium.

Chapter 2 analyses the consequences of sticky wages on short-run macroeconomic equilibrium. We first use fix-price equilibrium concepts to study the implications of nominal rigidities affecting both wages and prices within a simple aggregate model. Two kinds of involuntary unemployment may appear: Keynesian unemployment, on the one hand, where production is limited by sales constraints and where a rise in wages (or in public expenditures) is likely to improve employment, and classical unemployment, on the other hand, where it is low profitability which limits the hiring of new workers and where it is a drop in wage costs that can improve the employment level. Then, while addressing the labour market more specifically, we analyse the consequences of three alternate formulations of short-run wage rigidities, assuming that the output price is perfectly flexible. First, nominal wage rigidity in orthodox Keynesian theory; secondly, the wage indexation hypothesis, in which emphasis is put on contracts aiming at protecting workers' purchasing power from various types of shocks likely to perturbate the short-run equilibrium of the economy; and, thirdly, the rigidity of intertemporal expected real wages, where we focus on the difference between production and consumption real wages and on intertemporal substitution effects.

Chapters 3 and 4 focus on the fix-price approach. Chapter 3 examines the consequences of real wage rigidities on the relationship between inflation and unemployment. We consider a dynamic model where prices and wages are sticky in the short-run and likely to change over time as a function of excess demand and expected inflation, but also tending towards a target real wage. The model emphasizes the potential conflict between firms' investment behaviour which determines an appropriate real wage so that a balanced full-employment steady state can exist and the more or less important rigidity of real wages which limits output profitability. We show that the kind of long-term disequilibrium which the economy is led to, as well as the intensity of the inflation–unemployment dilemma or the natural unemployment rate, crucially depend on the gap between the target real wage and the appropriate real wage.

Chapter 4 extends the model presented in chapter 2 to an open economy with domestic and foreign goods which are imperfect substitutes. This allows for a wider range of short-run economic policy instruments, including the exchange rate or trade policy variables. In a variant of the model, we study the consequences of an oil shock, noting the difference between the short-run effects with nominal rigidities and the long-run effects with potential rigidities affecting real wages. We show here that an oil shock can lead to short-run Keynesian or classical unemployment. We also show that the long-run depression effect of an oil shock is deeper when real wages are highly sticky: the higher the wage indexation the weaker the economy facing such a shock.

Chapters 5 and 6 overview and assess the main mechanisms likely to account for the rigidity of real wages and long-lasting involuntary unemployment. Chapter 5 is dedicated to implicit contracts and to the role of unions. The implicit contract theory assumes that wages and employment result from long-run agreements leading to optimal risk-sharing between firms and their employees. It accounts for real wage rigidity when workers are risk-averse and firms are risk-neutral, but, as we shall see, it can only explain the existence of involuntary unemployment or socially inefficient underemployment by arbitrarily limiting the types of contracts a firm and its employees can sign, or through rather unconvincing specifications of the model. In the implicit contract approach, contingent contracts are signed on a competitive market *ex ante*, meaning, before the information about profitability of firms is revealed (whether in a symmetric or asymmetric way). Are the findings qualitatively different, if we assume that the contract market is imperfectly competitive, with a union on the one hand and one or several firms on the other? We will here review both main models based on unions' behaviour: the monopoly union model and the bilateral monopoly model. Assuming that a union has a utilitarist objective (it maximizes its members' expected welfare), we come to the conclusion that such models can explain involuntary unemployment and socially inefficient underemployment only if the type of contracts which can be signed is arbitrarily limited. Finally, the criticisms levelled at implicit contracts also apply to union models. However, the literature on unions suggests that maximizing the expected utility of a representative worker is a very poor image of unions' objectives, and that more realistic objective functions may deeply modify the implications of unions' behaviour. In this perspective, we show that the lay-off by seniority rule can account for real wage rigidity and involuntary unemployment when unions act in seniors' interest. We also show that, in an insider–outsider setting, the presence of bargaining between insiders and firms may lead to some kind of inefficient unemployment persistence, when the economy is subject to independently distributed productivity shocks.

Chapter 6 provides an overview of the efficiency wage theory. The main idea behind efficiency wage models is that workers' productivity (or the quality of their work) depends on the real wage they are paid. If a higher wage is associated with a higher quality of labour, then it may be profitable to pay higher wages than the reservation wages, and this explains the existence of involuntary unemployment. Initially contemplated in nutrition models applied to developing countries, the link between wages and productivity is usually justified within an imperfect information context. Some models are based on adverse selection mechanisms, in which firms have imprecise information about the ability of particular workers. If ability and workers' reservation wages are positively correlated, offering higher wages enables firms to attract job candidates of better average quality. In moral hazard models, effort on the job cannot be monitored: labour contracts then urge individuals not to shirk, either through clauses providing for the payment of a bonus when the firm perceives a good signal concerning the worker's activity or through the threat of dismissal if the worker is caught shirking. Such models account for the existence of long-lasting involuntary unemployment as well as for characteristics within the labour market such as discrimination against specific social groups or dual labour markets. This chapter ends with an examination of other versions of the efficiency wage theory: the labour turnover model and sociological models.

Chapters 7 and 8 are dedicated to extensions of efficiency wage models:

macroeconomic fluctuations and fiscal policy (chapter 7), employment subsidies and optimal taxation (chapter 8). In chapter 7, we build a temporary equilibrium model in which wages result from a very simple efficiency wage mechanism and where output fluctuations are due to variations in public expenditures. The main idea is that expected real wage rigidity and transitory shocks in real goods demand may cause variations in economic activity through intertemporal substitution in consumption. The model shows that low variations in real wages may go with high variations in the employment level and a low elasticity of labour supply. Furthermore, in such a model, normative analysis of public expenditures differs from the usual criteria within welfare economics: the government is tempted to encourage a transitory increase in public consumption beyond the long-run optimal level in order to benefit from a positive externality on employment associated with the increase in output prices and, consequently, the time consistent stationary level of public expenditures is higher than the long-run optimal level.

Chapter 8 explores the role of employment subsidies and commodity taxation policies in a general equilibrium model with a dual labour market. Individuals working in the primary sector receive higher real wages than those employed on the secondary market. We put here the emphasis on the necessity of a compromise between the efficiency objective which leads to subsidizing primary job creations and the redistributive cost of such a policy when lump-sum transfers are not possible. We show that an employment subsidy policy does not generally allow recovery of the first-best optimum and we describe the second-best Pareto-optimal policy.

1 Price rigidities and temporary equilibrium

The main distinction between Keynesian and neoclassical macroeconomic approaches probably lies in their different appraisals of the competitive markets' ability to spontaneously reach an efficient allocation of resources in the short run. Keynes himself conceded that in the long run the market's mechanisms may lead to a certain kind of efficiency but he contested the practical consequences of this proposition, since the regulating processes furthering such an hypothetic long-run optimum are often too weak or slow acting to be satisfactory.[1] The general equilibrium theory, as rigorously formulated by Arrow and Debreu (1954) and Debreu (1959), does not allow any distinction between the short and the long run that can be used directly when dealing with these issues. Indeed, the Arrow–Debreu model deals with an intertemporal economy but it brings forward hypotheses that make it pointless to distinguish between the short and the long run: for each product and each date, it is assumed that there exists a complete set of competitive contingent markets. Within such a context, under the usual assumptions of general competitive equilibrium theory, there exists an intertemporal equilibrium which is an *ex ante* Pareto optimum. In order to emphasize the disruptive factors and inefficiencies that might affect the economy in the short run, macroeconomic theory needs a much more realistic context, where some of the previous assumptions are not established and, more particularly, where time actually matters because markets are incomplete. In a given period, only a few of the markets are open and agents exchange goods and financial assets taking into account the expected evolution of markets in the following periods. This is the perspective of the temporary equilibrium approach introduced by Hicks (1946). Within this framework, households have to determine their labour supply, their current consumption and the part of their resources they will save and keep in the form of assets for a future consumption. Their decisions will be based on signals perceived in the current period (prices, interest rates, quantity constraints . . .), and also on their expectations concerning their future resources and the evolution of prices. Intertemporal allocation of resources also allows firms to make optimal decisions about their stocks and investments, taking into account the expected evolution of prices and the intensity of demand in the future.

Our purpose here is to present the basic concepts of the temporary equilibrium approach which will be useful in next chapters.[2] To remain as simple as possible, we will reason within the context of a pure exchange economy with a single asset (money). Though this is a very elementary structure, these concepts may be applied to more complex models. The first section of this chapter will address *Walrasian temporary equilibrium*, analysed according to Grandmont's approach (1983). In the current period, only spot markets are open; there is no future market and future prices are subject to expectations that may be uncoordinated and that result from some learning process. For each consumer, consumption and savings decisions result from intertemporal optimization which leads to determining an indirect utility index taking into account the money balances held at the end of the period and implicitly including the expectation-making process. Then the Walrasian temporary equilibrium is determined by the price vector that equates aggregate demand and supply on every market in the current period. As emphasized by Grandmont (1983), such an equilibrium can be achieved only if expected prices are relatively inelastic with respect to current prices. In fact, the real balance effect, associated with price variations must be reinforced by an intertemporal substitution process strong enough to allow a Walrasian temporary equilibrium.

Sections 2 and 3 are devoted to the fix-price approach of *disequilibrium theory*. The essential assumption of fix-price models is that nominal rigidities prevail in the short run and, in that sense, they are doubtless connected with the Keynesian tradition. We will contemplate an economy affected by unexpected shocks where prices react with delay to shifts in demand and supply. If a shock happens to disturb the supply and demand functions, and if, as we assume it, prices are not altered before the following period, the transactions desired by agents will be incompatible and the possible exchanges will be limited by *rationing constraints*. In Drèze's model (1975), addressed in section 2 such quantity constraints appear to be the outcome of a tâtonnement. On the contrary, in Bénassy's model (1975) addressed in section 3, the quantity constraints directly result from the exchange process and the incompatibility between supply and demand. These equilibria may be Pareto dominated, and, as shown in the next chapter, they create multiplier effects similar to those contemplated by Keynes.

In the literature on temporary equilibrium with nominal rigidities, two types of assumptions have been made to account for the price-setting mechanism. First of all, a number of fix-price disequilibrium models more or less explicitly hypothesize a competitive economy subject to unexpected shocks affecting productivity, labour supply or policy parameters. These disruptive factors do not cause prices to shift instantaneously up to the new Walrasian temporary equilibrium and, accordingly, the economy experiences a transitory disequilibrium phase during which markets are cleared through quantity rationing. In this perspective, Malinvaud (1977, pp. 88–97) contemplates a macroeconomic disequilibrium model where prices are set at an average level of competitive equilibrium prices. On the whole, this assumption does not differ very much from that of macroeconomic models with rational expectations, nominal rigidities and anticipatory price setting in which wages are set so as to adjust expected labour demand to expected labour supply or, more generally, where all prices are set at the expected Walrasian equilibrium.[3] Secondly, another approach consists in assuming that agents have some monopoly power in an economy where competition is imperfect. As soon as prices are set, the economy experiences some kind of discrepancy between supply and demand according to the underlying competition structure. This approach was brought in by Bénassy (1973, 1976a) and Grandmont and Laroque (1976) and is widely adopted in more recent literature.[4]

Whatever assumption we make to describe the price-setting mechanism, it remains to explain why prices respond slowly to real and monetary disturbances affecting the economy. Assuredly, our understanding of the phenomena that explain the rigidity of nominal prices, and accordingly the real effects of money, is still very imperfect. Besides, the stickiness of nominal prices certainly does not boil down to the existence of a single reason. For instance, producers acting as monopolistic competitors may choose not to adjust prices in response to transitory shifts in demand because it is much simpler for daily management to set prices for certain intervals of time and let demand determine output during those intervals, or because erratic pricing may penalize risk-averse customers, or because there is a cost of learning the real state of demand or even because modifying prices, printing new catalogues and changing labels is actually costly.

Models in which there is endogenous price stickiness have been developed in writings on *near-rationality* (Akerlof and Yellen, 1985) or *menu costs* (Mankiw, 1985) and, in a dynamic context, in models where price-setters change prices either at fixed intervals or as soon as they deviate too much from their desired value (see Blanchard and Fischer, 1989, chapter 8, for an overview). Note that keeping prices unchanged is a question of convenience in the near-rationality argument and a consequence of the small costs of changing prices in the models with menu costs or optimal staggering. However, to a certain extent, both reasons are equivalent. Assuming that firms are satisfied with a near-rational behaviour implicitly means that fully optimal decisions would entail extra management costs that would make them unprofitable. Symmetrically, why should one assume that prices rather than production are costly to change? Probably because firms find it simpler to change prices from time to time and to let output adjust to shifts in demand!

Section 4 will focus on the idea according to which agents may not lose much from not manipulating prices in the framework of the fix-price approach. For this purpose, following Hahn (1978), we will assume that agents conjecture the price vector at which they believe they must trade as a function of the transactions they wish to make. We will contemplate fix-price allocations located in the neighbourhood of the Walrasian equilibrium and we will establish that, for any consistent conjecture, not manipulating prices is near-rational. Likewise, it will be shown that, for such allocations, no bilateral, mutually advantageous trade exists if agents bear small bargaining costs.

1 Walrasian temporary equilibrium

Consider a pure exchange economy characterized as follows: the economy includes n consumption goods indexed $h = 1, \ldots, n$. Money will be used as numeraire, unique store of value and medium of exchange at the same time. The implicit structure of the model is that of an overlapping generation model. Time is divided into infinitely many discrete periods $t = 1, 2, \ldots$ and m agents indexed by $i = 1, \ldots, m$ are living during the current period (period 1). For simplicity's sake, we will assume that agents live only during two periods but the arguments may be easily extended to a greater number of periods. Thus, in the current period, agents' economic horizon is limited to the next period (period 2) and in that period there will be new agents coming into the market.

The notations used in this chapter are:

$p^t = (p_h^t)$:   price vector in period t

$\omega_i^t = (\omega_{hi}^t)$:   agent i's initial endowment vector in period t

$x_i^t = (x_{hi}^t)$:   agent i's consumption vector in period t

$z_i^t = (z_{hi}^t)$:   agent i's net demand vector in period t, that is

$$z_i^t = x_i^t - \omega_i^t$$

M_{i0}: Initial money balances, held by agent i at the beginning of period 1.

M_i: Final money balances, held by agent i at the end of period 1, and saved in the prospect of future consumption in period 2. Consumers are not allowed to borrow money, which implies $M_i \geq 0$. Agent i budget constraint yields

$$p^1 z_i^1 + M_i = M_{i0}$$

Agent i has an intertemporal utility function $U_i(x_i^1, x_i^2)$ over $R_+^n \times R_+^n$, which we assume is continuous and strictly quasi-concave. In the current period, agents observe the price vector p^1 and anticipate vector p^2 which will prevail in the following period. To simplify notations, we will assume that all agents have the same price expectation. Furthermore, the only information that the consumers have on the current state of the economy is the price vector p^1 and we will assume that price expectations depend on this price vector. We will write

$$p^2 = \varphi(p^1)$$

where φ is a continuous function, characterizing the subjective relationship between current prices and expected future prices. Note that expected prices also implicitly depend upon the traders' information on past history (they may incorporate some learning procedure), money holdings and current and future endowments of goods.

Our main concern is the equilibrium achieved in the current period (period 1). Traders' demand in that period are the result of the maximization of intertemporal preferences:

P_1 Maximize $U_i(\omega_i^1 + z_i^1, \omega_i^2 + z_i^2)$ with respect to z_i^1, z_i^2 subject to:

$$p^1 z_i^1 + \varphi(p^1) z_i^2 \leq M_{i0} \qquad (1.1)$$

$$p^1 z_i^1 \leq M_{i0} \qquad (1.2)$$

$$\omega_i^t + z_i^t \geq 0 \qquad t = 1, 2 \qquad (1.3)$$

The inequality (1.1) represents agent i's budget constraint for both periods. It means that total value of the net demands estimated on the basis of the current and expected prices, must not exceed the money resources initially available. (1.2) means that M_i, the money held at the end of period 1, must not be negative. Finally, (1.3) indicates that consumption in each period is not negative.

On the basis of this intertemporal maximization, the relation between the current transactions z_i^1 and the current price vector p^1, can be explained through a dynamic programming argument. For given values of z_i^1 and $M_i = M_{i0} - p^1 z_i^1$, the optimal future consumption z_i^2 maximizes $U_i(\omega_i^1 + z_i^1, \omega_i^2 + z_i^2)$ subject to:

$$\varphi(p^1) z_i^2 \leq M_i$$
$$\omega_i^2 + z_i^2 \geq 0$$

In this problem, the transactions z_{hi}^2 are the unknowns and z_i^1 and M_i, representing the decisions taken in the first period, are fixed parameters. Let $z_i^2 = \psi_i(z_i^1, M_i, p^1)$ be the optimal solution. Note that ψ_i is homogeneous of degree 0 in (M_i, p^1), when φ is homogeneous of degree 1, i.e., when the expected future prices are unit elastic with respect to current prices. The expected intertemporal optimal utility is

$$U_i = U_i(\omega_i^1 + z_i^1, \omega_i^2 + \psi_i(z_i^1, M_i, p^1))$$

and thus, it may be written in the form of a V_i function with variables z_i^1, M_i and p^1 as arguments

$$V_i = V_i(z_i^1, M_i, p^1)$$

Such a function defines an indirect utility of the money held at the end of the current period. Its justification shows that the utility of the money holdings results from an optimization programme taking into account the consumption decisions in both periods, as well as the evolution of prices expected by agents. Obviously, the argument may be extended to a larger number of periods: if consumers optimize over periods $t = 1, 2, \ldots, T$, the optimal expected utility can be written as a function of current transactions, current prices and final money balances for a given subjective relation between current prices and future prices.

When function φ is homogeneous of degree 1, function V_i is homogeneous of degree 0 with respect to (M_i, p^1). In that case, only real money balances enter the expected utility index. Moreover, as function U_i is strictly quasi-concave, function V_i is strictly quasi-concave with respect to (z_i^1, M_i).

In period 1, agents base their decisions concerning consumption and money holdings on the maximization of the expected utility index V_i. Thus, they solve the following problem:

P$_2$ Maximize $V_i(z_i^1, M_i, p^1)$ with respect to z_i^1 and M_i subject to:

$$p^1 z_i^1 + M_i = M_{i0}$$
$$z_i^1 + \omega_i^1 \geq 0 \qquad M_i \geq 0$$

For given initial money holdings M_{i0} and resources ω_i^1, the optimal demands depend on current prices: $z_{hi}^1 = z_{hi}^1(p^1)$ for all h.

A *Walrasian temporary equilibrium* is obtained when the current price vector achieves equality of supply and demand on all markets. It is thus defined as price vector p^* such that[5]

$$\sum_{i=1}^{m} z_{hi}^1(p^*) = 0 \text{ for all } h = 1, \ldots, n \qquad (1.4)$$

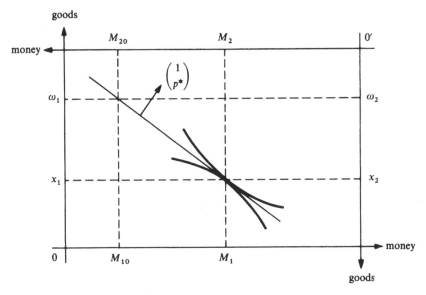

Figure 1.1   Walrasian temporary equilibrium

When the expected future prices are independent from the current prices, vector p^1 does not appear as an argument of the utility function V_i. Then, in the case of a one-good economy with two agents, the Walrasian temporary equilibrium can be represented in the traditional Edgeworth diagram.

This concept of Walrasian temporary equilibrium allows us to describe how agents may coordinate in the short run, while their price expectations may remain subjective and uncoordinated. However, as shown by Grandmont (1983), the existence of such an equilibrium is granted only when the expected future prices are relatively insensitive to the current prices. Precisely the image of function φ should be a bounded set, which excludes the unit elasticity case, for existence of equilibrium to be ensured. This can be easily explained with the example of a one-good economy: then p^1, p^2, ω_i^1, ω_i^2, x_i^1 and x_i^2 are positive real numbers. Note that the relationship between current price p^1 and current demand x_i^1 goes through two effects. First of all, when p^1 increases, the real value of the initial money holdings M_{i0} decreases which causes current demand to decrease if current consumption is a normal good. This is the real balance effect advanced by Pigou (1943) and Patinkin (1956). The second effect is the intertemporal substitution effect: when p^1 increases while p^2 remains stable or increases less, the real interest rate $r = p^1/p^2 - 1$ increases, and, for a given net income, alters the optimal ratio of the current consumption to the future consumption. The intertemporal substitution effect vanishes if the expected future price is unit elastic with respect to the current price. In such a case, p^2 is proportional to p^1 and r is a constant independent of p^1. Then, only the real balance effect remains. More generally, when the p^2/p^1 ratio varies within certain limits, variations in the real interest rate are limited and the intertemporal substitution effect is weaker. In such a situation, the real balance effect alone may not suffice to balance the goods market and an excess supply or demand might happen at any price. This possibility can be illustrated by the following example. Consider a one-commodity economy where all the consumers have the same utility function[6]

$$U_i(x_i^1, x_i^2) = (x_i^1)^\lambda + \delta(x_i^2)^\lambda$$

where λ and δ are parameters between 0 and 1. Assume also that the consumers have identical endowments and money holdings

$$\omega_i^1 = \omega^1, \omega_i^2 = \omega^2, M_{i0} = M_0 \text{ for all } i$$

One easily checks that individual demands satisfy $x_i^1 > \omega^1$ if and only if $p^1 < f(p^2)$ where

$$f(p) \equiv p^\lambda (p\omega^2 + M_0)^{1-\lambda}/\delta(\omega^1)^{1-\lambda}$$

Function f is increasing and invertible. As $p^2 = \varphi(p^1)$, there is an excess demand at any price p^1 if $\varphi(p^1) > f^{-1}(p^1)$ for all p^1 and an excess supply if $\varphi(p^1) < f^{-1}(p^1)$ for all p^1. In such cases, no Walrasian temporary equilibrium can exist.

2 Drèze fix-price equilibrium

We now assume that some degree of nominal rigidity prevails in the economy: after some exogenous perturbation affecting either the money holdings, initial endowments or price expectation schemes, current prices do not adjust immediately to the new Walrasian temporary equilibrium. Here, the simplest assumption is to assume that prices are given in the current period: they may differ from the temporary Walrasian equilibrium but they will adjust more or less rapidly in the following periods. The current price vector p^1 will thus be considered as exogenously given. In section 4, we will discuss a possible justification for this assumption concerning price rigidity in the short run.

If prices are fixed in the short run and if they actually differ from the Walrasian equilibrium, markets will not clear in the usual sense of the word. Nevertheless, the economy may achieve some kind of coherency through quantity rationing. A Drèze equilibrium (1975) may be viewed as the outcome of this coordination process. Agents perceive quantity constraints limiting the possible exchanges. These constraints satisfy a number of coherency conditions and they allow constrained demands and constrained supplies to be balanced in each market.

We will first describe agents' intertemporal optimization behaviours when facing such quantity constraints. Then, we will be able to define the Drèze equilibrium. And, finally, we will emphasize the inefficiency properties of this kind of equilibrium.

2.1   *Rationing constraints and agents behaviours*

The main innovation of the fix-price approach compared with the Walrasian equilibrium approach, lies in the fact that agents receive signals both in the form of prices and quantity constraints. These constraints determine the exchanges likely to be made by agents. Let us keep the same two-period model, and assume that agent i perceives the following constraints: $\bar{z}_i^t = (\bar{z}_{hi}^t) \in R_+^n$ and $\underline{z}_i^t = (\underline{z}_{hi}^t) \in R_-^n$, where $\bar{z}_{hi}^t$ $(-\underline{z}_{hi}^t)$ refers to the upper bound he perceives as limiting his purchases (his sales) in market h at period t, with $t = 1,2$. This gives

$$\underline{z}_{hi}^t \leq z_{hi}^t \leq \bar{z}_{hi}^t \text{ for } t = 1,2 \text{ and for all } h = 1, \ldots, n \tag{1.5}$$

Note that $\bar{z}_i^2$ and $\underline{z}_i^2$ are expected future constraints. We assume that these expected constraints depend on the current constraints and we write $\bar{z}_i^2 = \bar{\eta}_i(\bar{z}_i^1), \underline{z}_i^2 = \eta_i(\underline{z}_i^1)$ where $\bar{\eta}_i$ and η_i are continuous functions. More particularly, $\bar{z}_i^2 = +\infty$ and $\underline{z}_i^2 = -\infty$ when agent i perceives quantity constraints as transitory shifts from the Walrasian temporary equilibrium.

Agent i's intertemporal optimization programme can be obtained by adding the quantity constraints (1.5) to problem P_1 and by taking into account the expectation-making process described above. This leads to the following problem:

P_1' Maximize $U_i(\omega_i^1 + z_i^1, \omega_i^2 + z_i^2)$ with respect to z_i^1, z_i^2 subject to:
$p^1 z_i^1 + \varphi(p^1) z_i^2 \leq M_{i0}$
$p^1 z_i^1 \leq M_{i0}$
$\underline{z}_{hi}^1 \leq z_{hi}^1 \leq \bar{z}_{hi}^1$ for all $h = 1, \ldots, n$
$\eta_{hi}(\underline{z}_i^1) \leq z_{hi}^2 \leq \bar{\eta}_{hi}(\bar{z}_i^1)$ for all $h = 1, \ldots, n$
$\omega_i^t + z_i^t \geq 0$ $t = 1,2$

An expected utility index can now be defined as in section 1. Indeed, let us assume that agent i realizes the trades z_{hi}^1 in the first period and holds the amount of money M_i at the end of that period. Then, the optimal intertemporal utility is obtained by solving the following decision problem. Given z_i^1 and M_i:

Maximize $U_i(\omega_i^1 + z_i^1, \omega_i^2 + z_i^2)$ with respect to z_i^2 subject to:
$\varphi(p^1) z_i^2 \leq M_i$
$\eta_{hi}(\underline{z}_i^1) \leq z_{hi}^2 \leq \bar{\eta}_{hi}(\bar{z}_i^1)$ for all $h = 1, \ldots, n$
$\omega_i^2 + z_i^2 \geq 0$

In this problem, the unknowns are transactions z_{hi}^2 made in the second period. As the price vector p^1 is taken to be fixed, the optimal value of these transactions is a function of z_i^1, M_i, $\bar{z}_i^1$ and $\underline{z}_i^1$. We shall write these second-period transactions as

$$z_i^2 = \psi_i(z_i^1, M_i, \bar{z}_i^1, \underline{z}_i^1)$$

and the corresponding intertemporal utility, expected in period 1, is

$$U_i = U_i(\omega_i^1 + z_i^1, \omega_i^2 + \psi_i(z_i^1, M_i, \bar{z}_i^1, \underline{z}_i^1))$$

This intertemporal utility will be written $V_i(z_i^1, M_i, \bar{z}_i^1, \underline{z}_i^1)$. This defines an expected utility index depending on current transactions, final money holdings and quantity constraints perceived in the current period. Note that the strict quasi-concavity of U_i implies that V_i is strictly quasi-concave with respect to (z_i^1, M_i).

In period 1, consumer i maximizes his expected utility index V_i on the set of net trades which satisfy the budget constraint and the quantitative constraints:

P_2' Maximize $V_i(z_i^1, M_i, \bar{z}_i^1, \underline{z}_i^1)$ with respect to z_i^1, M_i subject to:
$$p^1 z_i^1 + M_i = M_{i0}$$
$$\underline{z}_{hi}^1 \leq z_{hi}^1 \leq \bar{z}_{hi}^1 \quad \text{for all } h = 1, \ldots, n$$
$$z_i^1 + \omega_i^1 \geq 0 \qquad M_i \geq 0$$

Given current prices p^1, the optimal transaction vector z_i^1 in problem P_2' (hereafter called *constrained demand*) only depends on the quantity signals $\bar{z}_i^1$ and $\underline{z}_i^1$. We will write it as $\hat{\xi}_i(\bar{z}_i^1, \underline{z}_i^1)$. As V_i is strictly quasi-concave in (z_i^1, M_i), constrained demand is uniquely determined.

We now are in position to define the Drèze equilibrium. In what follows, all the variables considered (prices, transactions, quantity constraints) are related to the current period and index 1 will be left out in order to lighten the notations.

2.2 *Drèze equilibrium*

Definition 1.1 A Drèze equilibrium consists of transactions z_i^* and quantity constraints $\bar{z}_i, \underline{z}_i$, for $i = 1, \ldots, m$, such that

(α) $z_i^* = \hat{\xi}_i(\bar{z}_i, \underline{z}_i)$ for all $i = 1, \ldots, m$

(β) $\sum_{i=1}^m z_i^* = 0$

(γ) for all $h, z_{hi}^* = \bar{z}_{hi}$ for some i implies $z_{hj}^* > \underline{z}_{hj}$ for all j; and $z_{hi}^* = \underline{z}_{hi}$ for some i implies $z_{hj}^* < \bar{z}_{hj}$ for all j

Therefore, a Drèze equilibrium consists of net trades combined with quantity constraints, such that net trades maximize utility under quantity constraints (requirement α) and are mutually compatible (requirement β). Furthermore, agents do not simultaneously perceive quantity constraints on both sides of a market (requirement γ). Only agents on one side of the market (supply or demand) can perceive constraints that actually limit exchanges, which means that the market is frictionless.

In a Drèze equilibrium, an agent is said to be *rationed on market h* if his utility increases when the constraint limiting his exchanges on this market is suppressed. In mathematical terms, let the sets S_{hi} be defined as follows

$$S_{hi} = \{(z_i, M_i) \mid pz_i + M_i = M_{i0}; \underline{z}_{ki} \leq z_{ki} \leq \bar{z}_{ki}, \text{ for all } k \neq h; z_i + \omega_i \geq 0, M_i \geq 0\}$$

Then agent i is rationed on market h if there exists $(\hat{z}_i, \hat{M}_i)$ in S_{hi} such that

$$V_i(\hat{z}_i, \hat{M}_i, \bar{z}_i, \underline{z}_i) > V_i(z_i^*, M_i^*, \bar{z}_i, \underline{z}_i)$$

where $M_i^* \equiv M_{i0} - pz_i^*$.

We can easily check that condition (γ) and the strict quasi-concavity of function V_i imply that all the rationed agents belong to the same side of the market: no seller is rationed if one buyer is rationed and vice versa. Therefore, it is unambiguous to refer to an excess supply on market h when the sellers are rationed and to an excess demand when the buyers are rationed.

In a nutshell, in a Drèze equilibrium, net trades maximize agents' preferences under such quantity constraints on each market so that supplies and demands are not simultaneously rationed.

When the expected quantity constraints are independent from current quantity constraints, $\bar{z}_i$ and $\underline{z}_i$ do not appear as arguments of the utility function V_i. Then, in the case of a one-good economy with two agents, the fix-price equilibrium is easily visualized in the Edgeworth diagram. In figure 1.2, point B represents the equilibrium allocation and the transactions made are $z_1^* = x_1^* - \omega_1$ and $z_2^* = x_2^* - \omega_2$. Agent 1 is rationed on the goods' market, where an excess supply prevails. He perceives a quantity constraints $\underline{z}_1$, while agent 2 is not rationed on this market.

In the definition of the Drèze equilibrium, it is neither specified how demand rationing is shared among purchasers, nor how rationing of supply is shared among sellers. The only requirement is that only one side of the market can be tightly constrained (supply or demand). In such a situation, a great number of equilibria can exist, at least when there are several constrained agents in the same market: these multiple equilibria correspond to the many ways rationing may share out among agents. Conversely, a more specific definition of the Drèze equilibrium can be given by setting in advance the sharing out of quantity constraints. For example, we may require that all the agents perceive the same quantity constraints on

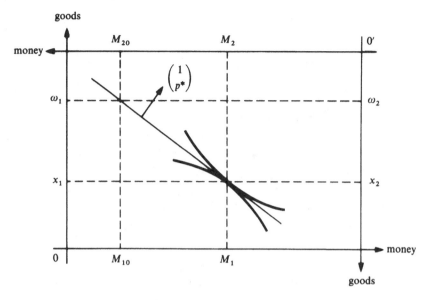

Figure 1.2   Fix-price equilibrium

each market, that is to say: $\bar{z}_i = \bar{z}; \underline{z}_i = \underline{z}$ for all i. (Existence of a Drèze equilibrium under uniform rationing is proved in appendix 1). We may also require that agents be rationed according to a pre-set order (priority rationing). In such cases, the equilibrium uniqueness is much more likely.

2.3   Fix-price equilibrium inefficiency

The basic characteristic of a competitive Walrasian equilibrium, true under fairly general hypotheses, is to be a Pareto optimum: using a price vector in all profit and utility maximizations, which induces compatible decisions, guarantees an efficient utilization of resources in the economy. Figure 1.3 shows that this fundamental proposition of welfare economics does not hold for a fix-price equilibrium: indeed, the equilibrium is at point B, and therefore, does not belong to the contract curve (E) representing the Pareto-optimal allocations.

In so far as the fix-price equilibria must be budget compatible for every agent, in a situation where prices are set a priori, they belong to a subset of physically feasible allocations. In figure 1.3, this subset is represented by line (D). We may question the Pareto optimality of the fix-price equilibria in this subset. Such an optimality would be a second-best Pareto optimality, that is to say a Pareto optimality within the subset of feasible states defined by the fix-price exchange constraint.

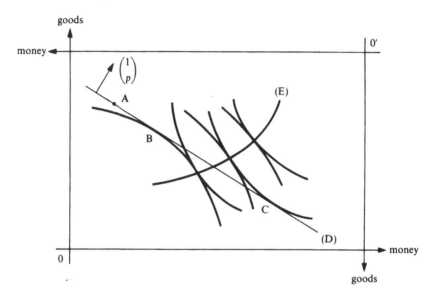

Figure 1.3   Fix-price equilibrium inefficiency

In figure 1.3, the set of second-best optima is the segment BC, which actually includes equilibrium B. However, as shown by Bénassy (1975), such a property is not generally true and a counterexample can easily be found to show the likelihood of fix-price equilibrium inefficiency within budget compatible allocations.

Consider a two-goods economy with two agents. For simplicity's sake, let us assume that the perceived constraints do not appear as arguments in the utility function V_i. Agent i utility becomes

$$V_i = V_i(z_{1i}, z_{2i}, M_i) \qquad i = 1, 2$$

Using the budget constraint

$$M_i = M_{i0} - p_1 z_{1i} - p_2 z_{2i}$$

the utility level of agent i can be written as a function of net trades

$$V_i = V_i(z_{1i}, z_{2i}, M_{i0} - p_1 z_{1i} - p_2 z_{2i})$$

which allows a simple graphical description of preferences. Indifference curves of agent 1 are drawn in figure 1.4. They are concentric and their saturation point E_1 stands for the usual Walrasian (unconstrained) demands. At this point, agent 1 buys good 1 and sells good 2.

Using a double-axis system we can represent a fix-price equilibrium, shown by point A in figure 1.5. At point A, agent 1 buys good 1 and sells good 2, while agent 2 sells good 1 and buys good 2.

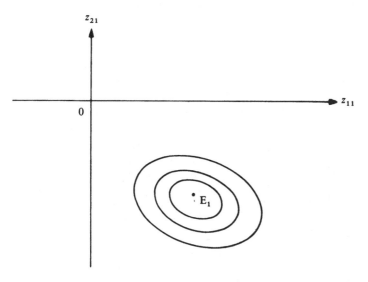

Figure 1.4   Agent 1's indifference curves

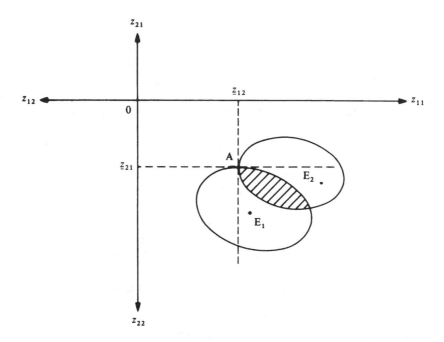

Figure 1.5   Fix-price equilibrium

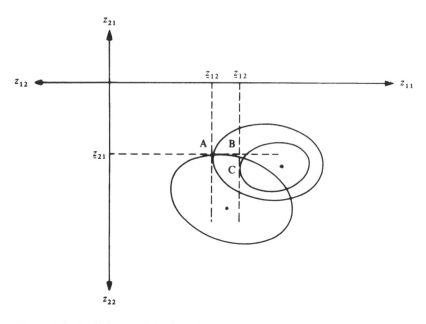

Figure 1.6   Inefficiency of the fix-price equilibrium

Agent 1 perceives constraint $\underline{z}_{21}$ on market 2. Utility maximization leads him to point A, where one of his indifference curves is tangent to the line $z_{21} = \underline{z}_{21}$. Similarly, agent 2 perceives constraint $\underline{z}_{12}$ which limits the quantity of good 1 likely to be sold. While maximizing his utility given the quantity constraint, he is also led to point A. However, such an equilibrium is not Pareto optimal within the set of budget compatible allocations. Indeed, any point located within the shaded area provides each agent with a utility strictly larger than the one achieved at point A.

Interpreting such an inefficiency is easier when focusing on the role of money as a medium of exchange. Indeed, let us assume that transactions are made market by market in the form of money/goods exchanges. For agent 1, buying an additional quantity of good 1 – by moving from point A to point B, for instance – lowers his satisfaction level and thus is not optimal. However, this is basically due to the fact that this agent does not know that the additional purchase will end up relaxing the constraint perceived by agent 2 on good 1 market. Relaxing the constraint, which would change from $\underline{z}_{12}$ to $\underline{z}'_{12}$, would urge agent 2 to increase his demand for good 2, and this would lead the economy to point C. There, both agents' utility levels are increased. Yet, such a scenario is rather unlikely. From agent 1's point of view the purchase of an additional quantity of good 1 primarily comes down to an exchange of goods for money, with given quantity constraints. Thus he does not spontaneously make a supplementary purchase though it would ultimately increase his satisfaction level.

This section introduced a fix-price equilibrium concept, where agents base their purchases and sales on the price system but also take into account the quantity constraints endogeneously defined. These constraints have the double property of making the transactions desired by agents coherent and not simultaneously rationing supply and demand. Yet, we may question the quantity signal-making process in such a model. The only answer is probably the hypothesis of a *tâtonnement* on quantity constraints, intervening prior to exchanges and organized by an auctioneer. Thus, a quantity tâtonnement leading to a fix-price equilibrium would substitute for a Walrasian tâtonnement leading to an equilibrium price system. Should the nature of the signals emitted by the auctioneer be altered, his role remains nonetheless vital in maintaining the logic coherency of the Drèze model. To a certain extent, the equilibrium concept suggested by Bénassy (1975), goes beyond the idea of a centralized market, with the auctioneer gathering and transmitting the information to all the agents.

3 Bénassy fix-price equilibrium

In Bénassy's approach, agents can make exchange propositions that exceed the quantity constraints prevailing on the market. These propositions will be referred to as *effective demands*. Effective demands are expressed independently on each market and they do not depend on the rationing constraint perceived on that market. They only depend on the constraints perceived on the other markets. Effective demands may be incompatible and therefore are different from the *ex post* trades. The incompatibility of effective demands makes agents perceive quantity constraints that limit the possible exchanges and these perceived constraints allow to define new effective demands. A Bénassy equilibrium (hereafter a K-equilibrium) is reached when these new effective demands coincide with the previous ones. It is a fixed point of the compound mapping: effective demands→perceived constraints→effective demands.

To begin with, the relationship between the effective demand expressed on the one hand and the transactions made and the perceived constraints on the other hand needs to be elaborated. Once the notion of a *non-manipulable rationing scheme* is introduced, we can clarify the agents' effective demand-making process. Then, we will be able to define a K-equilibrium, a terminology chosen by Bénassy (1975), in order to stress the relation between his equilibrium concept and previous writings, such as

Clower's (1965) and Leijonhufvud's (1968) that emphasized the importance of quantity rationing in the economics of Keynes.

3.1 *Effective demands, realized transactions and perceived constraints*

The K-equilibrium approach implies a distinction between the trade offers
(or effective demands) and the *ex post* trades (realized transactions).
We let:

$\tilde{z}_{hi}$ = agent i net effective demand for good h

z^*_{hi} = net transaction made by agent i on market h

Effective demands are exchange propositions and thus are not necessarily
mutually compatible. In other words, the total net demand for good h may
be different from 0

$$\sum_{i=1}^{m} \tilde{z}_{hi} \neq 0$$

Conversely, realized transactions satisfy

$$\sum_{i=1}^{m} z^*_{hi} = 0$$

Realized transactions can be associated with effective demands by
postulating the existence of *rationing schemes* given by the actual trading
and rationing rules on each market. Rationing schemes represent the
functioning of markets where the aggregate excess demand may differ from
zero and where nevertheless, exchanges take place. Formally, a rationing
scheme on market h is described by mappings $F_{hi}: R^m \rightarrow R$, such that

$$z^*_{hi} = F_{hi}(\tilde{z}_{h1}, \ldots, \tilde{z}_{hm}) \qquad \text{for all } i = 1, \ldots, m$$

Thus, the rationing scheme F_{hi} asssigns a transaction z^*_{hi} to consumer i,
that depends upon all effective demands expressed on market h. The
rationing schemes are supposed to satisfy the following conditions for all
$\tilde{z}_{h.} = (\tilde{z}_{h1}, \ldots, z_{hm})$ and all h, i:

(C_1) F_{hi} is continuous, non-decreasing in $\tilde{z}_{hi}$

(C_2) $\sum_i F_{hi}(\tilde{z}_{h.}) = 0$

(C_3) $\tilde{z}_{hi} F_{hi}(\tilde{z}_{h.}) \geq 0; |F_{hi}(\tilde{z}_{h.})| \leq |\tilde{z}_{hi}|$

(C_4) $F_{hi}(\tilde{z}_{h.}) = \tilde{z}_{hi}$ if $\tilde{z}_{hi}\left(\sum_{j=1}^{m} \tilde{z}_{hj}\right) \leq 0$

Condition C_1 means that realized transactions vary continuously with
effective demands and the larger the effective demand, the larger the
transaction made. Condition C_2 says that rationing schemes define feasible
transactions. C_3 stands for the voluntary exchange rule: the sign of an

agent's transaction cannot be reversed and no agent may be compelled to exchange more than he wants to. As for condition C_4, it means that only agents on the 'long side' of the market are likely to be constrained. For instance, with an excess supply of goods on market h, that is when $\sum_{j=1}^{m} \tilde{z}_{hj} < 0$ only suppliers – i.e., agents i such that $\tilde{z}_{hi} < 0$ – may be constrained. Such a condition is in accordance with the hypothesis of a frictionless market and is closely related to condition (γ) in the definition of a Drèze equilibrium. Note, however, that C_4 is not necessary for the definition of a K-equilibrium. If this condition does not hold, then both sides of a market can be rationed simultaneously. A priori, several rationing schemes can be contemplated and described by using functions F_{hi}, which meet the conditions above: uniform, priority or proportional rationing . . .

The comparison of effective demands with *ex post* transactions leads agents to perceive subjective quantity constraints. As in the Drèze model, these constraints will take the form of vectors $\bar{z}_i = (\bar{z}_{hi}) \in R^n_+$ and $\underline{z}_i = (\underline{z}_{hi}) \in R^n_-$, where $\bar{z}_{hi}$ ($-\underline{z}_{hi}$) stands for the quantity agent i thinks he can buy (sell) on market h. The constraints perceived by an agent on a market may be considered as functions of the whole set of effective demands expressed on this market. Thus we will write

$$\bar{z}_{hi} = \bar{G}_{hi}(\tilde{z}_{h\cdot}) \qquad \text{for all } i = 1, \ldots, m$$

and

$$\underline{z}_{hi} = \underline{G}_{hi}(\tilde{z}_{h\cdot}) \qquad \text{for all } i = 1, \ldots, m$$

where the functions $\bar{G}_{hi}$ and $\underline{G}_{hi}$ are assumed to satisfy the following conditions for all $\tilde{z}_{h\cdot}$ and all h, i:

(C_5) $\bar{G}_{hi}$ and $\underline{G}_{hi}$ are continuous

(C_6) $\underline{G}_{hi}(\tilde{z}_{h\cdot}) \leq F_{hi}(\tilde{z}_{h\cdot}) \leq \bar{G}_{hi}(\tilde{z}_{h\cdot})$

(C_7) $\bar{G}_{hi}(\tilde{z}_{h\cdot}) = F_{hi}(\tilde{z}_{h\cdot})$ if $\tilde{z}_{hi} > F_{hi}(\tilde{z}_{h\cdot})$

$\underline{G}_{hi}(\tilde{z}_{h\cdot}) = F_{hi}(\tilde{z}_{h\cdot})$ if $\tilde{z}_{hi} < F_{hi}(\tilde{z}_{h\cdot})$

Note that C_6 and C_7 are logical coherency conditions. In particular, C_7 requires that, when an agent is actually constrained on a market, the constraint he perceives (on purchases or sales) coincide with the transaction made. Thus, it is an objective constraint. On the other hand, when an agent is not constrained on a market, he may still perceive constraints stemming from his subjective appraisal of what he can buy or sell.

The following example illustrates these rationing scheme and perceived constraints notions. We consider a priority rationing on a given market h. We assume that agent 1 is the only supplier on this market (i.e., $\tilde{z}_{h1} < 0$). We also assume that demanders are served in a priority order: agent 2 is served first, then follows agent 3, then 4, . . .,m. When agent i meets the sole supplier, he enjoys the residual supply remaining after the other agents have made their transactions. The residual supply is equal to

$$\tilde{z}_{h1} + \sum_{j=2}^{i-1} z_{hj}^* = \text{Min}\left\{0, \tilde{z}_{h1} + \sum_{j=2}^{i-1} \tilde{z}_{hj}\right\}$$

We quite naturally assume that such a quantity stands for the constraint agent i perceives. In confirmity with the sign conventions adopted, we write

$$\bar{z}_{hi} = \text{Max}\left\{0, -\tilde{z}_{h1} - \sum_{j=2}^{i-1} \tilde{z}_{hj}\right\} \tag{1.6}$$

and the transaction made by agent i will be

$$z_{hi}^* = \text{Min}\{\tilde{z}_{hi}, \bar{z}_{hi}\}$$
$$= \text{Min}\left\{\tilde{z}_{hi}, \text{Max}\left(0, -\tilde{z}_{h1} - \sum_{j=2}^{i-1} \tilde{z}_{hj}\right)\right\} \tag{1.7}$$

Equations (1.6) and (1.7) illustrate the relationship existing between the effective demands expressed on a market, on the one hand, and, on the other hand, the realized transactions and the constraints perceived.

3.2   *Non-manipulable rationing scheme*

A rationing scheme is said to be *non-manipulable* if any agent perceives lower and upper constraints on the market, limiting the possible exchanges, and if these constraints cannot be altered when effective demand is altered. On the other hand, a rationing scheme is manipulable when an agent can, in case of rationing, alter the transactions he makes, by changing his effective demand. The priority rationing system, mentioned in the previous paragraph, is non-manipulable. Conversely, a rationing scheme where transactions are proportional to the effective demand expressed is manipulable.

These definitions can be formalized as follows. Let

$$\tilde{z}_h^i = (\tilde{z}_{h1}, \ldots, \tilde{z}_{h,i-i}, \tilde{z}_{h,i+1}, \ldots, \tilde{z}_{h,m})$$

and

$$\tilde{z}_{h\cdot} = (\tilde{z}_{hi}, \tilde{z}_h^i)$$

We also write

$$\bar{\phi}_{hi}(\tilde{z}_h^i) = \text{Max}\{\alpha \mid F_{hi}(\alpha, \tilde{z}_h^i) = \alpha\}$$
$$\underline{\phi}_{hi}(\tilde{z}_h^i) = \text{Min}\{\alpha \mid F_{hi}(\alpha, \tilde{z}_h^i) = \alpha\}$$

The function $\bar{\phi}_{hi}$ ($\underline{\phi}_{hi}$) defines the maximum quantity agent i can demand (supply) and buy (sell) without rationing, as a function of the effective demands expressed by the other agents. The rationing scheme F_{hi} is

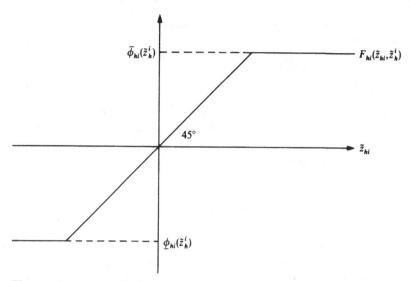

Figure 1.7   Non-manipulable rationing scheme

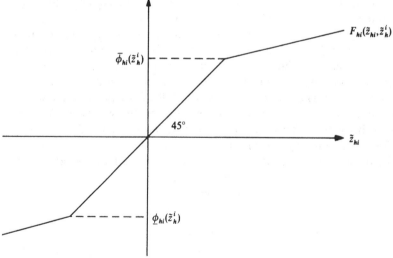

Figure 1.8   Manipulable rationing scheme

non-manipulable if it meets the following requirements

$$F_{hi}(\tilde{z}_{hi}, \tilde{z}_h^i) = \begin{cases} \text{Min}\{\tilde{z}_{hi}, \bar{\phi}_{hi}(\tilde{z}_h^i)\} & \text{if } \tilde{z}_{hi} \geq 0 \\ \text{Max}\{\tilde{z}_{hi}, \underline{\phi}_{hi}(\tilde{z}_h^i)\} & \text{if } \tilde{z}_{hi} \leq 0 \end{cases}$$

If not, the rationing scheme is manipulable. This is illustrated in figures (1.7) and (1.8).

When the rationing scheme is non-manipulable, a simple way to define $\bar{G}_{hi}$ and $\underline{G}_{hi}$ is

$$\bar{G}_{hi}(\tilde{z}_{hi}, \tilde{z}_h^i) \equiv \bar{\phi}_{hi}(\tilde{z}_h^i) \tag{1.8}$$

$$\underline{G}_{hi}(\tilde{z}_{hi}, \tilde{z}_h^i) \equiv \underline{\phi}_{hi}(\tilde{z}_h^i) \tag{1.9}$$

Obviously $\bar{G}_{hi}$ and $\underline{G}_{hi}$ satisfy C_5, C_6 and C_7. The constraints perceived by an agent on a market are then directly deduced from the exchange propositions made by other agents, independently from the demand expressed by the agent in question.

3.3 *Definition of the effective demands*

The most crucial assumption in Bénassy's model is the definition of the agents' trade offers (demands $\tilde{z}_{hi}$). Following Clower (1965), Barro and Grossman (1971) and Grossman (1971), he assumes that an agent expresses effective demand on market h, that results from the maximization of his utility, taking into account the quantity constraints perceived on all the markets *except* market h. Therefore, this effective demand differs from the constrained demand introduced in section 2.1, where all the perceived quantity constraints were taken into account. Here, on the contrary effective demand expressed on a market only takes into account the constraints perceived on the other markets. This definition of demand under quantity rationing is rather intuitive. When a consumer is rationed on the labour market in which he cannot sell the quantity of labour he would like to, he transfers the constraint onto the goods markets by reducing his demand. This corresponds to the 'dual decision rule' according to Clower's terminology. Similarly, the sales constraints a firm perceives will be passed on to the labour market or on to the intermediate goods markets through a decrease in the firm's demand.

This leads us to define effective demand $\tilde{z}_{hi}$ as the h-th component of the vector z_i, which solves the following problem:

Q_h Maximize $V_i(z_i, M_i, \bar{z}_i, \underline{z}_i)$ with respect to z_i, M_i
          subject to:
          $pz_i + M_i = M_{i0}$
          $\underline{z}_{ki} \leq z_{ki} \leq \bar{z}_{ki}$ for all $k \neq h$
          $z_i + \omega_i \geq 0$ $M_i \geq 0$

$\tilde{z}_i = (\tilde{z}_{1i}, \ldots, \tilde{z}_{ni})$ is a function of the perceived constraints and will be written as

$$\tilde{z}_i = \tilde{\xi}_i(\bar{z}_i, \underline{z}_i)$$

Clearly, *effective demand* $\tilde{z}_i$ differs from *constrained demand* $\xi_i(\bar{z}_i, \underline{z}_i)$ obtained by maximizing utility under the budget constraint and by taking into account *all* quantity constraints (as in the Drèze model).

When rationing schemes are non-manipulable, the effective demand definition given above may be deduced from agents strategies which aim at obtaining the most preferred consumption bundle through the trade offers they express. Indeed let us assume that the constraint perception functions $\bar{G}_{hi}$ and $\underline{G}_{hi}$ are defined by (1.8) and (1.9). Then, the constraints $\bar{z}_i$ and $\underline{z}_i$ do not depend upon the effective demands expressed by agent i, and the transaction he makes on market h, written z_{hi}^*, will be defined as follows

$$z_{hi}^* = \begin{cases} \text{Min}(\tilde{z}_{hi}, \bar{z}_{hi}) & \text{if } \tilde{z}_{hi} \geq 0 \\ \text{Max}(\tilde{z}_{hi}, \underline{z}_{hi}) & \text{if } \tilde{z}_{hi} \leq 0 \end{cases}$$

or

$$z_{hi}^* = \text{Min}\{\bar{z}_{hi}, \text{Max}(\tilde{z}_{hi}, \underline{z}_{hi})\} \tag{1.10}$$

Now, let us assume that agent i expresses demands z_{hi}^d on the different markets $h = 1, \ldots, n$ in order to maximize his utility, taking into account the rationing process described in the relation (1.10). These demands must be the solution of the following problem:

Q' Maximize $V_i(z_i, M_i, \bar{z}_i, \underline{z}_i)$ with respect to $z_{hi}^d, h = 1, \ldots, n, z_i$ and M_i
subject to:
$$pz_i + M_i = M_{i0}$$
$$z_i + \omega_i \geq 0 \qquad M_i \geq 0$$

with

$$z_{hi} = \text{Min}\{\bar{z}_{hi}, \text{Max}(z_{hi}^d, \underline{z}_{hi})\} \qquad \text{for all } h$$

Generally, problem Q' does not admit a unique optimal solution. This is illustrated in figure 1.9, in the case of a one-good economy with two agents: any demand expressed by agent 1 between AB and AC leads to equilibrium transactions at point B.

However, it can be shown that the effective demand vector $\tilde{z}_i$ belongs to the set of Q' optimal solutions. Therefore, expressing effective demands $\tilde{z}_{hi}$ allows us to realize the constrained plan, i.e., to optimize satisfaction in view of all the rationings experienced. Under the non-manipulability assumption, effective demands are thus optimal signals transmitted by agents to the market. This is expressed in the following proposition:

Proposition 1.1 Assume

$$\tilde{z}_i = \xi_i(\bar{z}_i, \underline{z}_i) \tag{1.11}$$

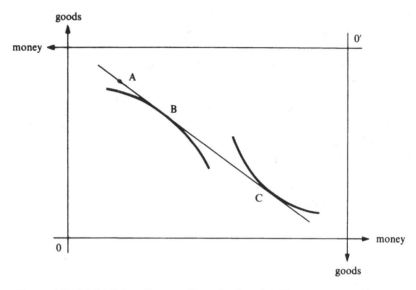

Figure 1.9   Multiplicity of agent 1's optimal trade offers

and

$$z_{hi}^* = \text{Min}\{\bar{z}_{hi}, \text{Max}(\tilde{z}_{hi}, \underline{z}_{hi})\} \qquad \text{for all } h = 1, \ldots, n \qquad (1.12)$$

Then

$$z_i^* = \hat{\xi}_i(\bar{z}_i, \underline{z}_i)$$

Proof[7]

Let $\tilde{z}_i$ and z_i^* be defined respectively by (1.11) and (1.12) and $\hat{z}_i = \hat{\xi}_i(\bar{z}_i, \underline{z}_i)$. Let us show that $z_{hi}^* = \hat{z}_{hi}$ for all h.

Assume first that $\tilde{z}_{hi} \in [\underline{z}_{hi}, \bar{z}_{hi}]$. This implies that $z_{hi}^* = \tilde{z}_{hi}$, but also that $\tilde{z}_{hi} = \hat{z}_{hi}$, and thus $z_{hi}^* = \hat{z}_{hi}$.

Assume now that $\tilde{z}_{hi} > \bar{z}_{hi}$. Then $z_{hi}^* = \bar{z}_{hi}$. Assume also that $z_{hi}^* \neq \hat{z}_{hi}$. This implies that $\hat{z}_{hi} < \bar{z}_{hi} < \tilde{z}_{hi}$ and that $\bar{z}_i^h \neq \hat{z}_i$, where $\bar{z}_i^h$ is the optimal solution of the problem Q_h. This gives

$$V_i(\bar{z}_i^h, M_{i0} - p\bar{z}_i^h, \bar{z}_i, \underline{z}_i) > V_i(\hat{z}_i, M_{i0} - p\hat{z}_i, \bar{z}_i, \underline{z}_i)$$

As V_i is strictly quasi-concave, the latter inequality contradicts $\hat{z}_{hi} < \bar{z}_{hi}$. We thus have $z_{hi}^* = \hat{z}_{hi}$.

The argument is exactly symmetrical for $\tilde{z}_{hi} < \underline{z}_{hi}$.

3.4 K-equilibrium

Definition 1.2 A K-equilibrium consists of transactions z_i^*, effective demands $\tilde{z}_i$ and quantity constraints $\bar{z}_i, \underline{z}_i$, such that for all $i = 1, \ldots, m$ and all $h = 1, \ldots, n$:

(α'): $z_{hi}^* = F_{hi}(\tilde{z}_{h\cdot})$

(β'): $\bar{z}_{hi} = \bar{G}_{hi}(\tilde{z}_{h\cdot})$

       $\underline{z}_{hi} = \underline{G}_{hi}(\tilde{z}_{h\cdot})$

(γ'): $\tilde{z}_i = \tilde{\zeta}_i(\bar{z}_i, \underline{z}_i)$

This definition is in accordance with the intuitive definition given at the beginning of this section: agents express effective demands that make them perceive quantity constraints and a K-equilibrium is reached when the perceived constraints lead them to express unchanged effective demands. This K-equilibrium concept requires some additional comments. First of all, the hypotheses made above ensure the existence of a K-equilibrium (see the proof in appendix 1). Furthermore, according to proposition 1.1, when the rationing scheme is non-manipulable the transactions made by agents at equilibrium maximize their utility under all perceived constraints. Thus we have

$$z_i^* = \hat{\xi}_i(\bar{z}_i, \underline{z}_i)$$

Therefore, the equilibrium transactions coincide with the constrained demands, proving the similarity between Drèze's and Bénassy's equilibrium concepts. Note that this property would not make sense if the rationing scheme were manipulable, since in that case the rationing constraints could be relaxed by overbidding, that is by expressing trade offers higher than desired transactions. Non-manipulability is thus a vital assumption for the consistency of Bénassy's equilibrium concept. Finally, remember that condition C_4 implies that only the agents on the long side of the market may be rationed. Such a property also relates the K-equilibrium concept to Drèze's model.

The difference between Drèze's and Bénassy's equilibria lies in the nature of the signals agents emit. While commenting upon Drèze model, we assumed the existence of a centralized mechanism emitting quantity signals and indicating to agents the exchanges they can realize. In Drèze's model, agents express their constrained demands on the market, i.e. demands that maximize their satisfaction in view of the whole set of quantity constraints. Moreover, at equilibrium, the constrained demands are mutually compatible, while in Bénassy's the quantity signals appear to be by-products of the exchange process: agents' effective demands may be incompatible and it is the resulting rationing mechanism that make them perceive quantity constraints. However, both concepts are still quite similar and have two common characteristics: for each agent the equilibrium allocation maximizes utility under the whole set of perceived quantity constraints and only one side of the market is rationed. This suggests that certain equivalences between Drèze's and Bénassy's equilibria may be demonstrated. Indeed, both the following propositions can be proved under the hypotheses mentioned previously (including the strict quasi-concavity of the utility functions).[8] We write $z^* = (z_i^*)$.

1 If transactions z^* are realized at a Drèze equilibrium, then there exist functions F_{hi}, $\bar{G}_{hi}$ and $\underline{G}_{hi}$ for all h and all i, meeting requirements C_1 to C_7, such that z^* is realized at a K-equilibrium.

2 Assume that functions V_i are differentiable and that conditions C_1 to C_7 are satisfied. If z^* is a K-equilibrium and if $M_{i0} - pz_i^* > 0$ for all i, then z^* is a Drèze equilibrium.

Thus, the transactions made at any Drèze equilibrium can be combined with rationing schemes and constraint–perception functions, such that the equilibrium appears to be a K-equilibrium. Conversely, any K-equilibrium is a Drèze equilibrium if agents' utility functions are differentiable and final money holdings are strictly positive at equilibrium.[9] Eventually, with few restrictions, both equilibrium concepts are equivalent.[10]

4   Fix-price equilibria, near-rationality and bargaining cost

4.1   *Preliminaries*

Disequilibrium fix-price models assume that nominal prices do not react to exogenous disturbances affecting the economy in the short run and this assumption needs to be somewhat justified. As previously indicated, the rigidity of nominal prices probably results from various causes like price-setters imperfect information about the state of demand, implicit contracts between buyers and sellers designed for sharing out risk, greater simplicity of management when firms do not lose much from not manipulating prices or actual cost of changing prices. The arguments in terms of *near-rationality* or *menu costs* focus on the two last reasons. Following Akerlof and Yellen (1985) and Mankiw (1985), it is usually formalized in an imperfect competition setting where monopolistic competitors choose the price of the goods they produce. This can be easily explained. Consider an economy under monopolistic competition where firms are price-setters. Let $\Pi(p,\bar{p},\theta)$ be the profit of a given firm as a function of its own price p, the price vector of its competitors $\bar{p}$ and a parameter θ that may represent for instance the money stock. $\Pi(.)$ is a reduced form that results from all the characteristics of the economy, including demand and technology.

At $\theta = \theta^*$, equilibrium prices $p = p^*, \bar{p} = \bar{p}^*$ satisfy

$$\frac{\partial \Pi}{\partial p}(p^*, \bar{p}^*, \theta^*) = 0$$

Assume that θ deviates from θ^*. Assume also that the competitors of the firm in question do not adjust their prices. Therefore, we still have $\bar{p} = \bar{p}^*$. Let $L(\theta)$ be the profit loss due to a stable price behaviour, that is

$$L(\theta) = \Pi(\tilde{p}(\theta), \bar{p}^*, \theta) - \Pi(p^*, \bar{p}^*, \theta)$$

where $\tilde{p}(\theta)$ maximizes $\Pi(p, \bar{p}^*, \theta)$ with respect to p. We have

$$\frac{dL}{d\theta} = \frac{\partial \Pi}{\partial p}(\tilde{p}(\theta), \bar{p}^*, \theta) \frac{d\tilde{p}}{d\theta} + \frac{\partial \Pi}{\partial \theta}(\tilde{p}(\theta), \bar{p}^*, \theta) - \frac{\partial \Pi}{\partial \theta}(p^*, \bar{p}^*, \theta)$$

From

$$\frac{\partial \Pi}{\partial p}(\tilde{p}(\theta), \bar{p}^*, \theta) = 0$$

and

$$\tilde{p}(\theta^*) = p^*$$

we obtain

$$\frac{dL}{d\theta}\bigg|_{\theta = \theta^*} = 0$$

This is nothing more than establishing the *envelope theorem*. At the first order the effect on the optimal profit of an increase in θ is equivalent to that obtained when the price p is not adjusted. Hence, for one producer, the opportunity cost of keeping his price unchanged in case of a change in θ of $\Delta\theta$ is of second order in $\Delta\theta$ provided the other producers do not adjust their prices. Consequently, if there are small costs to changing prices, it may be optimal not to adjust prices. Likewise, keeping prices unchanged is near-rational in so far as the loss for not adjusting is very low, i.e., second order with respect to disturbances that might have first-order effects on real magnitudes. Such an imperfect competition model, similar to that of Akerlof and Yellen (1985), is developed in appendix 2.

Of course, the main advantage of monopolistic competition models is that price-setters are clearly identified while the perfect competition approach assumes that prices are set by an invisible auctioneer. However, it is not to stick to reality that the monopolistic competition framework has been so frequently used in these models. The reason is probably much more prosaic. Indeed, the argument is based on the smoothness of functions relating profits to prices and these functions are actually differentiable in monopolistic competition models. However, in a macroeconomic perspective, perfect and imperfect competition have both advantages and drawbacks. There is no doubt that imperfect competition models, drawn from the theory of industrial organization, yield a much more realistic description of the mechanisms of specific markets, but, from a macroeconomic standpoint, they lead to an *embarras de richesse*: a one-shot Bertrand game in an economy where there is one seller and many demanders for each commodity and where goods are imperfect substitutes is one possible choice among many others! Besides, the global organization of market economies is often so complex and so diversified that an abstract competitive general equilibrium model may be helpful to describe all these interactions. Moreover, if one aims at highlighting rigidities that are purely nominal, it seems logical to contemplate a case without any real rigidity as a benchmark, and, in a sense, imperfect competition introduces some kind of real rigidity in the model.

The purpose of this section is just to look at the fix-price models of disequilibrium theory and the near-rationality menu cost argument, when the fix-price allocation is viewed as a transitory shift from the Walrasian equilibrium. For that purpose, following Hahn (1978), we will assume that agents have conjectures of how the perceived quantity constraint might be relaxed by offering a different price. Given a price-quantity signal, conjectures show the price vector at which an agent believes he must trade, as a function of the transactions he desires. Consistent conjectures correspond to higher bids, that is, to exchange terms that are less advantageous than current market prices when agents want to trade more. At a fix-price equilibrium, given their conjectures, agents on the long side of the market may find it profitable to manipulate prices so as to relax quantity constraints. However, it appears that, in the neighbourhood of the Walrasian equilibrium, for any consistent conjecture the opportunity cost of not manipulating prices is 'very small', namely it is second-order in the monetary shock that caused the departure from the Walrasian equilibrium. Yet, this shock will exert a first-order effect on real magnitudes. Equivalently, at a fix-price equilibrium, located in the neighbourhood of the Walrasian equilibrium, there do not exist any bilateral mutually advantageous transactions if bilateral trades entail small bargaining costs.

4.2 *Conjectures*

Consider a fix-price equilibrium (in the sense of Drèze or Bénassy) with equilibrium transactions z_i^* and quantity constraints $\bar{z}_i, \underline{z}_i$ for all i. Agent i perceives a price-quantity signal $q_i = (p, \bar{z}_i, \underline{z}_i)$. We let $Q = R_+^n \times R_+^n \times R_-^n$.

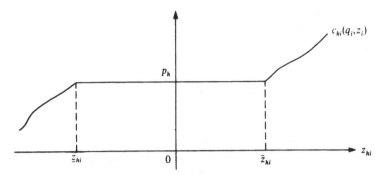

Figure 1.10 Consistent conjecture

Definition 1.3 A conjecture of agent i is a function $c_i = (c_{hi}): Q \times R^n \to R^n_+$ that specifies the prices $c_i(q_i,z_i)$ at which agent i thinks he is able to realize the transactions z_i given the information q_i. A conjecture c_i is said to be consistent if for all h, c_{hi} is non-decreasing in z_{hi} and

$$c_{hi}(q_i,z_i) = p_h \qquad \text{if } \underline{z}_{hi} \leq z_{hi} \leq \bar{z}_{hi}$$

for all $q_i = (p,\bar{z}_i,\underline{z}_i)$

Hence, for consistent conjectures, agents who are not rationed on a market take the price at which they must trade as given. Prices have to be raised if one aims at buying more than the quantity constraint and they must be lowered in order to be allowed to sell more than the constraint. A typical consistent conjecture is shown in figure 1.10.

Note that the consistency of conjectures implies that agents who are not rationed think that they are not in position to manipulate prices. This definition of consistency will be in accordance with the fact that constrained agents will not accept less advantageous prices: conjectures of unconstrained agents will thus be confirmed by the behaviour of those who are actually constrained.

4.3 *Near-rationality and bargaining cost*

We will first define the income variation that measures the opportunity cost of not manipulating prices. For simplicity's sake, we assume that expected utility V_i does not depend on $\underline{z}_i$ and $\bar{z}_i$. As indicated above, this makes sense in particular if fix-price equilibria are viewed as transitory shifts from the Walrasian equilibrium. We also assume that V_i is twice continuously differentiable over the set $z_i + \omega_i > 0, M_i > 0$. Given a conjecture $c_i(\cdot)$ and a signal q_i, the optimal transactions $z_i^c \equiv z_i^c(q_i, M_{i0})$ maximize $V_i(z_i, M_i)$ subject to the conjectural budget constraint

$$c_i(q_i, z_i)z_i + M_i = M_{i0}$$

and the feasibility conditions: $z_i + \omega_i \geq 0$ and $M_i \geq 0$.

Some notations have to be introduced. Let

$$V_i^c(q_i, M_{i0}) \equiv V_i(z_i^c, M_{i0} - c_i(q_i, z_i^c)z_i^c)$$

be the optimal conjectural utility of agent i.

Let $L_i^c \equiv L_i^c(q_i, M_{i0}, z_i)$ be the opportunity cost of choosing z_i rather than z_i^c in terms of income variation; L_i^c is given by

$$V_i^c(q_i, M_{i0} - L_i^c) = V_i(z_i, M_{i0} - c(q_i, z_i)z_i)$$

Let us consider a uniform monetary shock that leads to a proportional increase in money holdings

$$M_{i0} = (1 + \theta)\bar{M}_{i0} \qquad \text{for all } i$$

where θ belongs to Ω which is a neighbourhood of 0.

Let $p^* = (p_1^*, \ldots, p_n^*)$ be the price vector at the Walrasian equilibrium corresponding to $\theta = 0$. In this section, we investigate the properties of fix-price equilibria associated with p^* when θ deviates from zero. We assume that the fix-price equilibrium is unique (given $p = p^*$ and θ in Ω).[11] Given θ, this equilibrium is characterized by transactions $z_i^*(\theta)$, utility levels $V_i^*(\theta) \equiv V_i(z_i^*(\theta), (1 + \theta)\bar{M}_{i0} - p^* z_i^*(\theta))$ and quantity constraints $\bar{z}_i(\theta)$, $\underline{z}_i(\theta)$. Let $q_i(\theta) = (p^*, \bar{z}_i(\theta), \underline{z}_i(\theta))$ be the price–quantity signal perceived by agent i as a function of θ.

Any function $z_i(\cdot): \Omega \to R^n$ is called a *behaviour rule*. It describes agent i's transactions as a function of θ. In particular, $z_i^c(\theta) \equiv z_i^c(q_i(\theta), (1 + \theta)\bar{M}_{i0})$ and $z_i^*(\theta)$ are both behaviour rules. We will assume that $z_i^*(\theta)$ is continuous at $\theta = 0$ for all i, with right-hand side and left-hand side derivatives. Lastly, we note that $z_i^*(0) = z_i^c(0) = z_i^{**}$, where z_i^{**} stands for agent i's transactions in the Walrasian equilibrium, reached at $\theta = 0$. To simplify matters, we assume $z_{hi}^{**} \neq 0$ for all h and all i. We also assume $z_i^{**} + \omega_i > 0$ and $M_i^{**} = M_{i0} - p^* z_i^{**} > 0$ for all i.

Given a behaviour rule $z_i(\cdot)$, we can define the income variation

$$L_i^c(\theta) \equiv L_i^c(q_i(\theta), (1 + \theta)\bar{M}_{i0}, z_i(\theta))$$

which is the opportunity cost of following the rule $z_i(\theta)$ rather than $z_i^c(\theta)$. This leads to the following definition:

Definition 1.4 Given the conjecture c_i, the behaviour rule $z_i(\cdot)$ is *near-rational* if $L_i^c(0) = 0$ and $L_i^c(\theta)$ is second order in θ when θ tends to 0.

In other words, $z_i(\cdot)$ is a near-rational behaviour rule if, in the neighbourhood of $\theta = 0$, the opportunity cost of realizing transactions $z_i(\theta)$ rather than $z_i^c(\theta)$ is very small in comparison with the real effects of monetary shocks since these effects are first order in θ. This leads to proposition 1.2 which characterizes the near-rationality of fix-price equilibria.

> *Proposition 1.2* For all individuals $i = 1, \ldots, m$, the behaviour rules $z_i^*(\cdot)$ are near-rational for any consistent conjectures c_i.

Proof Let

$$\tilde{V}_i(p, M_{i0}) = \text{Max}\{V_i(z_i, M_i) \mid pz_i + M_i = M_{i0}; z_i + \omega_i \geq 0; M_i \geq 0\}$$

be the indirect utility function for a consumer who is not quantity constrained. Lastly, let

$$L_i^{c*}(\theta) \equiv L_i^c(q_i(\theta), (1 + \theta)\bar{M}_{i0}, z_i^*(\theta))$$

be the income variation corresponding to the behaviour rule $z_i^*(\cdot)$. We have

$$V_i^c(q_i(\theta), (1 + \theta)\bar{M}_{i0} - L_i^{c*}(\theta)) = V_i^*(\theta) \qquad (1.13)$$

Note that $L_i^{c*}(0) = 0$ since $z_i^*(0) = z_i^c(0)$ for all consistent conjectures c.

It remains to prove that $L_i^{c*}(\theta)$ is second order in θ. For all consistent conjectures, we have

$$V_i^c(q_i(\theta), (1 + \theta)\bar{M}_{i0} - L_i^{c*}(\theta)) \leq \tilde{V}_i(p^*, (1 + \theta)\bar{M}_{i0} - L_i^{c*}(\theta)) \qquad (1.14)$$

since individual i cannot do better than maximizing utility at prices p^* without facing any rationing constraint. From (1.13) and (1.14) we obtain

$$V_i^*(\theta) \leq \tilde{V}_i(p^*, (1 + \theta)\bar{M}_{i0} - L_i^{c*}(\theta))$$

As $\partial \tilde{V}_i / \partial M_{i0} > 0$, we deduce that $L_i^{c*}(\theta) \leq \bar{L}_i(\theta)$ for all consistent conjectures, $\bar{L}_i(\theta)$ being defined by

$$V_i^*(\theta) = \tilde{V}_i(p^*, (1 + \theta)\bar{M}_{i0} - \bar{L}_i(\theta)) \qquad (1.15)$$

Note that $\bar{L}_i(0) = 0$. Let us show that $\bar{L}_i(\theta)$ is second order in θ. For that purpose, consider the following problem:[12]

Maximize $V_i(z_i, M_i)$ with respect to z_i, M_i subject to:
$p^* z_i + M_i = (1 + \theta)\bar{M}_{i0} \qquad \lambda_i(\theta)$
$z_{hi} \geq z_{hi}^{**}(\theta)$ if $z_{hi}^{**} < 0 \qquad \mu_{hi}(\theta)$
$z_{hi} \leq z_{hi}^{**}(\theta)$ if $z_{hi}^{**} > 0 \qquad \mu_{hi}(\theta)$
$z_i + \omega_i \geq 0; M_i \geq 0$

where $\lambda_i(\theta)$ and $\mu_{hi}(\theta)$ for $h = 1, \ldots, n$, are Kuhn–Tucker multipliers.

Observe that $z_i = z_i^*(\theta), M_i = (1+\theta)\bar{M}_{i0} - p^*z_i^*(\theta)$ is an optimal interior solution to this problem. At $\theta = 0$, first-order optimality conditions are satisfied at $z_i = z_i^{**} = z_i^*(0), M_i = M_i^{**}$.

This gives

$$\frac{\partial V_i}{\partial z_{h_i}}(z_i^{**}, M_i^{**}) = \lambda_i(0)p_h^* + \mu_{h_i}(0) \text{ if } z_{h_i}^{**} < 0$$

$$\frac{\partial V_i}{\partial z_{h_i}}(z_i^{**}, M_i^{**}) = \lambda_i(0)p_h^* - \mu_{h_i}(0) \text{ if } z_{h_i}^{**} > 0$$

$$\frac{\partial V_i}{\partial M_i}(z_i^{**}, M_i^{**}) = \lambda_i(0)$$

At $(z_i, M_i) = (z_i^{**}, M_i^{**})$ the V_i partial derivative vector is proportional to vector $(p^*, 1)$. We thus have $\mu_{h_i}(0) = 0$ for all h and the multiplier $\lambda_i(0)$ is given by

$$\frac{\partial V_i}{\partial x_i}(z_i^{**}, M_i^{**}) = \lambda_i(0)p^*$$

Since functions $z_{h_i}^*(\theta)$ have left-hand side and right-hand side derivatives at $\theta = 0$ and multipliers are unique with $\mu_{h_i}(0) = 0$ for all h, we deduce that $V_i^*(\theta)$ is differentiable at $\theta = 0$ and that

$$\left.\frac{dV_i^*}{d\theta}\right|_{\theta=0} = \lambda_i(0)\bar{M}_{i0} \tag{1.16}$$

Furthermore $\tilde{V}_i$ is differentiable in M_{i0} at $(p, M_{i0}) = (p^*, \bar{M}_{i0})$ because V_i is twice continuously differentiable and $z_i^{**} + \omega_i > 0$ and we have

$$\left.\frac{\partial \tilde{V}_i}{\partial M_{i0}}\right|_{\substack{p=p^* \\ M_{i0}=\bar{M}_{i0}}} = \frac{\partial V_i}{\partial M_i}(z_i^{**}, M_i^{**}) = \lambda_i(0) \tag{1.17}$$

(1.15), (1.16) and (1.17) prove that $\bar{L}_i(\theta)$ is differentiable at $\theta = 0$ with

$$\left.\frac{d\bar{L}_i(\theta)}{d\theta}\right|_{\theta=0} = 0$$

$\bar{L}_i(\theta)$ is thus second order in θ at $\theta = 0$. Using $L_i^{c*}(\theta) \le \bar{L}_i(\theta)$ shows that $L_i^{c*}(\theta)$ is second order in θ for any consistent conjecture.

Proposition 1.2 states that, in the neighbourhood of $\theta = 0$, the expected gain of manipulating prices may be very low compared to the monetary shock that caused the shift from the Walrasian equilibrium. However, it should be noted that this expected gain (as well as the fix-price allocation itself) crucially depends on the rationing schemes on the various markets. If rationing is approximately uniform, confining oneself to a local argument in the neighbourhood of $\theta = 0$ makes sense since each agent is only marginally affected by shifts in quantity constraints that result from the global shock. In that case, the first-order effect of the shock on agents' utility levels may be considered as a reasonable approximation of the total effect. Then, from proposition 1.2, the opportunity cost of not manipulating prices may be actually insignificant for all agents, whereas it can be large for some agents and zero for others under priority rationing. This suggests that, in practice, our first-order/second-order result may explain why agents choose not to manipulate prices in so far as the effect of rationing is not borne by a small subset of agents. Note, however, that priority rationing exerts a much smoother welfare effect if it is contemplated in an intertemporal perspective where, in practice, it appears as an indefinite unemployment period on the labour market or as delivery delays on the goods markets. Furthermore, we can associate this nominal rigidity argument, which may be pertinent for some markets, with real rigidity assumptions on other markets, such as the rigidity of real wages on the labour market. We will come back to these issues in a later example.

Another way of highlighting our basic property is to establish that at the fix-price equilibrium associated with $p = p^*$ and $\theta \neq 0$, there does not exist any bilateral, mutually advantageous trade if there are small costs in bargaining over the terms of this trade. Here again, small means second order in θ. A possible interpretation of this approach is that, at a fix-price equilibrium, quantity constraints $\bar{z}_i, \underline{z}_i$ are transmitted to individual i, but this individual does not bear any cost for this information. Individual i may also conceivably try to meet another agent j so as to come to an agreement that would make them both better off, but then he would bear a cost that corresponds to search and bargaining time. For instance, job offers at market wages are transmitted to all individuals through employment bureau proposals or firms' advertisements. However, when involuntary unemployment prevails, a worker may also contemplate the possibility of directly searching for an employer likely to hire him at a lower wage, but this searching–bargaining period will be time consuming.

Consider a fix-price equilibrium where the transactions satisfy $z_{hi}^* \cdot z_{hj}^* < 0$ for some h and some i and j. A bilateral trade in market h between agents i and j corresponds to incremental transactions $\Delta z_{hi}, \Delta z_{hj}$ and bilateral payments t_i, t_j such that $\Delta z_{hi} + \Delta z_{hj} = 0, \Delta z_{hi} \cdot z_{hi}^* > 0$, $\Delta z_{hj} \cdot z_{hj}^* > 0$ and $t_i + t_j = 0$. Here, t_i (t_j) represents the additional net payment from i to j (from j to i).

Assume that the agents bear a fixed cost, equal to γ in utility terms, when bargaining so as to relax quantity constraints. At a fix-price equilibrium, where the signal $q_i(\theta)$ is perceived, the bilateral trade would lead to a welfare level $\bar{V}_i(\theta)-\gamma$ for agent $i, \bar{V}_i(\theta)$ being defined as the optimal utility level reached in the following problem:

Q(θ)   Maximize $V_i(z_i+\Delta z_i, M_i)$ with respect to z_i, M_i subject to:
$$p^* z_i + t_i + M_i = (1+\theta)\bar{M}_{io}$$
$$\underline{z}_{hi}(\theta) \leq z_{hi} \leq \bar{z}_{hi}(\theta) \text{ for all } h$$
$$\omega_i + z_i + \Delta z_i \geq 0; M_i \geq 0$$

where Δz_i is a n-dimensional vector with all coordinates equal to zero except the h-th which is equal to Δz_{hi}.

The bilateral trade is welfare-improving for agent i in state θ if $\bar{V}_i(\theta)-\gamma > V_i^*(\theta)$.

Proposition 1.3   There exists a function $\bar{\gamma}(\theta):\Omega \to R$, differentiable at $\theta=0$, such that $\bar{\gamma}(0)=0$ and $\bar{\gamma}'(0)=0$ for which, at the fix-price equilibrium associated with $p=p^*$ and θ, no bilateral, mutually advantageous trade exists if $\gamma > \bar{\gamma}(\theta)$.

Proof
Let us assume that $\Delta z_{hi}, t_i, \Delta z_{hj} = -\Delta z_{hi}, t_j = -t_i$ is advantageous for agents i and j in state θ. Assume for instance $z_{hi}^*(\theta) > 0$ and $z_{hj}^*(\theta) < 0$, which implies $\Delta z_{hi} > 0, \Delta z_{hj} < 0, t_i > 0, t_j < 0$. Four cases have to be considered.
Case 1: $z_{hi}^*(\theta) < \bar{z}_{hi}(\theta)$ and $z_{hj}^*(\theta) > \underline{z}_{hj}(\theta)$
In this case, agents i and j are not rationed in market h. V_i and V_j being quasi-concave, a necessary condition for the bilateral trade to be advantageous for agent i is that it corresponds to a lower unit cost than p_h^*, that is, $t_i/\Delta z_{hi} < p_h^*$. Symmetrically, it is necessary that $t_j/\Delta z_{hj} > p_h^*$ for the trade to be welfare-improving for agent j. Both conditions are contradictory.
Case 2: $z_{hi}^*(\theta) = \bar{z}_{hi}(\theta)$ and $z_{hj}^*(\theta) > \underline{z}_{hj}(\theta)$
Agent j is not rationed on market h. Thus $t_j/\Delta z_{hj} > p_h^*$ if the exchange makes agent j better off. This implies $t_i/\Delta z_{hi} > p_h^*$.
In problem Q(θ), agent i buys $z_{hi}' = z_{hi} + \Delta z_{hi}$ units of good h at a non-linear price schedule $\tilde{p}_h(z_{hi}')$ defined by

$$\tilde{p}_h(z_{hi}') = p_h^* + \frac{t_i - p_h^* \Delta z_{hi}}{z_{hi}'}$$

with

$$\underline{z}_{hi}(\theta) + \Delta z_{hi} \leq z_{hi}' \leq \bar{z}_{hi}(\theta) + \Delta z_{hi}$$

Since $t_i > p_h^* \Delta z_{hi}$, this non-linear price schedule is less advantageous than buying commodity h at price p_h^* without quantity rationing. This implies

$$\bar{V}_i(\theta) \le \tilde{V}_i(p^*, (1+\theta)\bar{M}_{io})$$

Hence, a necessary condition for the bilateral trade to be welfare-improving for individuals i and j is

$$\gamma_i(\theta) \equiv \tilde{V}_i(p^*, (1+\theta)\bar{M}_{io}) - V_i^*(\theta) > \gamma$$

Note that $\gamma_i(0) = 0$. Furthermore, we know from the proof of proposition 1.2 that $\gamma_i'(0) = 0$.

Case 3: $z_{hi}^*(\theta) < \bar{z}_{hi}(\theta)$ and $z_{hj}^*(\theta) = \underline{z}_{hj}(\theta)$

Case 3 is symmetrical to case 2: $\gamma_j(\theta) > \gamma$ is a necessary condition for the exchange to be welfare-improving for individuals i and j.

Case 4: $z_{hi}^*(\theta) = \bar{z}_{hi}(\theta)$ and $z_{hj}^*(\theta) = \underline{z}_{hj}(\theta)$

This fourth case is impossible in a Drèze equilibrium. In a K-equilibrium condition C_4 and the quasi-concavity of V_i and V_j imply that agents i and j cannot simultaneously benefit from relaxing their quantity constraint on market h. Thus, either $z_i^*(\theta)$ maximizes agent i's utility at price p^* with $\bar{z}_{hi} = +\infty$ (other quantity constraints being unchanged), or $z_j^*(\theta)$ maximizes agent j's utility at price p^* with $\underline{z}_{hj} = -\infty$ (other quantity constraints being unchanged). This leads us back to cases 2 and 3.

Let $\bar{\gamma}(\theta) = \text{Max}\{\gamma_1(\theta), \ldots, \gamma_m(\theta)\}$. We have $\bar{\gamma}(0) = 0, \bar{\gamma}'(0) = 0$ and there is no bilateral, mutually beneficial trade if $\gamma > \bar{\gamma}(\theta)$.

So far, we have restricted ourselves to fix-price equilibria viewed as departures from the Walrasian equilibrium. However, the basic idea highlighted in propositions 1.2 and 1.3 extend to situations where real rigidities prevail on some markets, while other markets are perfectly competitive. By way of example, let us consider a productive economy including H workers, N identical firms, labour being the input, and a unique consumption good sold at price p. We assume that workers do not bear any disutility when working and each of them supplies one unit of labour whatever the wage rate.

Assume that real wages are fixed at some exogenously given level, because for instance of one of the incentive mechanisms, which we will address in chapter 6 devoted to efficiency wage models. The real production cost of a firm writes as $C(y) = y^2/2$ where y stands for the output. Assume that aggregate demand for goods Y^d depends upon aggregate income $Y \equiv Ny$ and aggregate real money holdings M_0/p. We let

$$Y^d = cY + d\frac{M_0}{p} \qquad 0 < c < 1, d > 0$$

Let us assume that the money stock is fixed at $M_0 = \bar{M}_0$. Then the equilibrium on the goods market is obtained at a price

$$p^* = \frac{d\bar{M}_0}{(1-c)N}$$

At the same time, involuntary unemployment will prevail if H is large enough.

Now, let us assume that $M_0 = (1+\theta)\bar{M}_0$ and suppose that the price remains at $p = p^*$. Then the economy experiences fix-price equilibria with excess supply for goods when $\theta < 0$ and excess demand for goods when $\theta > 0$. Using a terminology that will be explained in chapter 2 (pp. 58–63), $\theta < 0$ corresponds to Keynesian unemployment and $\theta > 0$ to classical unemployment.

Let us assume that the rationing is uniform on the goods market. Then, under Keynesian unemployment, all firms perceive identical sales constraints and we have $y = 1 + \theta$. For all firms, real profit is

$$\Pi = y - \frac{y^2}{2} = 1 + \theta - \frac{(1+\theta)^2}{2}$$

The optimal profit $\Pi^* = 1/2$ is reached when $\theta = 0$. Firms do not choose to reduce their own prices to win customers and this leads to a loss in profit that is lower than $L = \Pi^* - \Pi = \theta^2/2$ which is second order in θ. However, the monetary shock θ exerts a first-order effect on output.

Under classical unemployment, firms reach the optimal profit Π^* and they enjoy an excess demand for their output. Nevertheless, they do not expect to be in position to make a profit out of this comfortable position by raising prices. If we had explicitly modelled the behaviour of consumers, we would have observed that the higher welfare gain consumers might have expected by bidding over p^* is second order in θ. Consumers thus do not lose much when they consider that the rationing of the demand for goods is a constraint they cannot manipulate (in practice, a delivery delay). Given this behaviour firms are right in believing that they cannot sell at prices higher than p^*. Equivalently at a fix-price equilibrium, be it Keynesian or classical, there does not exist any trade that would be profitable both to a firm and to a consumer, when bilateral bargaining entails a small cost.

This example allows us to illustrate the importance of the assumption made on the rationing scheme. Indeed, let us assume now that sales constraints are borne by a subset of N_1 firms, with $N_1 < N$ and $-N_1/N < \theta < 0$. Let y_1 and y_2 be the output, respectively for a constrained firm and an unconstrained firm. We have

$$y_1 = 1 + \frac{\theta N}{N_1}$$

$$y_2 = 1$$

For a constrained firm, the opportunity cost of not manipulating its price is given by

$$L = \frac{1}{2}\left(\frac{N\theta}{N_1}\right)^2$$

The smaller the subset of firms which are sales constrained, the larger the opportunity cost. For instance, in the case of a 10 per cent variation in aggregate output ($\theta = -1/10$), the relative opportunity cost L/Π^* is 1 per cent if $N_1/N = 1$, 4 per cent if $N_1/N = 1/2$ and 16 per cent if $N_1/N = 1/4$.

The results of this section also extend to situations where initially (i.e., before the money shock) prices on markets where no real rigidity prevails (the goods market in our example) may differ from Walrasian equilibrium prices. Indeed, consider the previous example. Assume now that $p \neq p^*$ and that the rationing is uniform on the goods market (i.e., $N_1 = N$).

Keynesian unemployment prevails when $p > (1 + \theta)p^*$ and then we have

$$y = (1 + \theta)\frac{p^*}{p}$$

There is classical unemployment with $y = 1$ when $p < (1 + \theta)p^*$.

Let $L(p, \theta)$ be the profit loss per firm due to the sales constraints. We have

$$L(p, \theta) = \frac{1}{2}\left[1 - \frac{p^*(1 + \theta)}{p}\right]^2 \qquad \text{if } p > (1 + \theta)p^*$$

$$L(p, \theta) = 0 \qquad \text{if } p \leq (1 + \theta)p^*$$

Now, let us assume that $\theta \in [-\alpha, +\alpha]$ with $0 < \alpha < a < 1$. Then, one easily checks that there exist functions $C(\alpha)$ and $\varepsilon(\alpha)$ such that $C(0) = 0$, $C'(0) = 0$, $\varepsilon(0) = 0$ and $C(\alpha) > 0$, $\varepsilon(\alpha) > 0$ for all α in $(0, a)$ that satisfy

$$L(p, \theta) < C(\alpha) \qquad \text{for all } \theta \text{ in } [-\alpha, +\alpha]$$

if

$$\left|\frac{p - p^*}{p^*}\right| < \varepsilon(\alpha)$$

Hence, when the initial price distortion $(p - p^*)/p^*$ is small enough, price cutting is unprofitable if there is a bargaining cost which is of second order with respect to the maximal possible variation in the money stock.

For instance, a possible choice is

$$C(\alpha) = \frac{k\alpha^2}{2}$$

$$\varepsilon(\alpha) = \frac{\alpha(\sqrt{k} - 1)}{1 - \alpha\sqrt{k}}$$

with $1 < k < 1/a^2$.

If $\alpha = 1/10$ and $k = 4$, we have $C = 0,02$ and $\varepsilon = 0,125$. In that case, the economy may experience 10 per cent output variations. If $(p - p^*)/p^*$ is lower than 12.5 per cent and the bargaining cost is greater than 2 per cent of desired sales, cutting prices is not profitable when Keynesian unemployment prevails.

Appendix 1 Existence theorems

I Existence of a Drèze equilibrium

Let λ_h, $h = 1, \ldots, n$, be real numbers such that $\lambda_h > \sum\limits_{i=1}^{m} \omega_{hi}$ and let

$$Q_h = [p_h - \lambda_h, p_h + \lambda_h]$$

$$Q = \prod_{h=1}^{n} Q_h$$

For $\tau_h \in Q_h$ and $\tau = (\tau_h) = (\tau_1, \ldots, \tau_n) \in Q$, let us define the following functions

$$\bar{z}_{hi}(\tau_h) = \begin{cases} \lambda_h & \text{if } \tau_h \in [p_h - \lambda_h, p_h] \\ \lambda_h + p_h - \tau_h & \text{if } \tau_h \in [p_h, p_h + \lambda_h] \end{cases}$$

$$\underline{z}_{hi}(\tau_h) = \begin{cases} p_h - \lambda_h - \tau_h & \text{if } \tau_h \in [p_h - \lambda_h, p_h] \\ -\lambda_h & \text{if } \tau_h \in [p_h, p_h + \lambda_h] \end{cases}$$

$$\bar{z}_i(\tau) = (\bar{z}_{1i}(\tau_1), \ldots, \bar{z}_{ni}(\tau_n))$$
$$\underline{z}_i(\tau) = (\underline{z}_{1i}(\tau_1), \ldots, \underline{z}_{ni}(\tau_n))$$
$$f_{hi}(\tau) = \hat{\xi}_{hi}(\bar{z}_i(\tau), \underline{z}_i(\tau))$$

$$f_h(\tau) = \sum_{i=1}^{m} f_{hi}(\tau)$$

where $\hat{\xi}_{hi}$ represents the h-th component of the constrained demand function $\hat{\xi}_i$.

Let Φ be the mapping from Q into Q, whose h-th component Φ_h is defined by

$$\Phi_h(\tau) = \tau_h + \frac{f_h(\tau)}{m}$$

Let us check that $\Phi_h(\tau) \in Q_h$ if $\tau \in Q$. Indeed, we have $\underline{z}_{hi}(\tau_h) \le f_{hi}(\tau_h) \le \bar{z}_{hi}(\tau)$. If $\tau_h \in [p_h, p_h + \lambda_h]$, then we have

$$-\lambda_h \le f_{hi}(\tau) \le \lambda_h + p_h - \tau_h$$

Hence

$$p_h - \lambda_h \le \tau_h - \lambda_h \le \tau_h + f_{hi}(\tau) \le \lambda_h + p_h$$

that is to say $\tau_h + f_{hi}(\tau) \in Q_h$. The argument is similar when $\tau_h \in [p_h - \lambda_h, p_h]$. Therefore, we have $\tau_h + f_{hi}(\tau) \in Q_h$ for all τ in Q. The convexity of Q_h implies that $\Phi_h(\tau) \in Q_h$ and thus $\Phi(\tau) \in Q$ if $\tau \in Q$. Therefore, Φ is a continuous mapping of the convex compact set Q into itself. Thus, according to Brouwer's theorem there exist τ^* in Q such that $\Phi(\tau^*) = \tau^*$.

One immediately checks that transactions z_{hi}^* and quantity constraints $\bar{z}_{hi}$ and $\underline{z}_{hi}$ defined by: $z_{hi}^* = f_{hi}(\tau^*)$, $\bar{z}_{hi} = \bar{z}_{hi}(\tau^*)$ and $\underline{z}_{hi} = \underline{z}_{hi}(\tau^*)$ meet conditions (α), (β) and (γ), therefore define a Drèze equilibrium (where all the agents perceive the same quantity constraints on each market).

II Existence of K-equilibrium

Let $\tilde{z} = (\tilde{z}_{hi})$ and $\bar{z} = (\bar{z}_{hi})$, $\underline{z} = (\underline{z}_{hi})$, with $h = 1, \ldots, n$ and $i = 1, \ldots, m$. Functions $\bar{G}_{hi}$ and $\underline{G}_{hi}$ express the perceived constraints $\bar{z}_{hi}$ and $\underline{z}_{hi}$ as a function of the effective demands $\tilde{z}_{hj}$, $j = 1, \ldots, m$. This allows us to write $(\bar{z}, \underline{z}) = G(\tilde{z})$, where G is a continuous mapping from R^{nm} into $R_+^{nm} \times R_-^{nm}$. From the maximum theorem, strict quasi-concavity of V_i implies that functions $\xi_i(\cdot)$ are continuous. We will write $\tilde{z} = \tilde{\xi}(\bar{z}, \underline{z})$, where $\tilde{\xi}$ is a continuous mapping from $R_+^{nm} \times R_-^{nm}$ into R^{nm}.

Let $\Gamma(\tilde{z}) = \tilde{\xi}[G(\tilde{z})]$ and

$$K_{hi} = \left[-\omega_{hi}, \frac{p\omega_i + M_{i0}}{p_h} \right] \quad \begin{array}{l} h = 1, \ldots, n \\ i = 1, \ldots, m \end{array}$$

$$K = \prod_{h,i} K_{hi}$$

We have $\tilde{\xi}_{hi}(\bar{z}_i, \underline{z}_i) \in K_{hi}$, for all h and all i. Consequently, the restriction of the function Γ to the convex compact set K is a continuous function from that set into itself. According to Brouwer's theorem, $\Gamma(\cdot)$ has a fixed point $\tilde{z}(*)$. This fixed point defines the effective demands to which corresponds to a K-equilibrium, characterized by transactions $z_{hi}^* = F_{hi}[\tilde{z}_h.(*)]$ and perceived constraints $\bar{z}_{hi} = \bar{G}_{hi}[\tilde{z}_h.(*)], \underline{z}_{hi} = \underline{G}_{hi}[\tilde{z}_h.(*)]$.

Appendix 2 A monopolistic competition model with near-rational behaviour

This appendix illustrates the near-rationality/menu cost argument with a simple monopolistic competition model due to Akerlof and Yellen (1985).

Let us consider an economy with m firms where each firm i chooses its price p_i and wage w_i. Let the demand curve facing firm i be

$$y_i = \left(\frac{p_i}{p} \right)^{-\sigma} \frac{M}{p} \quad \sigma > 1, i = 1, \ldots, m$$

where y_i = output of firm i, p_i = price of firm i, p = average price level, M = money stock per firm.

Firms produce output according to the production function

$$y_i = l_i^{1/a} \qquad a > 1$$

Furthermore, for incentive reasons, firms have to pay a constant real wage rate ω. We thus have

$$w_i = \omega p \qquad \text{for all } i$$

We will first define a long-run equilibrium where the money stock is fixed at $M = \bar{M}$ and each firm i chooses p_i and w_i given the average price level so as to maximize profits. It is assumed that the firms consider the average price level p as exogenously given (which makes sense if the economy includes a large number of firms) and that the demand for labour is lower than the supply.

The profit of firm i is

$$\Pi_i = p_i y_i - w_i l_i$$
$$= p_i y_i - w_i y_i^a$$

Using the demand curve and the real wage constraint allows to write the profit as a function of p_i, p, M

$$\Pi_i(p_i, p, M) = p_i \left(\frac{p_i}{p}\right)^{-\sigma} \frac{M}{p} - \omega p \left(\frac{p_i}{p}\right)^{-a\sigma} \left(\frac{M}{p}\right)^a$$

Maximizing Π_i with respect to p_i gives

$$(\sigma - 1) p_i^{1 + \sigma(a-1)} = \sigma a \omega p^{1 + \sigma(a-1)} \left(\frac{M}{p}\right)^{a-1}$$

From $p_i = p$ for all i, we obtain $p = \bar{p}$ when $M = \bar{M}$ with

$$\bar{p} = \left(\frac{\sigma a \omega}{\sigma - 1}\right)^{\frac{1}{a-1}} \bar{M}$$

Note that money is neutral in the long run: any increase in $\bar{M}$ is fully reflected in a proportional increase in all prices so that demand and output do not change.

Now, consider a transitory deviation of the money stock: $M \neq \bar{M}$. Assume that all the firms continue to charge the same price $\bar{p}$ and to pay the same money wage $\bar{w} = \omega \bar{p}$. In that case, $y_i = M/\bar{p}$ for all i: the monetary disturbance $M - \bar{M}$ thus exerts a first-order effect on the output levels when the firms do not adjust prices.

Let $L_i(M)$ be the opportunity cost of firm i for not adjusting its own price, given that all other firms do not adjust their prices and the money stock is M. We have

$$L_i(M) = \Pi_i(\tilde{p}_i(\bar{p},M),\bar{p},M) - \Pi_i(\bar{p},\bar{p},M)$$

where

$$\tilde{p}_i(p,M) = \mathrm{Arg}_{p_i}\mathrm{Max}\,\Pi_i(p_i,p,M)$$

A simple calculation yields

$$\frac{\tilde{p}_i}{\bar{p}} = \left(\frac{M}{\bar{M}}\right)^{\frac{a-1}{1+\sigma(a-1)}}$$

and

$$\Pi_i(\tilde{p}_i(\bar{p},M),\bar{p},M) = \frac{1+\sigma(a-1)}{\sigma a}\,M^{\frac{a}{1+\sigma(a-1)}}\,\bar{M}^{-\frac{(1-a)(1-\sigma)}{1+\sigma(a-1)}}$$

$$\Pi_i(\bar{p},\bar{p},M) = M - \frac{\sigma-1}{\sigma a}\,M^a(\bar{M})^{1-a}$$

Of course we have $L_i(\bar{M}) = 0$. We also deduce

$$L_i'(M) = \frac{1}{\sigma}\left(\frac{\bar{M}}{M}\right)^{\frac{(1-a)(1-\sigma)}{1+\sigma(a-1)}} - 1 + \frac{\sigma-1}{\sigma}\left(\frac{\bar{M}}{M}\right)^{1-a}$$

and thus $L_i'(\bar{M}) = 0$. Hence, the opportunity cost of not adjusting prices is second order with respect to the deviation $M - \bar{M}$: in that sense, not adjusting price is near-rational. Equivalently, if firm i bears a cost greater than $L_i(M)$ for adjusting its price, keeping its price unchanged is fully optimal.

2 Wage rigidity and short-run macroeconomic equilibrium

The aim of this chapter is to examine how wage rigidities may affect output and employment in the short run. We shall consider a simple macro-economic model and we shall explore the consequences of various assumptions going from generalized nominal rigidities postulated in the theory of fix-price equilibria to the real wage rigidity emphasized in many non-Walrasian microeconomic analyses of the labour market.

Indeed the theory of fix-price equilibria was the starting point of a macroeconomic analysis concerning the determinants of employment and the efficiency of public policies. These analyses, mainly due to Barro and Grossman (1971, 1976), Bénassy (1976b, 1977a) and Malinvaud (1977), have been carried out within a particularly simple aggregate model, that includes three commodities (a consumption good, labour and money) and usually three agents (a consumer, a firm and the government). Despite its simplicity, the model proves to be particularly relevant to the analysis of macroeconomic consequences of generalized nominal rigidities. Two kinds of unemployment may occur: Keynesian unemployment caused by a low demand for goods, and classical unemployment caused by an inadequate supply. This model provides a theoretical basis to Keynes-inspired stimulating fiscal policies, but it also shows that fiscal measures are inefficient should the unemployment be classical. Only a policy aiming at improving the profitability of the production sector is then likely to favourably affect employment. The first section of this chapter introduces the general hypotheses of this model, and shows how the fix-price analysis concepts can be applied to this particular situation. The second section analyses the different 'disequilibrium regimes' that may appear and emphasizes, among other things, the consequences of policies affecting public expenditures or real wages on the employment level.

However, the opposition between Keynesian and classical unemployments is, to a large extent, oversimplified. First, because it is based on the hypothesis of a symmetrical rigidity of prices and wages which is no doubt exaggerated, and also because the fix-price hypothesis does not allow a clear distinction between the implications of nominal or real wage rigidity. Therefore, the third section will focus on the consequences of wage rigidity when prices are flexible, considering in turn the money wage rigidity postulated by the orthodox Keynesian theory, the wage indexation hypothesis and finally the rigidity of intertemporal consumption real wages. In particular, enlarging slightly on our basic model, and following Akerlof and Yellen (1985) and Mankiw (1985), we will show that rigidity of money wages may occur in an imperfectly competitive economy with localized monopoly unions if these are satisfied with a 'near-rational' behaviour or, equivalently, if they bear small costs of changing wages. In this framework the usual results of orthodox Keynesianism hold, and in particular economic activity depends on shocks affecting the real goods demand or the money supply. On the contrary when intertemporal consumption wages are rigid in real terms, and the expectation-making process meets a few elementary rationality conditions, the monetary policy may become totally neutral but fiscal policy remains an efficient instrument to stimulate the economic activity owing to the intertemporal substitution effect caused by a transitory increase in public consumption. Finally, the wage indexation hypothesis, as examined by Gray (1976) and Fischer (1977b), allows us to contemplate intermediate cases between nominal and real rigidities and, more particularly, to characterize the implications of contractual wage rigidities when the economy is subject to different types of unexpected shocks.

1 The model

The economy includes three commodities: a consumption good, labour and money as the only store of value. There are three agents: a household, a firm and the government.

1.1 *Hypotheses on agents*

As in the previous chapter, the underlying structure of the economy is an overlapping generation model. The representative household[1] sells labour services and buys the consumption good. His income consists of wages and distributed profits. We will assume that the profits of the current period are distributed by the firm at the beginning of the following period. We let:

M_0: money held at the beginning of the current period, distributed profits included.

p: consumption good price,

m_0: initial real money holdings, defined by $m_0 = M_0/p$,

M: money held at the end of the period,

m: final real money holdings, defined by $m = M/p$,

x: consumption,

l: employment level in work-hours,

l_0: total available time for work/leisure trade-off,

s: money wage rate,

w: real wage rate, defined by $w = s/p$.

We saw in the previous chapter how to justify the existence of an indirect utility function, where the money held at the end of the period appears as an argument. In the present chapter, the utility function of the household is written as[2]

$$U = U(x, l_0 - l, m)$$

So, we assume that utility depends on consumption x, leisure time $l_0 - l$ and real final money holdings m. Function U is supposed to be strictly quasi-concave and twice continuously differentiable.

The household budget constraint writes as

$$x + m = wl + m_0$$

and means that the value of consumption and final money holdings is equal to the sum of wages and initial money holdings.

The firm uses labour as the only variable input to produce the consumption good, which is not meant to be stocked. At equilibrium, the quantity produced is thus equal to the quantity sold. The firm's technology is defined by the production function $y = f(l)$, where l is the employment level and y is the output. We assume that this function is twice continuously differentiable and satisfies the usual hypotheses: $f' > 0$, $f'' < 0$, $f(0) = 0$, $f'(l) \rightarrow 0$ when $l \rightarrow +\infty$ and $f'(l) \rightarrow \infty$ when $l \rightarrow 0$. The firm maximizes the current profit $py - sl$ which is saved in the form of a money balance for later distribution.

The government expresses a demand g on the goods market. For simplicity's sake, we assume for the moment that the household does not pay taxes and that public expenditures are exclusively financed by the creation of money. Taxes will be introduced in section 3.4.

Assuming that prices are fixed in the current period, fix-price equilibrium concepts, developed in the previous chapter, can be applied to this particular situation. We will use the K-equilibrium approach but using the Drèze equilibrium concept would lead to the same basic results. We will first define the constraints perceived by agents and the effective demands they express. Then we will demonstrate the existence of a unique fix-price equilibrium.

1.2 *Perceived constraints and effective demands*

As we saw in chapter 1, defining a fix-price equilibrium (K-equilibrium) requires us to specify how agents perceive quantity constraints on the different markets. Trade offers, referred to as effective demands, are expressed on these markets. When the offers are incompatible, that is to say, when the net excess demand is not equal to zero, actual transactions are different from effective demands and the agents perceive quantity constraints. We thus have to explain the relationship between effective demands and perceived constraints, and also to define the effective demands expressed by agents as a function of the constraints they perceived. This corresponds to the two stages of a mapping that can be symbolized as follows:

$$\begin{array}{ccccc} \text{effective} & & \text{perceived} & & \text{effective} \\ \text{demands} & \xrightarrow{\hspace{2cm}} & \text{constraints} & \xrightarrow{\hspace{2cm}} & \text{demands} \end{array}$$

A fixed point of this compound mapping defines a fix-price equilibrium.

Let us first specify the constraints perceived as a function of the effective demands.

1.2.1 **Perceived constraints**
We will write:

l_s: household's effective labour supply
l_d: firm's effective demand for labour
y_s: firm's effective supply of goods
x_d: household's effective demand for goods
y_d: total effective demand, which is the sum of private and public demands

$$y_d = x_d + g$$

A simple way to explain the quantity constraint perception process consists in assuming that each agent perceives a constraint equal to the maximum amount of goods he can actually exchange on a given market, with due account of the other agents' propositions.[3] We will adopt this hypothesis in the further developments. On the labour market, there is only one supplier (the household) and only one demander (the firm): the household perceives a constraint equal to the firm's effective demand l_d and the firm perceives a constraint equal to the household's effective supply l_s. On the consumption goods market, the firm is the only supplier and perceives a constraint equal to the quantity demanded y_d. There are two demanders, however, (the household and the government). For simplicity's sake, we assume that priority is given to the government, whose demand is never rationed.[4] The household perceives a constraint equal to the residual supply $y_s - g$.

1.2.2   Effective demands: the household

When the representative household does not perceive any rationing constraint, he solves the following programme, where the utility function U is maximized under the budget constraint:

P_0 Maximize $U(x, l_0 - l, m)$ with respect to $x \geq 0, m \geq 0$ and $0 \leq l \leq l_0$
subject to:
$$x + m = wl + m_0$$

Let (x_d^*, l_s^*, m^*) be the optimal solution to the programme P_0; this corresponds to Walrasian demands, also referred to as 'notional' in Clower's terminology (1965). x_d^*, l_s^* and m^* appear as functions of the real wage rate w and real money balances m_0

$$x_d^* = x_d^*(m_0, w)$$
$$l_s^* = l_s^*(m_0, w)$$
$$m^* = m^*(m_0, w)$$

These functions are differentiable (in the interior of their definition set) and we assume $\partial x_d^*/\partial m_0 > 0$, $\partial x_d^*/\partial w > 0$, $\partial l_s^*/\partial m_0 < 0$ and $\partial l_s^*/\partial w > 0$. A rise in the initial money stock m_0 makes the demand for goods increase and the labour supply decrease: consumption and leisure are normal goods, the demand for which increases along with the household's wealth. The labour supply is supposed to increase along with the real wage rate: when the latter increases the substitution effect, which tends to reduce leisure in favour of consumption, is greater than the income effect, which, on the contrary, tends to increase the demand for leisure. Finally, the demand for consumption is an increasing function of real wages, since both effects above-mentioned tend to cumulate.

The household's effective demand for goods is written as x_d. We obtain it by solving the following problem:

P_1 Maximize $U(x, l_0 - l, m)$ with respect to $x \geq 0, m \geq 0$ and $0 \leq l \leq l_0$
subject to:
$$x + m = wl + m_0$$
$$l \leq l_d$$

In that programme, the household maximizes his utility function under the budget constraint, taking into account the inequality $l \leq l_d$ representing the rationing constraint perceived on the labour market.

A convenient way to enhance the relation existing between notional demand x_d^* and effective demand x_d, is to introduce the following auxiliary problem, written $P_2(l)$, where the employment level l is fixed:

$P_2(l)$ Maximize $U(x,l_0-l,m)$ with respect to $x \geq 0$ and $m \geq 0$ subject to:
$$x+m = wl+m_0$$

Let $\tilde{x} = \tilde{x}(m_0,w,l)$ and $\tilde{m} = \tilde{m}(m_0,w,l)$ be the solution to $P_2(l)$.

$\tilde{x}$, referred to as the 'constrained demand' for consumption, is equal to the household's demand for goods when the employment level is taken into account as a given parameter, that is to say, when the household is actually constrained by the rationing prevailing on the labour market. We notice that constrained demand $\tilde{x}$ coincides with notional demand x_d^* when the employment level l is equal to the notional supply l_s^*. Hence

$$\tilde{x}(m_0,w,l_s^*(m_0,w)) = x_d^*(m_0,w) \tag{2.1}$$

The function $\tilde{x}$ is differentiable and we assume $\partial\tilde{x}/\partial m_0 > 0$, $\partial\tilde{x}/\partial w > 0$ and $\partial\tilde{x}/\partial l > 0$. Thus, constrained demand $\tilde{x}$ is supposed to increase along with the financial resources, owing to a rise in real money balances, real wages or the employment level.[5]

For fixed values of the parameters m_0 and w, the utility level achieved at the optimum of problem $P_2(l)$ is a function of the employment level, written $\varphi(l)$, and defined by

$$\varphi(l) = U(\tilde{x}(l),l_0-l,\tilde{m}(l))$$

Here, the parameters m_0 and w are taken to be fixed and do not explicitly appear as arguments of the functions $\tilde{x}$ and $\tilde{m}$. Function φ reaches its maximum on $[0,l_0]$ at the notional labour supply l_s^*. Moreover, the quasi-concavity of U implies that $\varphi(l)$ is a unimodal function: φ is increasing on $[0,l_s^*]$ and decreasing on $[l_s^*,l_0]$.[6]

By using problem $P_2(l)$, we can in two steps solve problem P_1, which defines effective demand x_d. We will first determine the optimal employment level, using function $\varphi(l)$ and by taking into account the rationing constraint imposed by the effective demand for labour l_d. We then, deduce the corresponding demand for goods, by using the function $\tilde{x}$.

The first step consists in solving the following problem:

Maximize $\varphi(l)$ with respect to $l \geq 0$ subject to:
$$l \leq \text{Min}\{l_0,l_d\}$$

Since $\varphi(l)$ is unimodal and reaches its maximum at $l = l_s^*$, the optimal value of l is equal to the minimum of l_s^* and l_d. Therefore, effective demand x_d is defined by

$$x_d = \tilde{x}(m_0,w,\text{Min}\{l_s^*,l_d\})$$

As constrained demand $\tilde{x}$ is an increasing function of the employment level, we can write

$$x_d = \text{Min}\{\tilde{x}(m_0,w,l_s^*),\tilde{x}(m_0,w,l_d)\}$$

Therefore, according to (2.1)

$$x_d = \text{Min}\{x_d^*(m_0,w),\tilde{x}(m_0,w,l_d)\} \tag{2.2}$$

The effective demand for consumption appears to be the minimum of the notional and constrained demands. If the effective demand for labour l_d is larger than the notional supply l_s^*, we have $x_d = x_d^* < \tilde{x}$: in this case, the effective demand for goods is equal to the notional demand. Otherwise, we have, $x_d = \tilde{x} < x_d^*$: the household is rationed on the labour market and this is reflected by a demand for goods lower than the notional demand. When unemployment prevails, the employment level is equal to the firms' demand l_d on the labour market. If production is efficient, employment and output are linked by the function f. Then, constrained demand $\tilde{x}$ is

$$\tilde{x} = \tilde{x}(m_0,w,f^{-1}(y))$$

We obtain a Keynesian-type consumption function, where the demand for goods depends on the variables m_0 and w but also on the aggregate income y.

Now, let us define the effective supply of labour l_s. It can be obtained by solving the following programme:

P_1' Maximize $U(x,l_0-l,m)$ with respect to $x \geq 0$, $m \geq 0$ and $0 \leq l \leq l_0$ subject to:
$x+m = wl+m_0$
$x \leq y_s - g$

In this programme, we maximize the utility function U, taking account of the rationing constraint prevailing on the consumer goods market. Let us define an auxiliary problem $P_2'(x)$, where consumption x is fixed and where the variables are m and l:

$P_2'(x)$ Maximize $U(x,l_0-l,m)$ with respect to $m \geq 0$ and $0 \leq l \leq l_0$ subject to:
$x+m = wl+m_0$

Let $\hat{l} = \hat{l}(m_0,w,x)$ and $\hat{m} = \hat{m}(m_0,w,x)$ be the solution to $P_2'(x)$. Thus, the 'constrained supply' $\hat{l}$ is equal to the labour supply when the household considers his consumption as given. When the consumption is equal to the notional demand x_d^*, $\hat{l}$ coincides with the notional supply l_s^*

$$\hat{l}(m_0,w,x_d^*(m_0,w)) = l_s^*(m_0,w) \tag{2.3}$$

The function $\hat{l}$ is differentiable and is supposed to satisfy $\partial\hat{l}/\partial m_0 < 0$, $\partial\hat{l}/\partial w > 0$ and $\partial\hat{l}/\partial x > 0$. In particular, larger consumption implies a larger constrained labour supply: an individual who is allowed to buy additional consumer goods because of less restrictive quantity rationing on goods markets will be willing to work more. For given values of the parameters m_0 and w, the utility level achieved at the optimum of problem $P'_2(x)$ is a function $\gamma(x)$ defined as follows

$$\gamma(x) = U(x, l_0 - \hat{l}(x), \hat{m}(x))$$

The function $\gamma(x)$ is unimodal and achieves its maximum at $x = x_d^*$.[7]

The problem P'_1 can be solved in two steps. First, we determine the optimal consumption level, evaluated on the basis of the function $\gamma(x)$, under the rationing constraint imposed by the residual effective supply $y_s - g$. Then, we deduce the effective labour supply by using function $\hat{l}$. This gives

$$l_s = \hat{l}(m_0, w, \text{Min}\{x_d^*, y_s - g\})$$

and

$$l_s = \text{Min}\{\hat{l}(m_0, w, x_d^*), \hat{l}(m_0, w, y_s - g)\}$$

From (2.3), we deduce

$$l_s = \text{Min}\{l_s^*(m_0, w), \hat{l}(m_0, w, y_s - g)\} \tag{2.4}$$

The effective labour supply is equal to the minimum value of the notional and constrained supplies. If the remaining goods supply $y_s - g$ is larger than the household's notional demand x_d^*, we have $l_s = l_s^* < \hat{l}$: effective labour supply is equal to notional supply. Otherwise, we have $l_s = \hat{l} < l_s^*$: the household experiences a rationing on the goods market which is reflected by a labour supply less than notional supply.

1.2.3 Effective demands: the firm

In the absence of quantity constraints, the maximization of the firm's profit is:

Maximize $y - wl$ with respect to $y \geq 0$ and $l \geq 0$ subject to:
$y = f(l)$

Let (y_s^*, l_d^*) be the solution to this programme. y_s^* is the notional supply of goods (or Walrasian supply) and l_d^* is the notional demand for labour. These transactions are defined by the equality of the marginal productivity of labour f' and the real wage rate w and we can write $y_s^* = y_s^*(w)$ with $dy_s^*/dw < 0$ and $l_d^* = l_d^*(w)$ with $dl_d^*/dw < 0$.

The notional goods supply and the notional demand for labour are only potential and do not necessarily intervene on the market as trade offers. On the contrary, when the firm perceives a quantity constraint on a given market it will take it into account to determine the effective demand (or supply) it will express on the other market.

We saw earlier that the firm perceives a constraint l_s on the labour market, defining the maximal quantity of labour services it may purchase; similarly, it experiences a demand constraint y_d on the goods market. Thus, effective demand for labour l_d results from the following problem:

Maximize $y - wl$ with respect to $y \geq 0$ and $l \geq 0$ subject to:
$y = f(l)$
$y \leq y_d$

The concavity of $f(.)$ implies that effective demand l_d is equal to the minimum of notional demand l_d^* and the quantity of labour necessary to meet the demand for goods, that is to say $f^{-1}(y_d)$

$$l_d = \text{Min}\{l_d^*(w), f^{-1}(y_d)\} \tag{2.5}$$

When demand y_d is lower than notional supply y_s^*, the rationing the firm experiences on the goods market spills over on to the labour market:[8] in this case, we have: $l_d = f^{-1}(y_d) < l_d^*$. Otherwise, the firm expresses a demand for labour equal to its notional demand. Similarly, the effective goods supply y_s can be obtained by solving the following problem:

Maximize $y - wl$ with respect to $y \geq 0$ and $l \geq 0$ subject to:
$y = f(l)$
$l \leq l_s$

where the quantity constraint falls on the available labour supply. The effective supply is equal to the minimum of the notional supply y_s^* and the quantity that can be produced with the available workforce, that is to say $f(l_s)$

$$y_s = \text{Min}\{y_s^*(w), f(l_s)\} \tag{2.6}$$

When the quantity of labour supplied l_s is lower than the notional demand l_d^*, the rationing prevailing on the labour market is passed on to the goods market; then, the effective goods supply is equal to the full-employment output $f(l_s)$. Otherwise, the goods supply is equal to the notional supply y_s^*.

1.3   Fix-price equilibrium

The previous developments lead us to the following results

$$l_s = \text{Min}\{l_s^*, \hat{l}(y_s - g)\}$$
$$l_d = \text{Min}\{l_d^*, f^{-1}(x_d + g)\}$$

$$y_s = \text{Min}\{y_s^*, f(l_s)\}$$
$$x_d = \text{Min}\{x_d^*, \tilde{x}(l_d)\}$$

For given values of p, s and M_0, notional supplies and demands are fixed. The four equations above form a system with four unknowns: l_s, l_d, y_s and x_d. A solution to this system defines a fix-price equilibrium.

The output y, the employment level l and the consumption level x satisfy the following equations[9]

$$y = \text{Min}\{y_s, y_d\}$$
$$l = \text{Min}\{l_s, l_d\}$$
$$x = \text{Min}\{y_s - g, x_d\}$$

From $x_d = y_d - g$ and $x = y - g$, we can explicitly define the fix-price equilibrium as a solution $(y_d, y_s, l_d, l_s, y, l)$ of the following equation system

$$l_d = \text{Min}\{l_d^*, f^{-1}(y_d)\} \tag{2.7}$$

$$y_d = \text{Min}\{x_d^* + g, \tilde{x}(l_d) + g\} \tag{2.8}$$

$$l_s = \text{Min}\{l_s^*, \tilde{l}(y_s - g)\} \tag{2.9}$$

$$y_s = \text{Min}\{y_s^*, f(l_s)\} \tag{2.10}$$

$$y = \text{Min}\{y_d, y_s\} \tag{2.11}$$

$$l = \text{Min}\{l_d, l_s\} \tag{2.12}$$

Equations (2.7) and (2.8) simultaneously determine the effective demands l_d and y_d; similarly, the equations (2.9) and (2.10) determine the effective supplies l_s and y_s. Finally, equations (2.11) and (2.12) define the level of transactions as the minimum of the supply and demand.

A priori, the equation system (2.7) to (2.12) is likely to admit several solutions and strong hypotheses would be necessary if we aimed at proving the existence and uniqueness of the fix-price equilibrium for any value of the parameters m_0 and w.[10] But, we will confine ourselves to a local reasoning, showing that with sensible hypotheses, a unique fix-price equilibrium exists in the neighbourhood of the Walrasian equilibrium.

Let us first define the Walrasian equilibrium. It is characterized by the equality of supply and demand on each market when the consumer and the firm express their notional supplies and demands. In such conditions, the variables m_0 and w are given by

$$l_s^*(m_0, w) = l_d^*(w) \tag{2.13}$$

$$y_s^*(w) = x_d^*(m_0, w) + g \tag{2.14}$$

Equations (2.13) and (2.14) can be represented in the (m_0, w) plane by respectively increasing and decreasing curves (see figure 2.1). Their

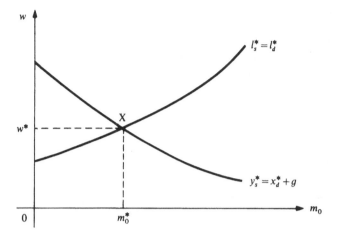

Figure 2.1   Walrasian equilibrium

intersection point is located at the Walrasian equilibrium X whose coordinates are m_0^* and w^*. In this case the price level and the money wage rate are $p^* = M_0/m_0^*$ and $s^* = w^*p^*$. The Walrasian price vector (p^*, s^*) is thus proportional to the initial money stock M_0.

Let $l^* \equiv l_s^*(m_0^*, w^*) \equiv l_d^*(w^*)$ and $y^* \equiv y_s^*(w^*) \equiv x_d^*(m_0^*, w^*) + g$ be the employment and output levels at the Walrasian equilibrium. We also define the following coefficients

$$\alpha^* = \frac{1}{w^*} \frac{\partial \tilde{x}}{\partial l}(m_0^*, w^*, l^*)$$

$$\beta^* = w^* \frac{\partial \tilde{l}}{\partial x}(m_0^*, w^*, l^*)$$

α^* may be interpreted as a marginal propensity to consume earned wages; similarly, β^* may be interpreted as a marginal propensity to supply labour services, when the rationing constraint prevailing on the consumer goods market is altered. Such marginal propensities are evaluated at the Walrasian equilibrium.

In order to establish the existence and unicity of the fix-price equilibrium in the neighbourhood of the Walrasian equilibrium, we will assume

Assumption A: $0 < \alpha^* < 1$; $0 < \beta^* < 1$

Thus, we assume that both propensities are positive and less than 1. Laroque (1978) has shown that assumption A is satisfied if and only if consumption, leisure and the final money holdings are substitutes, in the

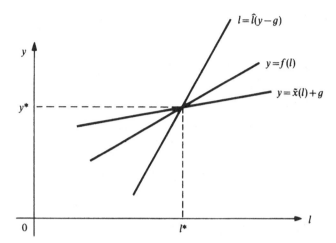

Figure 2.2 Linearization of curves $y=\tilde{x}(l)+g, l=\hat{l}(y-g)$ and $y=f(l)$

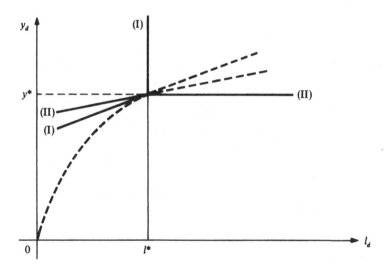

Figure 2.3 Linearization of curves (I) and (II)

conventional meaning of the word.[11] Using A, if $m_0=m_0^*$ and $w=w^*$, the curves $y=\tilde{x}(l)+g$, $l=\hat{l}(y-g)$ and $y=f(l)$, linearized at point (l^*,y^*) are positioned as shown in figure 2.2

Now, consider the curves (I) and (II) representing (2.7) and (2.8), whose intersection defines l_d and y_d. For $(m_0,w)=(m_0^*,w^*)$, the linearization of these curves at point (l^*,y^*) gives figure 2.3.

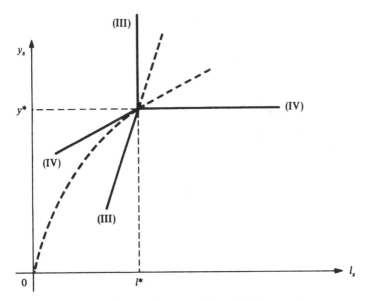

Figure 2.4   Linearization of curves (III) and (IV)

As the curves (I) and (II) move continuously with (m_0,w), their position implies that they admit a unique intersection point, if (m_0,w) is not too different from (m_0^*,w^*) and if we take only into account the intersection points located in the neighbourhood of the Walrasian transactions (l^*,y^*). It is the same for the curves (III) and (IV), representing (2.9) and (2.10), whose intersection determines l_s and y_s (figure 2.4).

The fix-price equilibrium is thus unique if (m_0,w) is not too different from (m_0^*,w^*) and if we impose $(l_d,y_d,l_s,y_s) \in v$ where v is a neighbourhood of the Walrasian solution (l^*,y^*,l^*,y^*). Other solutions for the system (2.7)–(2.12) may exist simultaneously, even with values of (m_0,w) close to (m_0^*,w^*), but the corresponding effective supplies and demands will not be included in the considered neighbourhood v. In that sense we can actually speak of the fix-price equilibrium local uniqueness.[12]

In this section, we have formally defined the fix-price equilibrium and we have also demonstrated its existence and local unicity. However, depending on the nature of the disequilibrium prevailing in the economy, markedly different situations may exist. We will now analyse the characteristics of the different 'disequilibrium regimes'.

2   Disequilibrium regimes

If we confine ourselves in analysing the main disequilibrium regimes, characterized by a strict excess supply or excess demand on each market, we may contemplate four situations. We will use the terminology introduced by Malinvaud (1977) to qualify the different disequilibrium regimes:

1st case: $l = l_d < l_s$ and $y = y_d < y_s$: Keynesian unemployment

2nd case: $l = l_d < l_s$ and $y = y_s < y_d$: classical unemployment

3rd case: $l = l_s < l_d$ and $y = y_s < y_d$: repressed inflation

The last case corresponds to the hypothesis $l_d > l_s$ and $y_d < y_s$, which is quite unlikely to be established. Indeed, it implies an excess demand on the labour market and an excess supply on the goods market: the firm would demand more labour services while the demand for consumption is lower than the supply. The firm would like to produce more than the available workforce allows, while the demand for goods would be perceived as too low. Such a situation is conceivable only if the firm aimed at increasing the volume of production in order to, for instance, stock and sell it in the following period.[13] However, since we assumed that the production sector keeps no stock and that production is meant to be sold in the current period, the situation above is unconceivable. We can easily prove it. Assume $l_d > l_s$ and $y_s > y_d$. From (2.6) and $y_s > y_d$ we obtain $l_s > f^{-1}(y_d)$. Likewise (2.5) and $l_d > l_s$ give $l_s < f^{-1}(y_d)$ which is at variance with the previous inequality. Therefore, only three situations are conceivable: the Keynesian unemployment, the classical unemployment and the repressed inflation. We can characterize these three regimes by writing the definition of employment and output as follows[14]

$$y = \mathrm{Min}\{y_d, y_s^*, f(l_s)\} \tag{2.15}$$

$$l = \mathrm{Min}\{f^{-1}(y_d), l_d^*, l_s\} \tag{2.16}$$

Both equations directly result from the relations (2.7) to (2.12) which define the fix-price equilibrium. Thus, the production y is equal to the minimum of the demand y_d, the notional supply y_s^* and the full-employment output $f(l_s)$. This comes down to saying that the transactions made by the firm maximize its profit under the constraints prevailing on the goods and labour markets.

When Keynesian unemployment prevails, we have $y = y_d$: the firm produces the quantity of goods demanded. For the classical unemployment regime, we have $y < y_d$ and $y < f(l_s)$ – from $l < l_s$ and $y = f(l)$ – which implies $y = y_s^*$: the output is equal to the notional goods supply. Finally, in the case of repressed inflation, we have $y = f(l_s)$: this is a full-employment production. Therefore the three regimes correspond to three possible volumes of production: y_d, y_s^* or $f(l_s)$. Let us now study each regime in detail.

2.1 *Keynesian unemployment*: $l_d < l_s$ and $y_d < y_s; y = y_d$

Keynesian unemployment is characterized by an excess supply on the labour and goods markets: the household is rationed on the labour market,

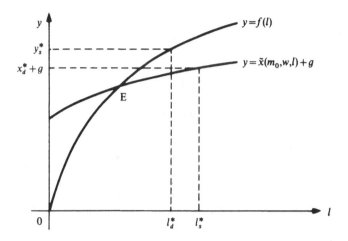

Figure 2.5   Keynesian unemployment equilibrium

owing to insufficient demand on the part of the firm, while the firm is rationed on the goods market because its output is limited by the demand.

In the *General Theory*, Keynes did not actually contemplate the underemployment problem within the context of a general excess supply. While reaffirming 'the first postulate of the classical theory', i.e., the hypothesis of an equal real wage rate and marginal labour productivity, Keynes confines himself to analysing labour market disequilibrium but dismisses the possibility of a disequilibrium on the goods market. However, as we shall see, the description of the disequilibrium regime given in this paragraph will allow us to come across the multiplier mechanism which is the cornerstone of Keynesian theory.

What are the characteristics of this equilibrium? The household, constrained on the labour market, expresses an effective demand equal to its constrained demand $\tilde{x}(m_0,w,l)$. Since, here, output is equal to demand, we have

$$y = \tilde{x}(m_0,w,l) + g \tag{2.17}$$

and also

$$y = f(l) \tag{2.18}$$

(2.17) and (2.18) simultaneously define the employment and output equilibrium values (point E in figure 2.5).

To interpret intuitively such a situation, assume that the fix-price equilibrium is the outcome of a quantity tâtonnement where one agent expresses effective demands at time t as a function of the constraints he

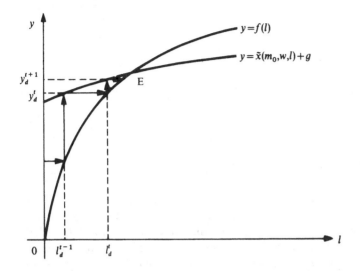

Figure 2.6 Keynesian equilibrium and quantity tâtonnement

perceives at time $t-1$. Assume, for instance, that the household expresses the demand for consumption x_d^t, at time t, taking into account the constraint he perceives on the labour market at time $t-1$, written l_d^{t-1}. Then we have

$$x_d^t = \tilde{x}(m_0, w, l_d^{t-1})$$

The demand for goods y_d^t, the firm perceives at time t, is defined by

$$y_d^t = \tilde{x}(m_0, w, l_d^{t-1}) + g$$

and the firm deduces its demand for labour by

$$l_d^t = f^{-1}(y_d^t)$$

The dynamic evolution of the system is represented in figure 2.6. The positions of the curves, implied by assumption A, ensures the convergence towards the Keynesian equilibrium point E.

Using (2.17) and (2.18), we have

$$y = \tilde{x}(m_0, w, f^{-1}(y)) + g \tag{2.19}$$

which defines the equilibrium output level y. Differentiating (2.19) and considering y as a function of m_0, w and g, we obtain

$$\frac{\partial y}{\partial m_0} = \sigma \frac{\partial \tilde{x}}{\partial m_0} \tag{2.20}$$

$$\frac{\partial y}{\partial w} = \sigma \frac{\partial \tilde{x}}{\partial w} \tag{2.21}$$

$$\frac{\partial y}{\partial g} = \sigma \tag{2.22}$$

where

$$\sigma = \frac{1}{1 - \frac{1}{f'}\frac{\partial \tilde{x}}{\partial l}} > 1$$

Note that σ plays the role of the autonomous demand multiplier of the traditional Keynesian models: for a variation dg in public consumption demand, the variation in the output is equal to σdg. According to (2.20) and (2.21), a rise in real money balances or in the real wage rate causes the equilibrium output level to increase: indeed, such a rise triggers an increased demand for goods on the part of the household, the global effect being obtained by applying the multiplier σ.

Keynesian unemployment occurs when an excess supply prevails on the goods and labour markets simultaneously. The situation is quite different when unemployment exists with an excess demand for goods. Such a fix-price equilibrium is referred to as a classical unemployment.

2.2 Classical unemployment: $l_d < l_s$ and $y_s < y_d; y = y_s^*$

When classical unemployment prevails, the representative firm is rationed on none of the markets: its demand is lower than the supply on the labour market, and its supply of goods is lower than the demand. The quantity constraints do not restrict the volume of the produced output, which is equal to the notional supply of goods. Similarly, the employment level is equal to the notional demand for labour

$$y = y_s^*(w) \qquad l = l_d^*(w) \tag{2.23}$$

The transactions made depend only on the real wage rate. The term 'classical', due to Malinvaud (1977), stems from such a property: a stimulating demand policy – through an increase in public expenditures for instance – is not likely to influence the employment level, because underemployment is due to wage rigidities which limit the profitability of the production sector.[15]

This leads us to distinguish between two clearly separate unemployment types: Keynesian unemployment caused by low aggregate demand, and classical unemployment due to insufficient profitability in the production sector. In this framework, the efficiency of any macroeconomic policy will entirely depend on the kind of unemployment prevailing in the economy: a rise in public expenditures or in households' money holdings will favourably affect the output and employment levels in a Keynesian unemployment situation but will be of no help should the unemployment be classical. With Keynesian unemployment, raising the real wage rate would improve the employment level while the effect is reversed under classical unemployment.

2.3 Repressed inflation: $l_s < l_d$ and $y_s < y_d; y = f(l_s)$

Unlike both other disequilibrium regimes, repressed inflation is characterized by an excess demand for labour. Full employment is achieved and firms are rationed on the labour market where the supply is insufficient. Also, demand exceeds supply on the goods market. We thus have a regime of generalized excess demand. As we shall see, the mechanisms characterizing such a regime are somehow symmetrical to those prevailing in Keynesian unemployment. The household is now constrained on the goods market. So, he expresses a supply of labour equal to his constrained supply $\hat{l}(m_0, w, y - g)$. The employment level l being equal to the labour supply, we have

$$l = \hat{l}(m_0, w, y - g) \tag{2.24}$$

Furthermore, we know that the transactions made (y, l) are linked by the production function

$$y = f(l) \tag{2.25}$$

(2.24) and (2.25) simultaneously determine the employment level l and output y. See figure 2.7, where the equilibrium is reached at point E'.

Here again, interpreting the fix-price equilibrium is easier if we assume that it results from a quantity tâtonnement. Assume that the household sets his supply of labour at time t according to the rationing constraint perceived on the labour market at time $t - 1$. If y_s^t is the goods supply and l_s^t the labour supply at time t, we will write

$$l_s^t = \hat{l}(m_0, w, y_s^{t-1} - g)$$
$$y_s^t = f(l_s^t)$$

Figure 2.8 shows the evolution of l_s^t and y_s^t. The position of the curves implied by assumption A, ensures their convergence towards the equilibrium point E'. At that point, the output level is such that the constraint perceived by the household on the goods market generates a sufficient

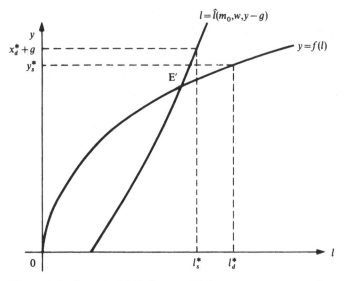

Figure 2.7   Repressed inflation equilibrium

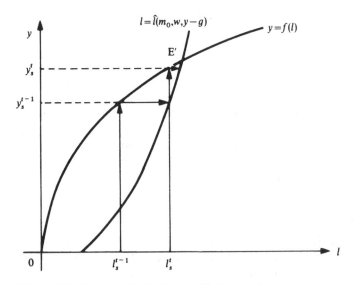

Figure 2.8   Repressed inflation equilibrium and quantity tâtonnement

labour supply to allow an output equal to the initial one. The constraints perceived by agents are then stationary.

(2.24) and (2.25) imply

$$l = \hat{l}(m_0, w, f(l) - g) \tag{2.26}$$

which defines the employment level l as a function of m_0, w and g. Differentiating (2.26) gives

$$\frac{\partial l}{\partial g} = -\rho \frac{\partial \hat{l}}{\partial x} \tag{2.27}$$

$$\frac{\partial l}{\partial m_0} = \rho \frac{\partial \hat{l}}{\partial m_0} \tag{2.28}$$

$$\frac{\partial l}{\partial w} = \rho \frac{\partial \hat{l}}{\partial w} \tag{2.29}$$

where

$$\rho = \frac{1}{1 - f' \dfrac{\partial \hat{l}}{\partial x}} > 1 \tag{2.30}$$

ρ can be considered as a supply multiplier: if we consider an exogeneous variation in the labour supply $d\hat{l}$, the resulting variation in employment is equal to $\rho \, d\hat{l}$. This is to be interpreted this way: a greater available workforce allows an increase in the volume of production which relaxes the rationing constraint on the goods market and therefore causes an additional rise in the labour supply.

Since $\partial \hat{l} / \partial x$ is positive, a rise in the public demand for goods increases the household's rationing which leads it to provide a lower supply of labour. As the sign $\partial \hat{l} / \partial m_0$ is negative, the employment level is a decreasing function of m_0: as consumption is fixed, due to the rationing prevailing on the goods market, a rise in money balances induces an additional demand for leisure and thus a decrease in the labour supply. Finally, a rise in the real wage rate exerts a positive effect on the labour supply and therefore on the employment level.

The repressed inflation regime is thus characterized by a transfer of rationing from demand for consumption to labour supply, creating a supply multiplier effect,[16] the symmetrical version of the demand multiplier in the Keynesian regime. It has been pointed out that the repressed inflation regime may fairly well describe the situation frequently encountered in planned economies such as existed in the USSR: the state's control over prices in addition to a low volume of production led to rationing the consumers, who responded by providing a lower – if not in quantity, at least in quality – supply of labour.[17]

Now that we have described the disequilibrium regimes and their basic properties, we have to determine which type of fix-price equilibrium will be actually achieved with the parameters w, m_0 and g. Thus, we will have to define the conditions of validity of the different disequilibrium regimes.

2.4   *The conditions of validity of the different regimes*

When the fix-price equilibrium belongs to the Keynesian unemployment regime, output satisfies equality (2.19). Since we have $y < y_s^*$ and $y < f(l_s^*)$, (2.19) and assumption A imply

$$y_s^* > \tilde{x}(m_0, w, l_d^*) + g \tag{2.31}$$

and

$$f(l_s^*) > x_d^*(m_0, w) + g \tag{2.32}$$

when (m_0, w) is located in the neighbourhood of the Walrasian equilibrium (m_0^*, w^*).

For a fix-price equilibrium in the classical unemployment regime, we have $y = y_s^* < y_d$ and $l = l_d^* < l_s$, which implies

$$y_s^* < \tilde{x}(m_0, w, l_d^*) + g \tag{2.33}$$

and

$$l_d^* < \hat{l}(m_0, w, y_s^* - g) \tag{2.34}$$

Finally, in the repressed inflation regime, the employment level l is given by (2.26). In this regime, we have: $l < l_d^*$ and $f(l) < x_d^* + g$; therefore the equality (2.26) and assumption A imply

$$l_d^* > \hat{l}(m_0, w, y_s^* - g) \tag{2.35}$$

and

$$f(l_s^*) < x_d^*(m_0, w) + g \tag{2.36}$$

Conditions (2.31) to (2.36) describe the three disequilibrium regimes. For a given public consumption g, they can be represented in the (m_0, w) plane. For that purpose, let us consider the following equalities

$$l_d^*(w) = \hat{l}(m_0, w, y_s^*(w) - g) \tag{2.37}$$

$$y_s^*(w) = \tilde{x}(m_0, w, l_d^*(w)) + g \tag{2.38}$$

$$f(l_s^*(m_0, w)) = x_d^*(m_0, w) + g \tag{2.39}$$

The curves representing the equations (2.37), (2.38) and (2.39) are respectively called C_1, C_2 and C_3; they cross each other at the Walrasian equilibrium $X = (m_0^*, w^*)$ and their slopes are

$$\left. \frac{dw}{dm_0} \right|_{C_1} = - \frac{\dfrac{\partial \hat{l}}{\partial m_0}}{\dfrac{\partial \hat{l}}{\partial w} + \dfrac{\partial l_d^*}{\partial w} \left(w \dfrac{\partial \hat{l}}{\partial x} - 1 \right)} > 0$$

$$\left. \frac{dw}{dm_0} \right|_{C_2} = - \frac{\dfrac{\partial \tilde{x}}{\partial m_0}}{\dfrac{\partial \tilde{x}}{\partial w} + \dfrac{\partial l_d^*}{\partial w} \left(\dfrac{\partial \tilde{x}}{\partial l} - w \right)} < 0$$

$$\left. \frac{dw}{dm_0} \right|_{C_3} = \frac{\dfrac{\partial x_d^*}{\partial m_0} - f' \dfrac{\partial l_s^*}{\partial m_0}}{f' \dfrac{\partial l_s^*}{\partial w} - \dfrac{\partial x_d^*}{\partial w}}$$

C_1 and C_2 are respectively increasing and decreasing but C_3 may be increasing or decreasing. In view of the characteristics of the disequilibrium regimes given above this leads to figure 2.9.

In figure 2.9 the Keynesian regime is characterized by low real money balances and low real wages, which explains the low demand for goods. While classical unemployment implies a high real wage rate, with unemployment being caused by the low profitability of the production sector. Finally, the economy is in the repressed inflation regime when real money holdings are high, while the real wage rate level is rather low: a good profitability and a large demand for goods encourage the firms to express a greater demand for labour than actually supplied.

We may also draw iso-employment curves, i.e., determine the locations of the points (m_0, w), where the employment level is constant. In the Keynesian unemployment regime, the production is defined by (2.19); thus, the iso-employment curve corresponding to an employment $\bar{l}$ is defined by

$$f(\bar{l}) = \tilde{x}(m_0, w, \bar{l}) + g$$

The pairs (m_0, w), which satisfy that quality, are lined up on a downward sloping curve. In the classical unemployment regime, the employment level depends only on the real wage rate. Therefore, in the (m_0, w) plane, the iso-employment curves are horizontal segments of line. Finally, in the repressed inflation regime, the employment level is defined by (2.26); then the iso-employment curve, corresponding to employment $\bar{l}$, writes as

$$\bar{l} = \hat{l}(m_0, w, f(\bar{l}) - g)$$

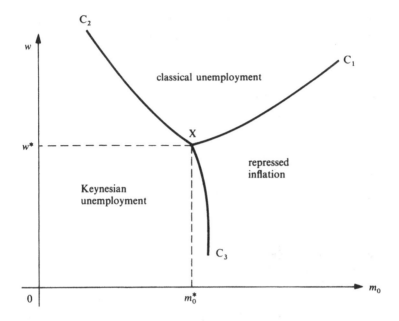

Figure 2.9   Disequilibrium regimes

and the pairs (m_0, w) which satisfy the last equality are lined up on an upward sloping curve.

Thus we obtain figure 2.10, with two iso-employment curves. The arrows indicate the direction of increasing employment, with the maximum level obtained at the Walrasian equilibrium X.

2.5   *Demand shocks and sticky prices*

Figure 2.9 allows us to evaluate the consequences of monetary or real demand shocks when nominal prices are sticky in the short run. Assume first that the economy is at a Walrasian equilibrium corresponding to a given money stock $\bar{M}_0$. This correspond to point X in figure 2.10. Suppose that p and s remain unchanged after an increase in the money supply (i.e., $M_0 > \bar{M}_0$): w is thus unchanged, but $m_0 = M_0/p$ increases. The economy then enters the repressed inflation regime. Conversely Keynesian unemployment prevails if $M_0 < \bar{M}_0$. When the money stock fluctuates around a mean value $\bar{M}_0$ and prices remain fixed at the Walrasian equilibrium corresponding to this mean value, the economy then alternately experiences

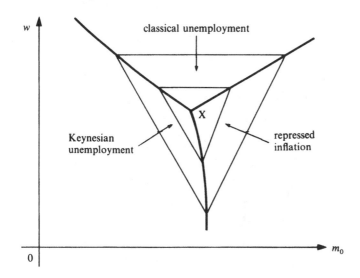

Figure 2.10 Iso-employment curves

repressed inflation and Keynesian unemployment, while the classical unemployment regime is never reached. On the contrary, assume that the real wage rate w is greater than w^* and the price p is such that supply and demand for goods are equal when $M_0 = \bar{M}_0$. Then, the economy undergoes the classical and Keynesian regimes in turn, when M_0 fluctuates in the neighbourhood of $\bar{M}_0$, prices and wages being unchanged.

Likewise, consider the consequences of transitory shocks in real demand[18] brought about say by fluctuations in public consumption around a mean value $\bar{g}$. Let $\bar{X}$ be the Walrasian equilibrium in the (m_0, w) plane that corresponds to $g = \bar{g}$. When g is increasing, C_1, C_2 and C_3 shift to the left. High public consumption thus leads to a new Walrasian equilibrium X_h. Conversely, C_1, C_2 and C_3 shift to the right when g is decreasing: the new Walrasian equilibrium is then at X_l (see figure 2.11). Assume that prices and wages remain at their mean value corresponding to $\bar{X}$ and that public consumption is alternately higher and lower than $\bar{g}$. When public consumption is high, $\bar{X}$ is in the repressed inflation regime while Keynesian unemployment prevails when public consumption is low. Finally, the economy alternately experiences the Keynesian and classical unemployment regimes if real wages were higher than w^* and the price p achieves equality of supply and demand on the goods markets when $g = \bar{g}$, as at point A in figure 2.11.

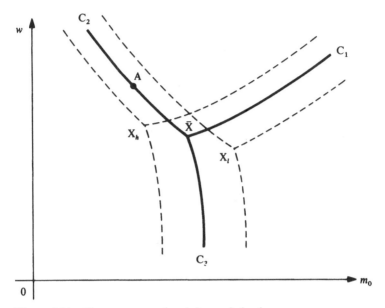

Figure 2.11   Consequences of real demand shocks

3   Wage rigidity and employment

Previously we have taken the money wage rate s and the general price level p to be inflexible: hypothetically, prices and wages were determined in the short run regardless of the tensions between demand and supply in the current period. We now focus on the case where only wages are sticky: the price p is flexible in the short run and makes demand for goods match with supply. If the nominal wage is fixed, an excess demand or supply may appear on the labour market, creating involuntary unemployment. Since that was the solution Keynes considered in the *General Theory*, we will refer to it as the orthodox Keynesian unemployment.

3.1   *Orthodox Keynesian unemployment*

Here, the nominal wage rate s is fixed in the short run, while the price p is set at a level where demand matches supply on the goods market. A simple diagram can show that this underemployment situation appears when the wage rate s is too high.

As $w = s/p = sm_0/M_0$, the pair (m_0, w) is located on a line OD with a slope s/M_0. The equilibrium is reached at the intersection between that line and the curves C_2 and C_3 where demand and supply for goods match. If s is

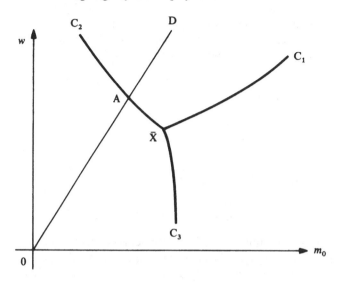

Figure 2.12   Orthodox Keynesian unemployment

larger than s^*, the line OD crosses the curve C_2, equilibrium is reached at point A, involuntary unemployment prevails and the output level is equal to $y_s^*(w)$.[19]

In a situation of orthodox Keynesian unemployment, the employment level depends on money balances and public expenditures: expansionary monetary or fiscal policies are efficient in downplaying unemployment. Indeed, the equilibrium price p is defined by the equality of supply and demand on the goods market, that is to say

$$y_s^*\left(\frac{s}{p}\right) = \tilde{x}\left(\frac{M_0}{p}, \frac{s}{p}, l_d^*\left(\frac{s}{p}\right)\right) + g \tag{2.40}$$

Differentiating this equality gives the variation of the price dp caused by a variation in the initial money holdings dM_0 or by a rise in public expenditures dg

$$\frac{dp}{dg} = \tau \quad \text{and} \quad \frac{dp}{dM_0} = \frac{\tau}{p}\frac{\partial\tilde{x}}{\partial m_0}$$

with

$$\tau = \frac{p^2}{s\dfrac{\partial\tilde{x}}{\partial w} + M_0\dfrac{\partial\tilde{x}}{\partial m_0} - s\dfrac{dy_s^*}{dw}\left(1 - \dfrac{1}{w}\dfrac{\partial\tilde{x}}{\partial l}\right)} > 0$$

A rise in the money stock or in public expenditures generates a rise in the equilibrium price and thus a drop in the real wage rate w. This ultimately stimulates the activity level and reduces involuntary unemployment. We obtain

$$\frac{dy}{dg} = \sigma' \text{ and } \frac{dy}{dM_0} = \frac{\sigma'}{p} \frac{\partial \tilde{x}}{\partial m_0}$$

where σ' is the public expenditure multiplier, defined by

$$\sigma' = \frac{1}{1 - \dfrac{\partial \tilde{x}/\partial l}{w} - \dfrac{(\partial \tilde{x}/\partial w)s + (\partial \tilde{x}/\partial m_0)M_0}{s \dfrac{dy_s^*}{dw}}} > 0$$

As in the Keynesian fix-price equilibrium, the multiplier is positive, but here it may be less or greater than 1. The efficiency of monetary or fiscal policies depends on mechanisms that are completely different in either case. With a Keynesian fix-price equilibrium, greater public expenditures or a rise in the money holdings relax the sales constraint the representative firm perceives. This mechanism is reinforced by the spillover effects on the labour and goods markets, and thus generates a multiplier greater than 1. A rise in the real wage rate would be beneficial, for it would contribute to stimulating the demand for goods. But, on the contrary, under orthodox Keynesian unemployment, monetary and fiscal policies are efficient only because they favour a price rise and thus a drop in the real wage.

3.2   *Rigidity of money wages, near-rationality and menu costs*

Nominal wage rigidity may arise when frequent wage negotiations are costly and detailed contingent wage contracts are unfeasible. In that case, it may be optimal for workers and firms to bargain over simple long-term contracts, that will specify nominal wages for several periods. As shown by Fischer (1977a) and Taylor (1979), the staggering of contract decisions will then entail a certain degree of nominal rigidity which will take a prominent part in the transmission of monetary impulses to economic activity. From this perspective, the literature on near-rationality (Akerlof and Yellen, 1985) and menu costs (Mankiw, 1985) suggests that nominal rigidity may in fact result from small barriers to perfect flexibility of wages or prices, either because inertia in price behaviour only involves small departures from full optimization or because agents bear small costs of changing prices. We will illustrate this approach by incorporating some imperfect competition features into the economy and by showing that price-making agents may conceivably not adjust nominal wages after monetary or real shocks.

We will assume that there exist a large number of localized labour markets. There also exist a continuum of identical firms and a continuum of identical worker-consumers (both of mass one), that are equally shared among the various labour markets. All firms produce the same commodity (whatever the labour market in which they are localized) and they behave competitively. As before, $l_d^*(s/p)$ and $y_s^*(s/p)$ stand respectively for (notional) labour demand and goods supply of a firm, and also for aggregate labour demand and aggregate goods supply when the same wage rate s prevails on all labour markets. Each worker supplies inelastically one unit of labour. The individual utility function is $u_1(x,m)$ if the worker is employed and $u_2(x,m)$ if he is unemployed, where, as before, x and m denote consumption and final real money holdings. For simplicity's sake, initial money holdings are uniformly shared among workers. Goods demand of an employed worker $\tilde{x}_1\left(\dfrac{M_0}{p}, \dfrac{s}{p}\right)$ is obtained from:

Maximize $u_1(x,m)$ with respect to $x \geq 0$ and $m \geq 0$ subject to:

$$x + m = \frac{s}{p} + \frac{M_0}{p}$$

Likewise, an unemployed worker's demand for goods $\tilde{x}_2\left(\dfrac{M_0}{p}\right)$ is given by:

Maximize $u_2(x,m)$ with respect to $x \geq 0$ and $m \geq 0$ subject to:

$$x + m = \frac{M_0}{p}$$

For any employment level l, such that $0 \leq l \leq 1$, the aggregate consumer demand $\tilde{x}$ is thus

$$\tilde{x}\left(\frac{M_0}{p}, \frac{s}{p}, l\right) \equiv l\tilde{x}_1\left(\frac{M_0}{p}, \frac{s}{p}\right) + (1-l)\tilde{x}_2\left(\frac{M_0}{p}\right)$$

The labour markets are supposed to be imperfectly competitive. On each labour market, a monopoly union unilaterally sets the nominal wage rate s. Unions consider the commodity price level as given, since total production of firms within its labour market makes up only an insignificant part of the aggregate output. We let W be the unions' objective function. W is supposed to depend on s, p and M_0. A possible interpretation is to suppose that unions maximize the expected welfare of their members, taking into account the effect of the wage level on the firms' hiring decisions. Assuming that all workers localized in a given labour market are members of the corresponding union, we have

$$W(s,p,M_0)=l_d^*\left(\frac{s}{p}\right)\tilde{u}_1\left(\frac{M_0}{p},\frac{s}{p}\right)+\left(1-l_d^*\left(\frac{s}{p}\right)\right)\tilde{u}_2\left(\frac{M_0}{p}\right)$$

where $\tilde{u}_1$ and $\tilde{u}_2$ respectively stand for the optimal utility level of employed and unemployed workers. Other definitions of the unions' objective function are however possible (see below). We only assume that W is continuously differentiable and also homogeneous of degree zero, so as to preclude any money illusion phenomenon.

Let $s_u(p,M_0)$ be the optimal wage rate chosen by a union, that is the nominal wage rate s that maximizes $W(s,p,M_0)$.

The goods' market equilibrium writes as

$$y_s^*\left(\frac{s}{p}\right)=\tilde{x}\left(\frac{M_0}{p},\frac{s}{p},l_d^*\left(\frac{s}{p}\right)\right)+g$$

This defines the equilibrium price p as a function of s and M_0 that we will write $p_e(s,M_0)$. Observe that $s_u(.)$ and $p_e(.)$ are both homogeneous of degree one.

If unions behave optimally, equilibrium prices and wages are defined by $s=s_u(p,M_0)$ and $p=p_e(s,M_0)$. We will assume that the solution (p,s) of this two-equation system is uniquely defined and satisfies $l_d^*\left(\frac{s}{p}\right)<1$. If (p,s) is an equilibrium associated with M_0, $(\lambda p,\lambda s)$ is also an equilibrium associated with λM_0 for all positive λ: variations in the money stock are thus reflected in proportional variations in equilibrium prices and wages.

Let us now consider a given expected money stock $\bar{M}_0$. We let $\bar{s}$ and $\bar{p}$ be the corresponding equilibrium prices, that is $\bar{s}=s_u(\bar{p},\bar{M}_0)$ and $\bar{p}=p_e(\bar{s},M_0)$. Suppose that an unexpected change in the money stock occurs so that M_0 differs from $\bar{M}_0$. We let ΔW be the welfare loss to a union that continues to choose $\bar{s}$ instead of maximizing W by taking into account the consequences of the shock. Let us show that it may be approximately rational for unions to follow such a rule of thumb (a sticky wage strategy) instead of fully maximizing W. Consider a deviation from an equilibrium where all unions choose $\bar{s}$. In such an equilibrium, we have $p=p_e(\bar{s},M_0)$. Due to the assumption of a large number of labour markets, a deviation from sticky wage behaviour by a single union has insignificant consequences on the equilibrium price level. Since a union that fully maximizes W chooses $s=s_u(p_e(\bar{s},M_0),M_0)$ we have

$$\Delta W = W(s_u(p_e(\bar{s},M_0),M_0),p_e(\bar{s},M_0),M_0) - W(\bar{s},p_e(\bar{s},M_0),M_0)$$

Considering ΔW as a function of M_0, we deduce

$$\left.\frac{d(\Delta W)/W}{dM_0/M_0}\right|_{M_0=\bar{M}_0} = \frac{\partial W}{\partial s}(\bar{s},\bar{p},\bar{M}_0)\frac{ds_u}{dM_0}(\bar{p},\bar{M}_0)\frac{\bar{M}_0}{W}$$

Furthermore, $\bar{s}$ is the optimal wage rate when the price level is $\bar{p}$ and the money stock is $\bar{M}_0$. We thus have

$$\frac{\partial W}{\partial s}(\bar{s},\bar{p},\bar{M}_0)=0$$

which gives

$$\left.\frac{d(\Delta W)/\Delta W}{dM_0/M_0}\right|_{M_0=\bar{M}_0}=0$$

The relative loss to a non-maximizing union over its maximum possible welfare level is thus of second order with respect to the relative variation in money holdings. This is the basis of the near-rationality argument developed by Akerlof and Yellen (1985): here, unions' inertial wage behaviour is suboptimal, but it is not very costly since it imposes very small welfare losses by comparison with full-optimizing behaviour. In that sense, inertial wage behaviour is near rational. Another possible interpretation is to assume that there is a small cost to the union of changing nominal wages (a menu cost). The unions' objective function is then $W(s,p,M_0)-CD$, where C is the menu cost and D is a dummy variable that indicates any change in nominal wages. Previous results then show that wage inertia is optimal for very small levels of the menu cost.

This is illustrated by the following simple example. Here, profits are supposed to be distributed to shareholders within the period so that we can interpret more easily the equilibria as deviations around a stationary equilibrium obtained when $M_0 = \bar{M}_0$. We let $u_1 = u_2 = x^\alpha m^{1-\alpha}, f(l) = l^\beta$ with $0 < \alpha < 1$ and $0 < \beta < 1$. We also assume that unemployed workers receive a compensation equal to $\bar{w}$ in real terms and financed through profit taxation. Finally, we let $g=0$. We then have

$$l_d^* = \left(\frac{s}{p\beta}\right)^{1/\beta-1} \qquad y_s^* = \left(\frac{s}{p\beta}\right)^{\beta/\beta-1}$$

The goods market equilibrium can be written as

$$(1-\alpha)y_s^*\left(\frac{s}{p}\right) = \alpha\frac{M_0}{p}$$

which gives

$$p_e(s,M_0) = \lambda s^\beta M_0^{1-\beta} \text{ with } \lambda = \beta^{-\beta} \left(\frac{\alpha}{1-\alpha}\right)^{1-\beta}$$

For computational simplicity, we will assume that unions maximize the expected labour income, that is

$$W(s,p,M_0) = \frac{s}{p} l_d^* \left(\frac{s}{p}\right) + \bar{w}\left(1 - l_d^*\left(\frac{s}{p}\right)\right)$$

which gives

$$s_u(p,M_0) = \mu p \text{ with } \mu = \bar{w}/\beta$$

We then obtain

$$\bar{p} = \lambda^{1/1-\beta} \mu^{\beta/1-\beta} \bar{M}_0$$
$$\bar{s} = \lambda^{1/1-\beta} \mu^{1/1-\beta} \bar{M}_0$$
$$p_e(\bar{s},M_0) = \lambda^{1/1-\beta} \mu^{\beta/1-\beta} \bar{M}_0^\beta M_0^{1-\beta}$$

Simple calculations then yield the relative welfare loss $\Delta W/W$ associated with inertial wage behaviour as a function of the unexpected rate of growth of the money stock ε, i.e., $M_0 = (1+\varepsilon)\bar{M}_0$. We obtain

$$\frac{\Delta W}{W} = \frac{(1+\varepsilon)^\beta - 1 - \beta\varepsilon}{1-\beta}$$

which gives

$$\left.\frac{d(\Delta W/W)}{d\varepsilon}\right|_{\varepsilon=0} = 0 \tag{2.41}$$

Furthermore, equilibrium real wages are given by

$$w = \frac{\bar{s}}{p_e(\bar{s},M_0)} = \mu(1+\varepsilon)^{\beta-1}$$

and the equilibrium employment level is

$$l = l_d^*(w) = \bar{w}^{1/\beta-1}\beta^{2/1-\beta}(1+\varepsilon) \tag{2.42}$$

From (2.41) and (2.42) the percentage loss in expected labour income $\Delta W/W$ due to non-maximizing unions' behaviour is of second order in terms of monetary shocks, but the employment level fluctuates proportionally to the size of the shocks. Assume for instance $\beta = 0.7$ and consider an increase of the money stock $\varepsilon = 10$ per cent. In that case, inertial wage behaviour entails a loss in expected labour income less than 0.4 per cent.

Assuming a small shift from full maximization or equivalently small menu costs, money shocks may thus generate large business cycles with sticky nominal wages.

3.3 *Wage indexation*

When workers and firms sign long-term contracts, partial or full indexation involves some degree of real wage rigidity and this changes deeply the effects of monetary and real shocks in comparison with an orthodox Keynesian model where wage rigidities are purely nominal. The importance of wage indexation became particularly important in the 1970s when western countries experienced large supply shocks which they had not been accustomed to during the previous decades. Previously, wage indexation had been more or less considered a favourable mechanism. First of all, because it allowed workers to be protected from excessive variations in their purchasing power, but also because it contributed to lessening the macroeconomic real effects of nominal fluctuations. The perspective changed in the 1970s when it became visible that indexation could also exacerbate the instability of economies faced with large supply shocks.

The effects of wage indexation in an economy subject to shocks of different types have been examined by Gray (1976) and Fischer (1977b). They assume that wages are set one period in advance so as to equalize expected labour supply and expected labour demand, but also labour contracts include an indexation clause to be enforced if the actual price does not coincide with the expected one. In their models, indexation always increases the volatility of the price level (measured by its variance) but the effect of indexation on the variance of output depends on the nature of the shocks. Indexation increases the response of output to a productivity shock, because indexing reduces the stabilization effect of real wage flexibility. On the contrary, indexation decreases the real effect of a nominal shock, brought about by an unexpected variation in the money supply, because of its effect on the output price. Thus, if one aims at minimizing the variance of output, wage indexation should be discouraged if the economy mostly experiences real shocks. More generally, there exists an optimal degree of indexation which is a decreasing function of the variance of real shocks relative to that of nominal shocks.

In Gray and Fischer's models, the economy may periodically experience excess labour demand as well as excess labour supply. As we shall see, similar results obtain when involuntary unemployment prevails because nominal wages are chosen so as to reach an exogenously given real wage rate that is larger than the Walrasian level.[20] This will be examined under the following assumptions. The production function of the representative firm is

$$y = \theta l^{\beta} \qquad 0 < \beta < 1$$

where θ is a random productivity shock.

For any variable x, we let $\hat{x} = \text{Log } x$. This gives

$$\hat{l}_d^* = -\frac{1}{1-\beta}\hat{w} + \frac{1}{1-\beta}u + a$$

$$\hat{y}_s^* = -\frac{\beta}{1-\beta}\hat{w} + \frac{1}{1-\beta}u + a$$

where a is a constant and $Eu = 0$, $\text{Var } u \equiv \sigma_u^2$

As in the example of the previous section, assume

$$y_d = \alpha\left(y + \frac{M_0}{p}\right) \qquad 0 < \alpha < 1$$

$$l_s = 1$$

The equilibrium price is then

$$\hat{p} = \beta\hat{s} + (1 - \beta)\hat{M}_0 - u + c \tag{2.43}$$

where c is a constant.

The nominal wage s is chosen one period in advance so as to obtain a given real wage rate w_0 for given price expectations p^e_{-1}. However, wages are allowed to respond to unexpected price variations. This can be written as

$$\hat{s} = \hat{w}_0 + \hat{p}^e_{-1} + \lambda(\hat{p} - \hat{p}^e_{-1}) \tag{2.44}$$

where the coefficient λ is the degree of indexation with $0 \leq \lambda \leq 1$. There is full indexation when $\lambda = 1$ and no indexation when $\lambda = 0$.

The money stock $\hat{M}_0$ is supposed to fluctuate around an average value $\bar{\mu}$. We let

$$\hat{M}_0 = \bar{\mu} + v$$

where v is a random shock such that $Ev = 0$ and $\text{Var } v \equiv \sigma_v^2$.

Lastly, to preclude any exogenous nominal rigidity due to systematic forecasting errors, expectations held in the previous period are supposed to be rational, which gives

$$\hat{p}^e_{-1} = E(\hat{p})$$

Substituting (2.44) into (2.43) and solving for the price level and output gives

$$\hat{p} = \bar{p} + \frac{(1-\beta)v - u}{1 - \beta\lambda} \tag{2.45}$$

$$\hat{y} = \bar{y} + \frac{\beta(1-\lambda)v + u}{1 - \beta\lambda} \tag{2.46}$$

where

$$\bar{p} = \frac{\beta\hat{w}_0 + (1-\beta)\bar{\mu} + c}{1 - \beta}$$

$$\bar{y} = \frac{(1-\beta)a - \beta\hat{w}_0}{1 - \beta}$$

From equation (2.45), a higher indexation (a larger value of λ) increases the variance of the price level whatever the type of shock. Equation (2.46) shows that the effect of indexation on output depends on the nature of the shocks: indexation decreases the real effects of money on output, but it increases the response of output to supply shocks. In particular, full indexation totally annihilates the real response of output to monetary policy, be it expected or not.

To define the optimal degree of indexing, assume that one aims at minimizing the variance of $\hat{y}^* - \hat{y}$, where $\hat{y}^*$ is the output target taken as the Walrasian equilibrium level, that is

$$\hat{y}^* = u - \beta a + a$$

Observe that

$$E(\hat{w}^*) = a(1-\beta)$$

where $\hat{w}^*$ stands for the Walrasian real wage rate. This gives

$$\hat{y}^* - \hat{y} = \frac{\beta}{1 - \beta}[\hat{w}_0 - E(\hat{w}^*)] - \frac{\beta(1-\lambda)v + \beta\lambda u}{1 - \beta\lambda} \tag{2.47}$$

(2.47) provides a decomposition of $\hat{y}^* - \hat{y}$ in two terms: the first one is proportional to the difference between target real wages $\hat{w}_0$ and expected Walrasian real wages $E(\hat{w}^*)$. The second depends on unexpected shocks and on the degree of indexing. Assuming that u and v are uncorrelated, we have

$$\mathrm{Var}(\hat{y}^* - \hat{y}) = \frac{\beta^2(1-\lambda)^2\sigma_v^2 + \beta^2\lambda^2\sigma_u^2}{(1 - \beta\lambda)^2}$$

which is minimized at

$$\lambda^* = \frac{(1-\beta)\sigma_v^2}{(1-\beta)\sigma_v^2 + \sigma_u^2} \tag{2.48}$$

This defines the optimal degree of indexation λ^* which is a decreasing function of the variance of real shocks relative to that of nominal shocks.

3.4   Real wage rigidity and price expectations

Let us now consider the case where it is the intertemporal consumption real wage ω which is fixed in the short run. In our initial model this rate is defined by

$$\omega = \frac{s}{I(p,p^e)} \tag{2.49}$$

where $I(p,p^e)$ stands for a price index, that depends on the current price p and the price p^e which is expected to prevail in the following period. The function $I(.)$ is homogeneous of degree zero and depends on the household's preferences. ω stands for the purchasing power of wages evaluated by consumers, and it is assumed to be rigid in the short run: ω is thus a parameter exogeneously determined. For the moment we will not explain the mechanisms responsible for such a rigidity. In chapter 7, we will develop a similar model where the rigidity of consumption real wages is caused by incentive mechanisms.

Moreover, up to now we have assumed that the expected future price p^e is proportional to the current price p. According to that hypothesis the household's welfare depends on the final money holdings M deflated by the current price p. In general, as shown in chapter 1, the household's welfare depends on the ratio M/p^e, while the expected price p^e depends on the current price p and, possibly, on the other variables observed by households. In this more general setting, we will write consumer utility function as

$$U = U(x,l_0 - l,\bar{m}) \text{ with } \bar{m} = M/p^e$$

where p^e is defined by the function ψ of p and possibly other variables

$$p^e = \psi(p, \ldots)$$

In what follows, we will assume that the expected price depends on the going price but also on the nominal value of the money stock at the beginning of the following period. Therefore, p^e will depend on p but also on $M_1 \equiv (1+\pi)M_0$, where π is the money supply growth rate

$$p^e = \psi(p,M_1) \equiv \psi(p,(1+\pi)M_0) \tag{2.50}$$

We will assume that ψ is homogeneous of degree one, differentiable and increasing with respect to p and M_1. We will also assume that $\psi(p,M_1)/p$ is a non-increasing function of p which means that the expected price elasticity, with respect to the current price, does not exceed one.

A possible explanation of this relation is as follows. Let M_t be the money holdings at the beginning of any period t, and $\pi_t = (M_{t+1} - M_t)/M_t$. Assume that agents believe that at each period t, the equilibrium price p_t is proportional to M_{t+1}, with a coefficient of proportionality X_t which depends on the real conditions of the economy at that period. This coefficient may depend on shocks affecting the firms' productivity, individuals' preferences or public consumption. As we shall see, the proportionality relation will be verified in the current period (i.e., $t=0$): if we multiply M_1 by an arbitrary positive real number μ (by modifying M_0 or π), the equilibrium price $p = p_0$ will be multiplied by μ. Hypothetically, agents believe in the existence of a relation such that

$$p_t = X_t M_{t+1} = X_t(1 + \pi_t)M_t$$

for each period t. In period t, they observe p_t, M_t and π_t and they deduce X_t, but they do not know the exact value of X_{t+1}. At period t, agents will subjectively consider the parameter X_{t+1} as a random variable, whose distribution may be correlated to X_t owing to possible correlations between the shocks affecting technology, preferences or public consumption. Given this belief, if agents have rational expectations, we have

$$p_{t+1}^e = E(X_{t+1} \mid X_t)(1 + \pi_{t+1}^e)M_{t+1}$$

where $E(. \mid X_t)$ stands for the operator of conditional mathematical expectation and p_{t+1}^e and π_{t+1}^e respectively represent the equilibrium price at period $t+1$ and the growth rate of the money holdings from $t+1$ to $t+2$, expected at period t. For each period t, we have

$$p_{t+1}^e = (1 + \pi_{t+1}^e)E\left(X_{t+1} \,\middle|\, \frac{p_t}{M_{t+1}}\right)M_{t+1}$$

At the current period $t=0$, we have: $p = p_0$, $p^e = p_1^e$, $\pi^e = \pi_1^e$ and

$$\psi(p, M_1) = (1 + \pi^e)E\left(X_1 \,\middle|\, \frac{p}{M_1}\right)M_1$$

Thus the function $\psi(.)$ implicitly includes the rate π^e and is homogeneous of degree one. If we assume

$$0 \le \frac{\partial \mathrm{Log}\, E(X_1 \mid X_0)}{\partial \mathrm{Log}\, X_0} \le 1$$

our assumptions on $\psi(\cdot)$ are satisfied and, in particular, the elasticity of price expectations with respect to the current price is inferior or equal to one.[21] This interpretation suggests that the elasticity of price expectations with respect to the current price should be less than one if movements in the current price are due to transitory shocks affecting the real parameters of the economy.

If we let $q = p^e/p$, the consumer's budget constraint writes as

$$x + q\bar{m} = wl + m_0'$$

where m_0' stands for the initial real money holdings after deduction of taxes. The government's budget constraint is

$$M_1 - M_0 = pg - T$$

where T stands for taxes. This gives

$$T = pg - \pi M_0$$

and we have

$$m_0' = m_0 - \frac{T}{p} = (1 + \pi)m_0 - g$$

When unemployment prevails, the constrained consumption demand $\tilde{x}(m_0', w, q, l)$ is obtained by maximizing $U(x, l_0 - l, \bar{m})$ under the budget constraint, considering the employment level as given. We will assume

$$0 < \frac{\partial \tilde{x}}{\partial m_0'} < 1 \; , \; 0 < \frac{1}{w}\frac{\partial \tilde{x}}{\partial l} < 1.$$

Equilibrium on the goods market gives

$$y_s^*(w) = \tilde{x}((1 + \pi)m_0 - g, w, q, l_d^*(w)) + g \tag{2.51}$$

with

$$q = \psi(1, (1 + \pi)m_0) \tag{2.52}$$

$$w = \omega\Gamma(1, (1 + \pi)m_0) \tag{2.53}$$

where function Γ is homogeneous of degree 1 and is defined by

$$\Gamma(p, M_1) \equiv I(p, \psi(p, M_1))$$

(2.51), (2.52) and (2.53) define w, m_0 and q. To ensure the existence and uniqueness of an equilibrium, we assume that the excess demand for goods is a decreasing function of the current price, that is

$$D \equiv \frac{\partial \tilde{x}}{\partial m_0} + \psi_2'\frac{\partial \tilde{x}}{\partial q} + \omega\Gamma_2'\left[\frac{\partial \tilde{x}}{\partial w} - \frac{dy_s^*}{dw}\left(1 - \frac{\partial \tilde{x}/\partial l}{w}\right)\right] > 0$$

with $\Gamma_2' \equiv \partial\Gamma/\partial M_1$ and $\psi_2' \equiv \partial\psi/\partial M_1$.

We can easily check that, in such a model, *a larger creation of money is totally neutral*: if M_0 or π increases the equilibrium price increases so that m_0 and w remain unchanged.[22] Contrary to the orthodox Keynesian unemployment case and to the partial indexation case, monetary shocks do not affect the activity level in this model. In the absence of nominal rigidity, a purely monetary expansionary policy has no effect on the real variables. While, on the other hand, fiscal policy is likely to increase output if the increase in public consumption is perceived as (totally or partially) transitory. We have

$$\frac{dm_0}{dg} = \frac{1}{D(1+\pi)}\left(\frac{\partial \tilde{x}}{\partial m_0'} - 1\right) < 0$$

$$\frac{dw}{dg} = \frac{1}{D}\left(\frac{\partial \tilde{x}}{\partial m_0'} - 1\right)\omega\Gamma_2' \le 0$$

Thus $dw/dg < 0$ if the expected price elasticity with respect to the current price is less than 1 which is a reasonable assumption if the fiscal impulse is transitory. Under this hypothesis, the rise in public expenditures leads to a drop in the real wage rate and ultimately to a rise in the employment level.

Therefore, when the intertemporal consumption real wage rate is rigid, a transitory rise in public expenditures stimulates economic activity. However, the reasons behind the fiscal policy efficiency are quite different from the Keynesian mechanisms. As in neoclassical market clearing models, the efficiency of the fiscal policy is due to the intertemporal substitution effect generated by the increase in public consumption, since, as long as this increase is perceived as transitory, the expected future price does not rise as much as the current price. After a fiscal shock, the production real wage rate decreases and, consequently, the employment level increases even though the intertemporal consumption real wage rate remains stable.

3 Real wages and the inflation–unemployment dilemma

The relationship between inflation and unemployment has been one of the most recurrent themes in the neo-Keynesian macroeconomic literature. In elementary Keynesian models, inflation may result from excess aggregate demand, that can be controlled through manipulating short-run fiscal and monetary policies, thus allowing the avoidance of both alternating disequilibria: unemployment and inflation. The analyses that postulate the existence of a stable Phillips relationship go along the same lines: Phillips' viewpoint (1958), theorized by Lipsey (1960), was that there exists an inverse relationship between unemployment and wage inflation, which only depends on structural parameters related to the degree of imperfection of the labour market. This leads to a relation between the unemployment rate and inflation which takes into account the growth rate of labour productivity, assuming that the share of wages in GNP is constant (Samuelson and Solow, 1960). Therefore, in this framework, economic policies have a double function: in the long run, they can change the terms of the inflation–unemployment dilemma, through structural measures which improve the mobility of workers and provide better information to agents. In the short run, the Phillips' curve defines the price to be paid, in terms of inflation, in order to achieve a certain employment level.

The monetarists were the first to emphasize the inadequacy of this theory, by stressing the instability of the Phillips relationship. In Friedman (1968) and Phelps (1968) analyses, the position of the Phillips curve depends on agents' expectations of the inflation path. In this context, the inflation–unemployment dilemma only intervenes in the short run, that is to say, for given inflation expectations. In the long run, expected and actual inflation rates coincide and the unemployment rate equals the natural rate, which depends on various market imperfections, such as the cost of gathering information about job vacancies and labour availabilities, the cost of mobility or the stochastic variability in demands and supplies. In this respect, reducing the unemployment level at the expense of higher inflation is possible only in the short run, owing to agents price expectations being incorrect. Assuming that agents determine their price expectations by using the available information at best, the rational expectations hypothesis has led the economists of the new classical school – Lucas (1972, 1975), Sargent and Wallace (1975), Barro (1976) – to deny the efficiency of any expansionary policy that can be expected: the output shifts from its equilibrium level, to which corresponds the natural level of unemployment, only if the change in economic policy is unexpected. Even if this rational expectations hypothesis is questionable, because it postulates that agents are endowed with very strong cognitive abilities, it is certainly realistic to assume that agents cannot be systematically fooled, and that their expectations should be fulfilled in the long run. However, we may challenge the assumption, crucial in the new classical approach, according to which competitive prices constantly balance the markets thus maintaining a Walrasian equilibrium. As a matter of fact, the fix-price equilibrium theory, well in accordance with the Keynesian paradigm, refutes such perfect flexibility of prices in the short run. As Tobin (1980) emphasized, it is that issue rather than the expectation-making hypotheses that radically divides the new classical and neo-Keynesian approaches.

If we refute the Walrasian postulate, and we assume that nominal rigidities prevail in the short run, expected macroeconomic policies may be efficient. Furthermore, the non-accelerating inflation rate of unemployment (NAIRU) should also depend on actual mechanisms which determine the intertemporal dynamics of prices and wages. Traditional neoclassical analysis considers this dynamics to be the result of tensions between demand and supply only, which is no doubt oversimplified. In this chapter, we will emphasize the role of real wage rigidity in this dynamics. Besides the empirical observation that real wages are relatively inflexible (typically, they only vary slightly in the business cycle in relation to the fluctuations in output and employment), there are a great deal of theoretical justifications for the insensibility of the real wage rate to the ups and downs of the economy. We will study them in detail in chapters 5 and 6: some are due to the risks shared by employers and workers; others emphasize the incentive role of labour contracts in a context of imperfect information; others contemplate labour contracts as resulting from bargaining between firms and trade unions. Lastly, wages' evolution may also result from decisions taken in the framework of an incomes policy, through the adoption of a minimum legal wage for instance.

If we accept the hypothesis of fixed prices in the short run, likely to vary between periods, there are still interesting questions we should address: What will be the intertemporal trend of macroeconomic equilibria? Will Keynesian or classical unemployment prevail in the long run? What observations can be made about the relationship between inflation and unemployment in an economy with some degree of real wage rigidity? What will be the role of price and income policies in the inflation regulating process?

In the following pages, we will emphasize capital accumulation dynamics and more particularly the relationship between profitability and investment, a question Malinvaud (1980), among others, addressed within a similar context. As we shall see, and it is the main theme of this chapter, wages may run counter to the profitability requirements for a rate of capital accumulation compatible with full employment. In this situation, the wages dynamics is at variance with investors' behaviours and may induce persistent disequilibria. We thus present in the same context short-run disequilibria caused by nominal rigidities and the disequilibria that may result in the long run from the investment behaviour of firms and from the more or less high rigidity of real wages.

We will analyse these mechanisms on the basis of a specific model presented in the first section of this chapter.[1] The second section will discuss the different types of fix-price equilibria likely to prevail in the short run. And the third section addresses the dynamic analysis and the analysis of long-run equilibria.

1   The model

We consider a macroeconomic model with three commodities: money, labour and a single good, which will be alternately regarded as a consumption good and a capital good. There are four types of agents: households, a production sector, a banking sector and the government.

1.1   *Households*

Households will be considered as a single aggregated agent whose behaviour is described by the following equations

$$C = c Y^D + d \frac{M}{p} \qquad 0 < c < 1, d > 0 \tag{3.1}$$

$$Y^D = wL + \Pi - T \tag{3.2}$$

$$L_s = L_0 e^{nt} \tag{3.3}$$

where:
C = real consumption demand,
Y^D = real disposable income,
M = nominal money balances,
p = money price of output,

$w=$ real wage rate,
$L=$ employment level,
$\Pi=$ distributed profits,
$T=$ income taxes,
$L_s=$ labour supply.

In relation (3.1), real consumption demand is postulated to depend linearly on disposable income Y^D together with real money balances M/p. Equation (3.2) defines real disposable income, which consists of wages and distributed profits minus income taxes. (3.3) means that the labour supply grows at a constant rate n.

1.2   The production sector

Here we will assume that returns are constant, and that capital and labour are complementary factors. Let α be the quantity of labour necessary to produce one unit of good and β the output that can be produced with one unit of capital: the production function of the representative firm may thus be written $Y=\text{Min}(L/\alpha,\beta K)$, where output Y depends on employment L and capital stock K.

Let Y_d be the effective demand for goods; Y_d includes consumption demand C, investment demand I and government demand G, so that

$$Y_d=C+I+G$$

Let Y_s and L_d be respectively the effective supply of goods and the effective demand for labour by the representative firm. The firm expresses an effective demand (or supply) on a given market by maximizing its profit, subject to the technological constraint (here the production capacity) and the quantity constraint perceived on the other markets. We also assume that the firm perceives as a constraint the quantity it can actually trade on this market. When the real wage is lower than the productivity of labour, this assumption implies

$$Y_s=\text{Min}\left\{\beta K,\frac{L_s}{\alpha}\right\} \qquad (3.4)$$

$$L_d=\text{Min}\{\alpha Y_d,\alpha\beta K\} \qquad (3.5)$$

If the labour supply L_s is important enough to allow a full utilization of the production capacity $(L_s>\alpha\beta K)$, Y_s is equal to the production capacity βK; otherwise, Y_s is equal to the full-employment output L_s/α. Similarly, if the effective demand for goods Y_d is greater than the production capacity βK, L_d corresponds to an output equal to βK; otherwise, the effective demand for labour corresponds to a production level equal to the effective demand for goods Y_d.

Let us consider now the investing behaviour of the firm. We assume that the firm finances its investment expenditures by borrowing funds from a banking sector at a constant interest rate r, which is exogenously fixed by the monetary authorities. We also define desired production $\bar{Y}$ by

$$\bar{Y} = \text{Min}\{Y_d, L_s/\alpha\} \tag{3.6}$$

$\bar{Y}$ can be interpreted as the quantity the firm wishes to produce – when the wage rate is lower than the productivity of labour: $w < 1/\alpha$ – taking into account the demand for its products and the labour supply but ignoring its production capacity. The investment demand will be assumed to depend on the desired output $\bar{Y}$, the capital stock K and the cost variables w, r

$$I = I(\bar{Y}, K, w, r) \tag{3.7}$$

with $I'_1 > 0, I'_2 < 0, I'_3 < 0, I'_4 < 0$. Function $I(.)$ is supposed to be homogeneous of degree one with respect to $(\bar{Y}, K)$, such that $I(\bar{Y}, K, w, r) > 0$ only if $w < 1/\alpha$ (a positive investment may occur only when the real wage rate is lower than the productivity of labour, and thus profits are positive). In relation (3.7), the variables $\bar{Y}$ and K define a lack of production capacity (when $\bar{Y} > \beta K$) or an overcapacity state (when $\bar{Y} < \beta K$), while the variables w and r characterize the profitability of investment. For unchanged values of $\bar{Y}$, K and r, an increase in the real wage decreases the demand for investment. Note that a positive investment $(I > 0)$ may be compatible with overcapacity $(\bar{Y} < \beta K)$ if w and r have low enough values.

These hypotheses were justified by Malinvaud (1980) in a model with uncertainty about future goods demand and future labour supply. In Malinvaud's model, when profitability is attractive enough, investing firms more easily run the risk of excess capacity in the future. This justifies the influence of profitability (and thus of the real wage rate) on investment, and explains why the firm is interested in investing in new equipment, even if it has an excess capacity in the current period. Malinvaud's result is presented in appendix 1. This appendix also develops another justification for relation (3.7). We assume that the production sector consists of a great number of identical firms presenting indivisibilities and it is possible to create new firms. In this case, the investment mechanism is based on a non-cooperative decision-making process by investors: even with an excess production capacity, creating new firms can be individually profitable if the real wage rate and the cost of capital are sufficiently low.

1.3   *The government and the banking sector*

Let G be government consumption demand. To finance its expenditures the government collects taxes and issues new money. The government budget constraint may then be written

$$G = T + \dot{M}_G/p$$

where $\dot{M}_G$ is the money creation necessary to finance the government budget deficit.

We assume that private investments are exclusively financed by borrowing funds from the banking sector. Hence, we have

$$\dot{M}_I/p = I - D$$

where $\dot{M}_I/p$ is the net money creation (in real terms) corresponding to the financing of private investment and D is the amount of interest payments of the current debt.

The total money creation may then be written as

$$\frac{\dot{M}}{p} = \frac{\dot{M}_G}{p} + \frac{\dot{M}_I}{p} = G + I - (T + D) \tag{3.8}$$

For simplicity's sake, we will assume that the government chooses the income tax rate to stabilize the total deduction from private revenue $T + D$ at a given proportion τ of the output Y. This assumption implies

$$\dot{M}/p = G + I - \tau Y \tag{3.9}$$

The distributed profits Π are equal to the output Y minus the wages wL and the interest payments D

$$\Pi = Y - wL - D$$

The disposable income is thus defined by

$$Y^D = wL + \Pi - T = Y - (D + T) = (1 - \tau)Y$$

For given values of the investment demand I and the output Y, the government can either fix the level of its expenditures G, or the total money creation $\dot{M}/p$. We shall assume that the government chooses a constant nominal growth rate of the money balances $\theta = \dot{M}/M$. From (3.9) the firms and the government's total demand for goods is then endogenously defined by

$$I + G = \tau Y + \theta \frac{M}{p} \tag{3.10}$$

Relation (3.10) implies

$$Y_d = C + I + G = [c(1 - \tau) + \tau]Y + (\theta + d)\frac{M}{p}$$

so that the government controls 'autonomous demand' by controlling the growth rate of the money balances θ.

2   Fix-price equilibria

In the previous section we defined the effective demands and supplies on labour (L_d,L_s) and on goods markets (Y_d,Y_s). Now, we assume that the transactions made on each market are equal to the minimum of demand and supply

$$Y = \text{Min}\{Y_d,Y_s\} = \text{Min}\{Y_d,\beta K,L_s/\alpha\} \tag{3.11}$$

$$L = \text{Min}\{L_d,L_s\} = \text{Min}\{\alpha Y_d,\alpha\beta K,L_s\} \tag{3.12}$$

Three disequilibrium regimes may occur: Keynesian unemployment, classical unemployment and repressed inflation.[2]

2.1   Keynesian unemployment: $Y = Y_d$

In the Keynesian case, there is an excess supply on both markets: $Y_d \leq Y_s$ and $L_d \leq L_s$. Consumers are rationed on the labour market and the firms on the goods market; Y is defined by

$$Y = C + I + G = c(1-\tau)Y + d\frac{M}{p} + \tau Y + \theta\frac{M}{p}$$

Let $\sigma = 1/[1 - c(1-\tau) - \tau]$ be the Keynesian multiplier. We have

$$Y = \sigma(d+\theta)\frac{M}{p} \tag{3.13}$$

The conditions of validity of Keynesian unemployment are defined by the requirements $Y \leq Y_s, L \leq L_s$, which can be written here as

$$\sigma(d+\theta)\frac{M}{p} \leq \beta K \tag{3.14}$$

$$\sigma(d+\theta)\frac{M}{p} \leq \frac{L_s}{\alpha} \tag{3.15}$$

2.2   Classical unemployment: $Y = \beta K$

Classical unemployment prevails when there is an excess demand on the goods market and an excess supply on the labour market: $Y_s \leq Y_d$ and $L_d \leq L_s$. Thus consumers are rationed on both markets, and the output level is equal to the production capacity βK.

In the case of classical unemployment, effective demand Y_d is defined by

$$Y_d = [c(1-\tau)+\tau]\beta K + (d+\theta)\frac{M}{p}$$

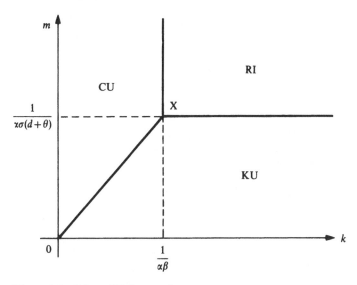

Figure 3.1   Disequilibrium regimes

The conditions of validity of classical unemployment, namely $Y \leq Y_d$ and $L \leq L_s$, may then be written as follows

$$\sigma(d+\theta)\frac{M}{p} \geq \beta K \tag{3.16}$$

$$\alpha\beta K \leq L_s \tag{3.17}$$

2.3   Repressed inflation: $Y = L_s/\alpha$

In the regime of repressed inflation, there is an excess demand on both markets: $Y_s \leq Y_d$ and $L_s \leq L_d$. Firms are rationed on the labour market, and consumers on the goods market. Repressed inflation implies $Y \leq Y_d$ and $L \leq L_d$, two conditions that can explicitly be written as

$$\alpha\sigma(d+\theta)\frac{M}{p} \geq L_s \tag{3.18}$$

$$\alpha\beta K \geq L_s \tag{3.19}$$

In order to represent the conditions of validity of the different regimes, we define variables per capita by $k = K/L_s$ and $m = M/pL_s$. Using conditions (3.14) to (3.19), the regions of Keynesian unemployment (KU), classical unemployment (CU) and repressed inflation (RI) can be represented in the (k,m) plane (see figure 3.1). Keynesian unemployment corresponds to high

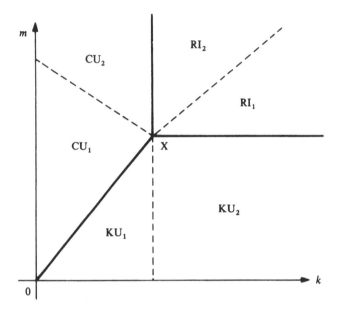

Figure 3.2   Sub-regimes

values of capital stock and to low values of real money balances, so that unemployment prevails with an excess capacity of production because of an insufficient demand for goods. Classical unemployment corresponds to the symmetrical case: there is an excess demand on the goods market because of an insufficient stock of capital and important money balances. Repressed inflation involves high values of the stock of capital and households' money holdings.

It will be useful, for what follows, to distinguish sub-regimes in KU, CU and RI, according to the values of Y_s, L_d and $\bar{Y}$ (see figure 3.2).

In KU, we always have $L_d = \alpha Y_d$ and $\bar{Y} = Y_d$, but Y_s may be equal to βK or L_s/α. We shall introduce two sub-regimes in the Keynesian region KU by

$$KU_1 = \{(m,k) \in KU, k \le 1/\alpha\beta\}$$
$$KU_2 = \{(m,k) \in KU, k \ge 1/\alpha\beta\}$$

The effective supply of goods Y_s is equal to the production capacity βK in KU_1 and to a full-employment production in KU_2.

In CU, we always have $Y_s = \beta K$ and $L_d = \alpha\beta K$, but $\bar{Y}$ may be equal to Y_d or to L_s/α; in CU, Y_d is defined by

$$Y_d = c'\beta K + (d + \theta)\frac{M}{p} \text{ with } c' = c(1 - \tau) + \tau$$

The sub-regimes CU_1 and CU_2 may then be defined by

$$CU_1 = \{(m,k) \in CU, c'\beta k + (d+\theta)m \le 1/\alpha\}$$
$$CU_2 = \{(m,k) \in CU, c'\beta k + (d+\theta)m \ge 1/\alpha\}$$

The desired output $\bar{Y}$ is equal to Y_d in CU_1 and to L_s/α in CU_2. Finally, in RI, we always have $Y_s = \bar{Y} = L_s/\alpha$, but L_d may be equal to $\alpha\beta K$ or to αY_d. In RI, Y_d is defined by

$$Y_d = \frac{c'L_s}{\alpha} + (d+\theta)\frac{M}{p}$$

and RI_1, RI_2 are defined by

$$RI_1 = \{(m,k) \in RI, c'/\alpha + (d+\theta)m \le \beta k\}$$
$$RI_2 = \{(m,k) \in RI, c'/\alpha + (d+\theta)m \ge \beta k\}$$

L_d is equal to αY_d in RI_1 and to $\alpha\beta K$ in RI_2.

In figures 3.1 and 3.2, point X defines a Walrasian equilibrium, where demand and supply are equal on both markets and no agent is rationed.

3 Dynamic analysis

The model will be formulated in continuous time, and for any variable depending on time $x(t)$, we will write $\dot{x} \equiv dx/dt$. The adjustment conditions for prices and money wages will be specified as follows

$$\frac{\dot{s}}{s} = \lambda\left(\frac{L_d - L_s}{L_d}\right) + \gamma_1\pi + \delta(w_0 - w) \quad \lambda > 0, 0 \le \gamma_1 \le 1, \delta > 0 \tag{3.20}$$

$$\frac{\dot{p}}{p} = \mu\left(\frac{Y_d - Y_s}{Y_d}\right) + \gamma_2\pi \quad \mu > 0, 0 \le \gamma_2 \le 1 \tag{3.21}$$

where s stands for the money wage rate and π is the expected inflation rate.

As in traditional neo-Keynesian macroeconomic models, the tensions between the supply and demand as well as the expected inflation rate intervene as variables explaining the price and wage dynamics. Furthermore, the money wage rate is assumed to evolve so that the real wage rate w gets closer to a certain objective real wage w_0. In the equation (3.20), $\delta(w_0 - w)$ thus introduces a non-competitive mechanism expressing some degree of real wage rigidity.

Since the real wage rate w is equal to s/p, we have

$$\frac{\dot{w}}{w} = \lambda\left(\frac{L_d - L_s}{L_d}\right) + \delta(w_0 - w) - \mu\left(\frac{Y_d - Y_s}{Y_d}\right) + (\gamma_1 - \gamma_2)\pi \tag{3.22}$$

We will assume that the expected inflation rate π is equal to the long-run inflation rate. Expectations are thus rational in the long run. In what follows, such an inflation rate will be equal to the growth rate of the money balances (per capita), so that we have

$$\pi = \theta - n \tag{3.23}$$

Let us introduce notations per capita by

$$y = \frac{Y}{L_s}, y_s = \frac{Y_s}{L_s}, y_d = \frac{Y_d}{L_s}, \bar{y} = \frac{\bar{Y}}{L_s}, l_d = \frac{L_d}{L_s}$$

Dynamics is then characterized by[3]

$$\dot{w} = w \left[\lambda \left(\frac{l_d - 1}{l_d} \right) + \delta(w_0 - w) - \mu \left(\frac{y_d - y_s}{y_d} \right) + (\gamma_1 - \gamma_2)(\theta - n) \right] \tag{3.24}$$

$$\dot{m} = m \left[(1 - \gamma_2)(\theta - n) - \mu \left(\frac{y_d - y_s}{y_d} \right) \right] \tag{3.25}$$

$$\dot{k} = k \left[I \left(\frac{\bar{y}}{k}, 1, w, r \right) - n \right] \tag{3.26}$$

All terms in the right-hand side of (3.24), (3.25) and (3.26) can be regarded as continuous functions of (w, m, k), and this system can be written as follows

$$\dot{w} = R(w, m, k)$$
$$\dot{m} = S(w, m, k) \qquad (S)$$
$$\dot{k} = T(w, m, k)$$

where R, S and T are continuous functions.[4]

A balanced growth path will correspond to a stationary point of (S); at this point the stock of capital K and real money balances M/p (and thus the output and the employment level) are growing at the natural rate n, and the real wage rate is constant. So, on a balanced growth path, real variables are growing at the same rate while relative prices are constant, a definition corresponding to the concept of the generalized quasi-equilibrium introduced by Hansen (1951).

A general characterization of these stationary states is provided in appendix 2. In this section, we will confine ourselves to two extreme cases: in proposition 3.1, expected inflation is supposed to be completely transferred into money wage and price increases ($\gamma_1 = \gamma_2 = 1$). The opposite case is considered in proposition 3.2 where we assume $\gamma_1 < 1$ and $\gamma_2 < 1$. In each case, we give a sufficient condition for the existence and uniqueness of the stationary state; we also characterize the corresponding fix-price equilibrium. Finally proposition 3.3 gives a sufficient condition for the stability of the balanced growth path. In these propositions, we introduce

$\bar{w}(r)$, a value of the real wage rate defined by

$$I(\beta,1,\bar{w}(r),r)=n$$

$\bar{w}(r)$ is the value of the real wage rate for which the investment rate I/K is equal to the natural growth rate n, when the desired output $\bar{Y}$ is equal to the production capacity βK.[5] As in Malinvaud's model (1980), where a similar parameter is introduced, $\bar{w}(r)$ defines an *appropriate income distribution* as a consequence of investment behaviour.

> *Proposition 3.1* Assume $\gamma_1=\gamma_2=1$. If w_0 belongs to a neighbourhood of $\bar{w}(r)$, (S) has a unique stationary point $s^*=(w^*,m^*,k^*)$, which coincides with the Walrasian equilibrium $(\bar{w}(r),X)$ when $w_0=\bar{w}(r)$. Furthermore,
>
> when $w_0>\bar{w}(r)$, $(m^*,k^*)\in KU\cap CU$
> when $w_0<\bar{w}(r)$, $(m^*,k^*)\in KU\cap RI$
>
> *Proposition 3.2* Assume $\gamma_1<1$ and $\gamma_2<1$. If (θ,w_0) belongs to a neighbourhood of $(n,\bar{w}(r))$, (S) has a unique stationary point $s^*=(w^*,m^*,k^*)$, which coincides with the Walrasian equilibrium $(\bar{w}(r),X)$ when $(\theta,w_o)=(n,\bar{w}(r))$. Furthermore,
>
> when $w_0>\bar{w}(r)$, $(m^*,k^*)\in KU$ if $\theta\leq n$
>
> $(m^*,k^*)\in CU$ if $\theta\in\left[n,n+\dfrac{\delta(w_0-\bar{w}(r))}{1-\gamma_1}\right]$
>
> $(m^*,k^*)\in RI$ if $\theta\geq n+\dfrac{\delta(w_0-\bar{w}(r))}{1-\gamma_1}$
>
> when $w_0\leq\bar{w}(r)$, $(m^*,k^*)\in KU$ if $\theta\leq n$
> $(m^*,k^*)\in RI$ if $\theta\geq n$

Proofs of propositions 3.1 and 3.2 are given in appendix 2.

When the expected rate of inflation has a unit coefficient in the price and wage adjustment equations, proposition 3.1 states the existence and uniqueness of a stationary state – for values of w_0 not too different from $\bar{w}(r)$ – and characterizes the corresponding fix-price equilibrium. In this case, when the target real wage rate w_0 is greater than the appropriate real wage rate $\bar{w}(r)$, the steady state lies on the boundary between KU and CU, so that an excess supply prevails on the labour market while the goods market is balanced. Full employment is realized when w_0 is inferior or equal to $\bar{w}(r)$; then the stationary state is located on the boundary between KU and RI, and both markets are cleared. So, in this first case, the relative positions of

w_0 and $\bar{w}(r)$ are sufficient to characterize the stationary state and this characterization does not depend on the growth rate of the money supply.

Proposition 3.2 presents the case where coefficients γ_1 and γ_2 are strictly less than 1. Then, for values of (θ, w_0) not too different from $(n, \bar{w}(r))$, a unique quasi-equilibrium still exists. However, unlike the previous case, the characterization of the corresponding fix-price equilibrium now depends on the growth rate of the money supply: the monetary policy is no longer neutral and determines the disequilibrium regime which prevails in the long run. The stationary state coincides with the Walrasian equilibrium $(\bar{w}(r), X)$ when $\theta = n$ and $w_0 = \bar{w}(r)$. When w_0 is greater than $\bar{w}(r)$, the balanced growth path corresponds to Keynesian unemployment for a low growth rate of the money balances θ; for intermediate values of θ, it corresponds to a situation of classical unemployment and the region of the repressed inflation is reached only with high values of θ. Furthermore, the more important is the gap between w_0 and $\bar{w}(r)$, the higher is the minimum value of θ at which a stationary situation of full employment occurs. When w_0 is less than $\bar{w}(r)$, no stationary point appears in the region of classical unemployment, and the balanced growth path is either in the Keynesian unemployment region (when $\theta \le n$) or in the repressed inflation region (when $\theta \ge n$). These results confirm the idea according to which classical unemployment occurs when the target real wages are 'too high', a conclusion which rests here upon the investment mechanism and character-izes the stationary states of a dynamic model.

We now turn to the question of the stability of balanced growth paths. System (S) is of order 3, and a complete study of its stability would be complex. However, proposition 3.3 gives a simple sufficient condition for asymptotic stability when the stationary state lies in the neighbourhood of the Walrasian equilibrium $(\bar{w}(r), X)$.

> *Proposition 3.3*   If $\lambda < \mu$, and if (θ, w_0) belongs to a neighbourhood of $(n, w(r))$, any interior[6] stationary point of (S) is asymptotically stable.

Proof   See appendix 2.

In proposition 3.3, the assumption that $\lambda < \mu$ illustrates the idea according to which *wages are relatively more rigid than prices*: an increase in excess demand has a more important effect on the growth rate of the output price (in case of a demand for goods) than on the growth rate of money wages (in the case of a demand for labour). This assumption allows us to prove the asymptotic stability of stationary equilibria that do not differ too much from the Walrasian equilibrium.

So far, we have studied the different types of balanced growth paths that can prevail in the economy, and we have given a sufficient condition for their stability in the neighbourhood of the Walrasian equilibrium. We now turn to an analysis of the relation between the inflation rate and the unemployment rate, evaluated at these steady states. For the sake of brevity, we shall consider only the case $w_0 > \bar{w}(r)$. We first assume $\gamma_1 < 1$ and $\gamma_2 < 1$. We know from proposition 3.2 that unemployment stationary states may occur in KU or CU, according to the growth rate of the money supply. However, we can be more precise and show the following results:

(a) If $\lambda < -I_1' \beta \delta / I_3'$, the stationary state belongs to the sub-regime KU_1 when $\theta \le n$.

(b) The stationary state belongs to the sub-regime CU_1 (CU_2) when $n \le \theta \le \hat{\theta}$ (when $\hat{\theta} \le \theta \le n + [\delta(w_0 - \bar{w}(r))]/(1 - \gamma_1)$), where $\hat{\theta}$ satisfies $n < \hat{\theta} < n + [\delta(w_0 - \bar{w}(r))]/(1 - \gamma_1)$.

Assertions (a) and (b) are proved in appendix 2 (see remarks 2 and 3). In what follows, we will assume $\lambda < -I_1' \beta \delta / I_3'$, so that the stationary state belongs successively to KU_1, CU_1, CU_2 and RI when the growth rate of the money supply is increasing. The relationship between the inflation rate and the unemployment rate will be evaluated separately for each regime. Then, using (a) and (b), we will be able to describe the global inflation–unemployment trade-off that characterizes the economy.

On a balanced growth path, the inflation rate π is equal to $\theta - n$. Using the relations (3.23), (3.25) and the condition $\dot{m} = 0$, we deduce

$$\pi = \frac{\mu}{1 - \gamma_2} \left(\frac{y_d - y_s}{y_d} \right) \tag{3.27}$$

Let $u = 1 - l$ be the unemployment rate, evaluated at the stationary state. In KU or CU, we have $l = l_d$. Using (3.24), (3.27) and the condition $\dot{w} = 0$, we obtain

$$\pi = -\frac{\lambda}{1 - \gamma_1} \left(\frac{u}{1 - u} \right) + \frac{\delta}{1 - \gamma_1} (w_0 - w) \tag{3.28}$$

Consider a balanced growth path located in KU_1 or CU_1. From (3.27) and $y_s = \beta k$, we have

$$\frac{y_d}{k} = \frac{\mu \beta}{\mu - (1 - \gamma_2)\pi} \tag{3.29}$$

Since in this case $\bar{y} = y_d$, we deduce from (3.26), (3.29) and condition $\dot{k} = 0$ that

$$I\left[\frac{\mu \beta}{\mu - (1 - \gamma_2)\pi}, 1, w, r \right] = n \tag{3.30}$$

By eliminating w in (3.28)–(3.30) we deduce

$$I\left[\frac{\mu\beta}{\mu-(1-\gamma_2)\pi},1,w_0-\frac{\lambda}{\delta}\left(\frac{u}{1-u}\right)-\frac{(1-\gamma_1)\pi}{\delta},r\right]=n \qquad (3.31)$$

which results in a relation between u and π that writes as

$$\pi=\hat{\pi}_1(u) \qquad \text{with } \hat{\pi}'_1<0$$

Let us now examine the case of a balanced growth path located in CU_2. In this case, $\bar{y}=1/\alpha$; using (3.26) and condition $\dot{k}=0$, we obtain

$$I\left(\frac{1}{\alpha k},1,w,r\right)=n \qquad (3.32)$$

and $u=1-l=1-\alpha\beta k$ implies

$$I\left(\frac{\beta}{1-u},1,w,r\right)=n \qquad (3.33)$$

By eliminating w in (3.28)–(3.33), we obtain

$$I\left[\frac{\beta}{1-u},1,w_0-\frac{\lambda}{\delta}\left(\frac{u}{1-u}\right)-\frac{(1-\gamma_1)\pi}{\delta},r\right]=n \qquad (3.34)$$

which results in a relation between u and π that writes as

$$\pi=\hat{\pi}_2(u) \qquad \text{with } \hat{\pi}'_2<0$$

By using (a) and (b), we obtain a global Phillips curve through a 'patching up' of the curves corresponding to $\hat{\pi}_1$ and $\hat{\pi}_2$.

When $\pi=0$, the balanced growth path lies on the frontier between KU_1 and CU_1; the unemployment rate is then equal to $\bar{u}$, with

$$\bar{u}=\hat{\pi}_1^{-1}(0)=\frac{\delta[w_0-\bar{w}(r)]}{\lambda+\delta[w_0-\bar{w}(r)]} \qquad (3.35)$$

When $\gamma_1\rightarrow1$ and $\gamma_2\rightarrow1$, the Phillips curve turns round the point $(\bar{u},0)$, and is vertical when $\gamma_1=\gamma_2=1$: in such a situation, a change in the growth rate of the money supply exerts no influence on the real economic activity in the long run, and there is no more trade-off between unemployment and inflation. As shown in (3.35), the long-run unemployment rate is an increasing function of the difference between target and appropriate wages $w_0-\bar{w}(r)$.

Intermediate cases are represented in figures 3.4 and 3.5. When $\gamma_1<1$ and $\gamma_2=1$, condition $\dot{m}=0$ is equivalent to $y_d=y_s$, so that any unemployment steady state is located on the boundary between KU_1 and CU_1. In such a case, the Phillips curve is defined by the function $\hat{\pi}_1$ for any value of the

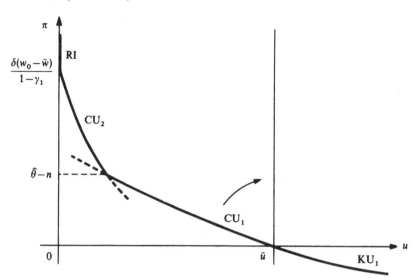

Figure 3.3 Phillips curve

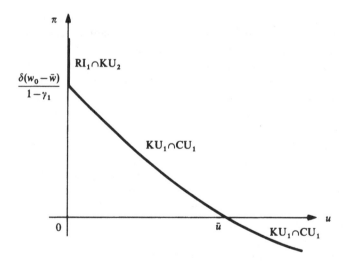

Figure 3.4 Case $\gamma_1 < 1$; $\gamma_2 = 1$

unemployment rate. Lastly, when $\gamma_1 = 1$ and $\gamma_2 < 1$, the Phillips curve is vertical when the steady state belongs to CU_2 and the repressed inflation regime can no longer be reached.

This shows how the long-run coexistence of inflation and unemployment can result from the incompatibility between the goals of an incomes policy

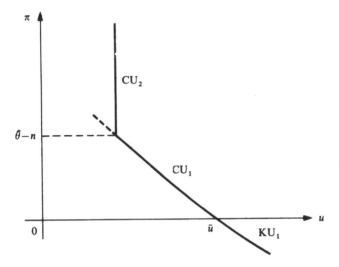

Figure 3.5   Case $\gamma_1 = 1$; $\gamma_2 < 1$

(which amounts here to the choice of the target real wage rate w_0) and investors' behaviours. In this model, the intensity of the dilemma between inflation and employment, represented by the Phillips' curve, is directly related to the difference between the target real wage and the appropriate wage. When inflation expectations do not completely affect the wage rate growth ($\gamma_1 < 1$), the minimum inflation rate we have to accept, in order to obtain a balanced full-employment growth path, is actually equal to $\delta(w_0 - \bar{w})/(1 - \gamma_1)$; when the coefficients γ_1 and γ_2 are equal to 1 unemployment is at its natural level $\bar{u}$ for any value of the inflation rate, but this natural level is an increasing function of the wage gap $w_0 - \bar{w}(r)$. In that case, $w = \bar{w}(r)$ at the stationary equilibrium so that the only long-run effect of a rise in target real wages w_0 (or in the adjustment speed coefficient δ) would be an increase in the long-run unemployment rate $\bar{u}$, without any durable wage/profit redistributive effect.

Thus, this model shows how important it is to concieve coherent income and monetary policies respectively symbolized by w_0 and θ and r. Of course, constraints limit planners in their choices of the target wage and the interest rate. As a matter of fact, in market economies the standard wage w_0 generally results more from labour contracts, freely negotiated between employers and employees than from public income policies. Similarly, various constraints that could be elaborated on in a more complex model, actually limit planners' choices concerning the interest rate. Therefore, it is not really easy to reduce the gap between the target wage w_0 and the appropriate wage $\bar{w}(r)$, but this should certainly be a priority for any long-run macroeconomic policy.

Appendix 1 Investment and profitability

We can adopt Malinvaud's approach (1980) to justify the investment function postulated in this chapter. It consists of describing the behaviour of the firm in a situation of uncertainty, assuming that it is imperfectly informed of the quantity constraint (goods demand and labour supply) that will limit its output in the future.

For simplicity's sake, we will here drop the continuous time formulation. Let us suppose that the capital goods acquired in period t become productive only in period $t+1$: thus, we have $K^{t+1} = K^t + I^t$. Let us also assume that the investment is financed by a bank loan at a rate r, and reimbursed the following period.

The firm is supposed to be risk-neutral: in period t investment I^t is chosen in order to maximize the expected profit of period $t+1$. This future profit is written Π^{t+1} in real terms. By adding the disposable capital to the profit margin obtained in period $t+1$, we have

$$\Pi^{t+1} = (1 - \alpha w_e^{t+1}) Y_e^{t+1} - rK^{t+1} \tag{3.36}$$

where w_e^{t+1} and Y_e^{t+1} stand respectively for the real wage rate and the output of period $t+1$ as expected at period t. We have

$$Y_e^{t+1} = \text{Min}\{ \bar{Y}_e^{t+1}, \beta K^{t+1} \}$$

where $\bar{Y}_e^{t+1}$ stands for the expected desired output of period $t+1$. We assume that, in period t, $\bar{Y}_e^{t+1}$ is a random variable whose distribution depends on the output desired in the current period $\bar{Y}^t = \text{Min}\{ Y_d^t, L_s^t/\alpha \}$. For simplicity, we assume that the firm does not expect any variations in the real wage rate, thus we have: $w_e^{t+1} = w^t$, with probability one. Expected profit can be written

$$E\Pi^{t+1} = (1 - \alpha w^t) E[\text{Min}\{ \bar{Y}_e^{t+1}, \beta K^{t+1} \} \mid \bar{Y}^t] - rK^{t+1}$$

where $E[. \mid \bar{Y}^t]$ stands for the conditional mathematical expectation operator. Let us assume that $\bar{Y}_e^{t+1}$ has a conditional density $f(. \mid \bar{Y}^t)$ and a cumulative distribution $F(. \mid \bar{Y}^t)$. This gives

$$E\Pi^{t+1} = (1 - \alpha w^t) \int_0^{\beta K^{t+1}} u f(u \mid \bar{Y}^t) \, du$$

$$+ \beta(1 - \alpha w^t) K^{t+1} [1 - F(\beta K^{t+1} \mid \bar{Y}^t)] - rK^{t+1} \tag{3.37}$$

The firm choses I^t so as to maximize $E\Pi^{t+1}$. The optimal investment is given by

$$\beta(1-\alpha w^t)[1-F(\beta(K^t+I^t)|\ \bar{Y}^t)]=r \qquad (3.38)$$

Equation (3.38) can be easily interpreted. An incremental unit of capital allows an additional profit margin $\beta(1-\alpha w^t)$, provided the demand for goods and the full-employment output are greater than the capacity $\beta(K^t+I^t)$. This is realized with a probability $1-F(\beta(K^t+I^t)|\ \bar{Y}^t)$. In (3.38), the left-hand side is thus the expected additional profit margin and, at the optimum, this must be equal to the cost of capital, that is to say here, to the interest rate.

Equation (3.38) implicitly defines I^t as a function of $\bar{Y}^t$, K^t, w^t and r^t

$$I^t=I(\bar{Y}^t,K^t,w^t,r^t)$$

with $I'_2<0$, $I'_3<0$ and $I'_4<0$. The function $I(.)$ will be homogeneous of degree 1 in $(\bar{Y}^t,K^t)$ if $F(\lambda u|\lambda\bar{Y})=F(u|\bar{Y})$ for every positive λ. In terms of probability, this means that the expectation $\bar{Y}_e^{t+1}$ is *unit elastic* with respect to $\bar{Y}^t$. This hypothesis also implies that $F(.|y_0)$ dominates $F(.|y_1)$ in the sense of first-order stochastic dominance when y_0 is larger than y_1 and, consequently, $I(.)$ is increasing in $\bar{Y}^t$.

Quite differently, the hypotheses concerning function $I(.)$ can also be justified by assuming that aggregate investment results from an entry process of new firms on the market. Let us assume that the production sector – so far considered as a single representative firm – corresponds in fact to a uniform continuum of identical firms, indexed by v, $v\in[0,K]$. We assume that there are indivisibilities in production capacities, so that each firm v corresponds to one unit of capital. K may then be regarded as the aggregate value of the stock of capital.

We assume that a uniform rationing prevails in both markets: firm v perceives a demand for its product equal to Y_d/K and a labour supply L_s/K. The previous definition of the goods' supply Y_s and of the labour demand L_d at the aggregate level – equations (3.4) and (3.5) – are compatible with this assumption. The goods supply of firm v is equal to $\text{Min}\{\beta,L_s/\alpha K\}$ for all firm v, and the aggregate goods supply Y_s writes as

$$Y_s=\int_0^K \text{Min}\left\{\beta,\frac{L_s}{\alpha K}\right\}dv=\text{Min}\left\{\beta K,\frac{L_s}{\alpha}\right\}$$

Likewise, the demand for labour is equal to $\text{Min}\{\alpha(Y_d/K),\alpha\beta\}$ for all v, and the aggregate demand for labour L_d is defined by

$$L_d=\int_0^K \text{Min}\left\{\alpha\frac{Y_d}{K},\alpha\beta\right\}dv=\text{Min}\{\alpha Y_d,\alpha\beta K\}$$

Within this context, investment corresponds to the entry of new firms on the market, and, in fact, we have to explain why investors decide to create firms. If we assume that entry to the market is free, a logical requirement would be that an investor decides to create a firm only if its expected profit is positive. For simplicity, we shall assume myopic foresight of real wages. Since a firm corresponds to one unit of capital, the expected discounted profit of a new firm is then equal to

$$\frac{(1-\alpha w)}{r} q_y^e - 1$$

where q_y^e is its expected production level.

Now, let us assume that investors evaluate q_y^e by looking at the production level which prevails for existing firms. This production level is equal to Y/K, where Y is the aggregate output. Let us assume that the potential investors expect to produce the same output as the existing firms. We also assume that the number of firms grows at a rate which is proportional to the expected discounted profit of the new firm. In continuous time, this gives

$$\frac{\dot{K}}{K} = a \left[\frac{1-\alpha w)}{r} \frac{Y}{K} - 1 \right] \qquad \text{with } a > 0$$

Then, the corresponding investment function can be written as

$$I = a[x(w,r)Y - K] \qquad \text{with } x(w,r) = \frac{1-\alpha w}{r}$$

or

$$I = a[x(w,r)\text{Min}\{\bar{Y}, \beta K\} - K]$$

Such an investment function satisfies our assumptions.

Appendix 2   Proofs

This appendix gathers the proofs of propositions 3.1 to 3.3. First, let us note

$$a = (1 - \gamma_1)(\theta - n) - \delta(w_0 - \bar{w})$$
$$b = (1 - \gamma_2)(\theta - n)$$
$$z = w - \bar{w}$$

with $\bar{w} = \bar{w}(r)$.

A stationary state $s^* = (w^*, m^*, k^*)$ is defined by conditions $\dot{m} = \dot{w} = \dot{k} = 0$, and thus by

$$b = \mu \left[\frac{y_d(*) - y_s(*)}{y_d(*)} \right] \tag{3.39}$$

$$a = \lambda \left[\frac{l_d(*) - 1}{l_d(*)} \right] - \delta z \tag{3.40}$$

$$I \left[\frac{\bar{y}(*)}{k^*}, 1, \bar{w} + z, r \right] = n \tag{3.41}$$

with the definitions and equilibrium relations

$$l_d(*) = \text{Min}\{\alpha y_d(*), \alpha \beta k^*\}$$
$$y_s(*) = \text{Min}\{1/\alpha, \beta k^*\}$$
$$y_d(*) = c'y(*) + (\theta + d)m^* \text{ with } c' = c(1 - \tau) + \tau,$$
$$\bar{y}(*) = \text{Min}\{y_d(*), 1/\alpha\},$$
$$y(*) = \text{Min}\{y_d(*), y_s(*)\},$$

where we note $y(*), y_d(*) \ldots$ the values of production, effective demand for goods ... evaluated at s^*.

Let us also define KU', CU' and RI' by

$$KU' = \{(w,m,k) \in R_+^3 \mid \sigma(d + \theta)m \le \beta k \text{ and } \alpha\sigma(d + \theta)m < 1\}$$
$$CU' = \{(w,m,k) \in R_+^3 \mid \sigma(d + \theta)m > \beta k \text{ and } \alpha\beta k < 1\}$$
$$RI' = \{(w,m,k) \in R_+^3 \mid \alpha\sigma(d + \theta)m \ge 1 \text{ and } \alpha\beta k \ge 1\}$$

KU', CU' and RI' define a partition of R_3 and can be characterized by the following sign conditions

$$KU': y_d \le y_s \text{ and } l_d < 1$$
$$CU': y_d > y_s \text{ and } l_d < 1$$
$$RI': y_d \ge y_s \text{ and } l_d \ge 1$$

Remark 1

Let s^* be a stationary state of (S) and $z^* = w^* - \bar{w}$. If $s^* \in CU'$, we have $\bar{y}^* > \beta k^*$ and (3.41) implies then $z^* > 0$. Inversely, if $s^* \notin CU'$, we have $\bar{y}^* \le \beta k^*$, and thus $z^* \le 0$.

Proofs of propositions 3.1 and 3.2 will directly result from two preliminary lemmas.

Let us define sets E_1, E_2 and E_3 as follows:

$$E_1 = \{(a,b) \mid a \ge 0 \text{ and } b \ge 0\},$$
$$E_2 = \{(a,b) \mid a < 0 \text{ and } b > 0\},$$
$$E_3 = \{(a,b) \mid b < 0 \text{ or } b = 0 \text{ and } a < 0\}$$

E_1, E_2 and E_3 define a partition of R_2.

LEMMA 1   Let s^* be a stationary state of (S). Then

$s^* \in RI'$ iff $(a,b) \in E_1$
$s^* \in CU'$ iff $(a,b) \in E_2$
$s^* \in KU'$ iff $(a,b) \in E_3$

Proof

If $s^* \in RI'$, we have $y_d(*) \geq y_s(*)$ and $l_d(*) \geq 1$; (3.39) and (3.40) then imply

$$b \geq 0 \text{ and } a \geq -\delta z^*$$

In this case, we have $z^* \leq 0$ (see remark 1) and thus $a \geq 0$. We obtain $(a,b) \in E_1$.

If $s^* \in CU'$, we have $y_d(*) > y_s(*)$ and $l_d(*) < 1$. Consequently, we deduce from (3.39) and (3.40)

$$b > 0 \text{ and } a < -\delta z^*$$

Then we have $z^* > 0$, and thus $a < 0$, which implies $(a,b) \in E_2$.

If $s^* \in KU'$, we have $y_d(*) \leq y_s(*)$ and $l_d(*) < 1$. If $y_d(*) < y_s(*)$, (3.39) implies $b < 0$. If $y_d(*) = y_s(*)$, (3.39) and (3.40) imply

$$b = 0 \text{ and } a < -\delta z^*$$

Since, in this case, we have $z^* = 0$, we obtain $a < 0$. So, in this third case, $(a,b) \in E_3$.

Furthermore, we have

$$E_1 \cap E_2 = E_1 \cap E_3 = E_2 \cap E_3 = \emptyset$$

Consequently, if there exists a stationary state, it belongs respectively to RI', CU' or KU', when (a,b) belongs to E_1, E_2 or E_3.

LEMMA 2 If (a,b) belongs to a neighbourhood U of $(0,0)$, system (S) has a unique stationary state.

Proof

(1) First assume that $(a,b) \in E_1$. In such a case, lemma 1 implies that any stationary state belongs to RI'. Let us show that a unique stationary state actually exists in this regime.

In RI', conditions (3.39), (3.40) and (3.41) may be written as follows

$$b = \mu \left[\frac{\alpha y_d(*) - 1}{\alpha y_d(*)} \right] \qquad (3.42)$$

$$a = \lambda \left[\frac{\text{Min}\{\alpha y_d(*), \alpha \beta k^*\} - 1}{\text{Min}\{\alpha y_d(*), \alpha \beta k^*\}} \right] - \delta z^* \qquad (3.43)$$

$$I\left[\frac{1}{\alpha k^*},1,\bar{w}+z^*,r\right]=n \qquad (3.44)$$

Since we have $I(\beta,1,\bar{w},r)=n$, $I'_1>0$ and $I'_3<0$, relation (3.44) implicitly determines k^* as a function of z^*, when $|z^*|\leq\varepsilon_1$ with $\varepsilon_1>0$. So we write

$$k^*=\phi(z^*) \text{ with } \phi'<0,\phi(0)=1/\alpha\beta \qquad (3.45)$$

Equation (3.43) may be rewritten as

$$a=\lambda\,\mathrm{Min}\left\{\frac{\alpha y_d(*)-1}{\alpha y_d(*)},\frac{\alpha\beta k^*-1}{\alpha\beta k^*}\right\}-\delta z^*$$

Using (3.42) and (3.45), we deduce

$$a=\lambda\,\mathrm{Min}\left\{\frac{b}{\mu},\frac{\alpha\beta\phi(z^*)-1}{\alpha\beta\phi(z^*)}\right\}-\delta z^* \qquad (3.46)$$

Equation (3.46) determines a unique value of z^*, which establishes $|z^*|\leq\varepsilon_1$ if $(a,b)\in A_1$, where A_1 is a neighbourhood of $(0,0)$.

k^* is then determined by (3.45), and (w^*,m^*) by

$$w^*=z^*+\bar{w} \qquad (3.47)$$

$$m^*=\frac{y_d(*)-c'/\alpha}{\theta+d} \text{ with } y_d(*)=\frac{\mu}{\alpha(\mu-b)} \qquad (3.48)$$

This stationary state is unique; it actually belongs to RI' if $l_d(*)\geq1$ and $y_d(*)\geq y_s(*)$. (3.39) and (3.40) imply that these conditions are equivalent to $b\geq0$ and $a+\delta z^*\geq0$.

Condition $b\geq0$ is established by assumption. Furthermore, if z^* is strictly negative, we have $\phi(z^*)>1/\alpha\beta$, and (3.46) implies $a+\delta z^*\geq0$. If z^* is not strictly negative, assumption $a\geq0$ implies $a+\delta z^*\geq0$.

(2) Assume $(a,b)\in E_2$. From lemma 1 any stationary state belongs to CU' and we have to show that a unique stationary state actually exists in this regime.

In CU' stationarity conditions (3.39), (3.40) and (3.41) may be written as follows

$$b=\mu\left[\frac{y_d(*)-\beta k^*}{y_d(*)}\right], \qquad (3.49)$$

$$a=\lambda\left(\frac{\beta k^*-1/\alpha}{\beta k^*}\right)-\delta z^*, \qquad (3.50)$$

$$I\left[\frac{\mathrm{Min}\{y_d(*),1/\alpha\}}{k^*},1,\bar{w}+z^*,r\right]=n. \qquad (3.51)$$

Equations (3.49) and (3.51) imply

$$I\left[\text{Min}\left\{\frac{\mu\beta}{\mu-b},\frac{1}{\alpha k^*}\right\},1,\bar{w}+z^*,r\right]=n \tag{3.52}$$

and (3.50) implies

$$\frac{1}{\alpha k^*}=\frac{\beta(\lambda-a-\delta z^*)}{\lambda} \tag{3.53}$$

Using (3.52) and (3.53), we see that z^* is determined by

$$I\left[\text{Min}\left\{\frac{\mu\beta}{\mu-b},\frac{\beta(\lambda-a-\delta z^*)}{\lambda}\right\},1,\bar{w}+z^*,r\right]=n \tag{3.54}$$

When $a=b=0$, (3.54) has a unique solution $z^*=0$. This solution still exists and is unique if $(a,b)\in A_2$, where A_2 is a neighbourhood of $(0,0)$.

$y_d(*)$ and k^* are then determined by (3.49) and (3.50). Furthermore, we have

$$w^*=z^*+\bar{w}, \tag{3.55}$$

$$m^*=\frac{y_d(*)-c'\beta k^*}{\theta+d} \tag{3.56}$$

(w^*,m^*,k^*) actually belongs to CU' if we have $l_d(*)<1$ and $y_s(*)<y_d(*)$, or – using (3.39) and (3.40) – $a+\delta z^*<0$ and $b>0$.

Condition $b>0$ is established by assumption. Furthermore we have assumed $a<0$; consequently, we have to establish the inequality $a+\delta z^*<0$ only if z^* is strictly positive. In such a case, (3.51) implies

$$\frac{\text{Min}\{y_d(*),1/\alpha\}}{k^*}>\beta$$

and thus

$$1/\alpha>\beta k^*$$

Using (3.50), we deduce $a+\delta z^*<0$.

(3) Assume $(a,b)\in E_3$. Let us show that a unique stationary state exists in KU'.

In KU', stationarity conditions may be written as follows

$$b=\mu\left[\frac{y_d(*)-\text{Min}\{\beta k^*,1/\alpha\}}{y_d(*)}\right] \tag{3.57}$$

$$a=\lambda\left[\frac{\alpha y_d(*)-1}{\alpha y_d(*)}\right]-\delta z^* \tag{3.58}$$

$$I\left[\frac{y_d(*)}{k^*}, 1, \bar{w} + z^*, r\right] = n \tag{3.59}$$

Relation (3.59) implicitly defines $k^*/y_d(*)$ as a function of z^*, when $|z^*| \leq \varepsilon_2$. So we write

$$\frac{k^*}{y_d(*)} = \psi(z^*) \text{ with } \psi' < 0, \ \psi(0) = 1/\beta$$

Using (3.57) and (3.58), we obtain

$$b = \mu\left[1 - \text{Min}\left\{\beta\psi(z^*), \frac{\lambda - a - \delta z^*}{\lambda}\right\}\right] \tag{3.60}$$

When $a = b = 0$, (3.60) has a unique solution $z^* = 0$. A unique solution for z^* still exists and establishes $|z^*| \leq \varepsilon_2$ if $(a,b) \in A_3$, where A_3 is a neighbourhood of $(0,0)$.

Then (3.57) and (3.58) determine $y_d(*)$ and k^*. Furthermore, we have

$$w^* = z^* + \bar{w} \tag{3.61}$$

$$m^* = \frac{y_d(*)(1-c')}{\theta + d} \tag{3.62}$$

(w^*, m^*, k^*) belongs to KU' if we have $y_d(*) \leq y_s(*)$ and $l_d(*) < 1$, or – using (3.39) and (3.40) – $b \leq 0$ and $a + \delta z^* < 0$.

Let us consider two cases in order to show that these conditions are met when $(a,b) \in E_3$.

First case $b < 0$
Then (3.58) implies

$$a + \delta z^* = \lambda\left[\frac{y_d(*) - 1/\alpha}{y_d(*)}\right] \leq \lambda\left[\frac{y_d(*) - \text{Min}\{\beta k^*, 1/\alpha\}}{y_d(*)}\right]$$

Hence, from (3.57), we have

$$a + \delta z^* \leq \frac{\lambda}{\mu} b < 0$$

Second case $b = 0$ and $a < 0$
Then (3.57) implies

$$y_d(*) \leq \beta k^*$$

and, from (3.59), we have $z^* \leq 0$ which implies $a + \delta z^* < 0$. In both cases, we have $b \leq 0$ and $a + \delta z^* < 0$, so that $(w^*, m^*, k^*) \in KU'$. Let $U = \cap_{i=1}^{3} A_i$. If $(a,b) \in U$, there exists a unique stationary state.

Q.E.D.

Remark 2 When $(a,b) \in E_2$, the stationary state belongs to CU'; it will belong to the sub-regime CU_1 if and only if $y_d(*) \leq 1/\alpha$. Calculations show that this condition is equivalent to

$$I\left[\frac{\mu\beta}{\mu-b}, 1, \bar{w} - \frac{a}{\delta} - \frac{\lambda b}{\delta(\mu-b)}, r\right] \leq n$$

or, using the definition of a and b

$$I\left[\frac{\mu\beta}{\mu-(1-\gamma_2)(\theta-n)}, 1, w_0 + \frac{\lambda-(1-\gamma_1)(\theta-n)}{\delta}\right.$$
$$\left. -\frac{\mu\lambda/\delta}{\mu-(1-\gamma_2)(\theta-n)}, r\right] \leq n$$

Let $\Gamma(\theta)$ stand for the left-hand side of this last inequality. Assume $\gamma_1 \neq 1$ and $\gamma_2 \neq 1$. Then we have $\Gamma' > 0$ and

$$\Gamma(n) < n$$

$$\Gamma\left[n + \frac{\delta}{1-\gamma_1}(w_0 - \bar{w})\right] > n$$

(by using condition $w_0 > \bar{w}$ which results from the inequalities $a < 0$ and $b > 0$). Consequently, if $\gamma_1 \neq 1$ and $\gamma_2 \neq 1$, the stationary state belongs to the sub-regime CU_1 (CU_2) if $\theta \leq \hat{\theta}$ ($\theta \geq \hat{\theta}$) where $\hat{\theta}$ is defined by $\Gamma(\hat{\theta}) = n$ and satisfies

$$\hat{\theta} \in \left[n, n + \frac{\delta(w_0 - \bar{w})}{1-\gamma_1}\right]$$

Remark 3 The stationary state belongs to KU' when $(a,b) \in E_3$. It will belong to the sub-regime KU_1 if and only if z^* – which is here determined by (3.60) – establishes

$$\beta\psi(z^*) < \frac{\lambda - a - \delta z^*}{\lambda}$$

This requirement is met – with a suitable choice of A_3 – when we have

$$\lambda < \frac{-I_1'\beta\delta}{I_3'}; a \leq 0$$

Remark 4 In this proof we have implicitly assumed that the equilibrium value of the wage rate w^* was less than the productivity of labour $1/\alpha$. Since we have $\bar{w}(r) < 1/\alpha$, we also have $w < 1/\alpha$ if (a,b) is not too different from $(0,0)$, which will be achieved with a suitable choice of A_1, A_2, and A_3.

Proof of Proposition 3.1   We assume $\gamma_1 = \gamma_2 = 1$. The existence and unicity of the stationary state s^* result from Lemma 2. If $w_0 = \bar{w}$, we can check that (w_0, X) is a stationary state. If $w_0 > \bar{w}$, we have $a < 0$ and $b = 0$. So that $(a,b) \in E_3$ and, from Lemma 1, $s^* \in KU'$. Condition $b = 0$ and relation (3.39) imply $y_d(*) = y_s(*)$, thus $s^* \in KU \cap CU$. If $w_0 < \bar{w}$, we have $a > 0$ and $b = 0$, so that $(a,b) \in E_1$ and, from Lemma 1, $s^* \in RI'$. Condition $y_d(*) = y_s(*)$ implies $s^* \in KU \cap RI$.

Proof of Proposition 3.2   The existence and unicity of the stationary state result from Lemma 2. Its characterization results from Lemma 1 when applied to the case $\gamma_1 < 1, \gamma_2 < 1$.

Proof of Proposition 3.3   Let $s^* = (w^*, m^*, k^*)$ be a stationary point of (S) located in the interior of one of the different regions $KU_i, CU_i, RI_i, i = 1,2$; let A be the Jacobian matrix of (S) evaluated at s^*

$$A = \begin{bmatrix} R'_w & R'_m & R'_k \\ S'_w & S'_m & S'_k \\ T'_w & T'_m & T'_k \end{bmatrix}$$

s^* will be asymptotically stable if the eigenvalues of A have negative real parts. To prove this result, we use the Routh–Hurwicz conditions. Let

$$F(x) = x^3 + a_1 x^2 + a_2 x + a_3,$$

be the characteristic polynomial of A. If $a_1 > 0$; $a_2 > 0$ $a_3 > 0$ and $a_1 a_2 - a_3 > 0$, then all the zeros of $F(x)$ have negative real parts. We know that the stationary point s^* satisfies

$$w^* = w_0 \; ; m^* = \frac{1}{\alpha\sigma(d+\theta)} \; ; k^* = \frac{1}{\alpha\beta}$$

when $(\theta, w_0) = (n, \bar{w}(r))$. Therefore, to prove proposition 3.3, we evaluate A at this point for the different regimes, and we show that the stability conditions are satisfied for each regime if $\lambda < \mu$.

Consider the Jacobian matrix of (S), relative to KU_1, evaluated at (w_0, X). At this point we have

$$R'_w = -\delta w_0$$
$$R'_m = \alpha\sigma(\lambda - \mu)(d+\theta)w_0$$
$$R'_k = \mu\beta\alpha w_0$$
$$S'_w = 0$$
$$S'_m = -\mu$$
$$S'_k = \mu\beta/\sigma(d+\theta)$$

$$T'_w = I'_3/(\alpha\beta)^2$$
$$T'_m = I'_1\sigma(d+\theta)/\alpha\beta$$
$$T'_k = -I'_1/\alpha$$

After a tedious calculation, we obtain the coefficients of $F(x)$

$$a_1 = \delta w_0 + I'_1/\alpha + \mu > 0$$
$$a_2 = \delta w_0\mu + \delta w_0 I'_1/\alpha - \mu w_0 I'_3/\alpha\beta > 0$$
$$a_3 = -w_0\lambda\mu I'_3/\alpha\beta > 0$$

Furthermore, we have $a_1 > \mu$; $a_2 > -\mu I'_3 w_0/\alpha\beta$ and hence

$$a_1 a_2 > -\mu^2 I'_3 w_0/\alpha\beta$$

This last term will be greater than a_3 if $\mu > \lambda$, which gives a sufficient condition for the stability conditions to be realized in this first case. It is left to the reader to check that the stability conditions are also satisfied in the other regimes.

If $\mu > \lambda$, the stability conditions remain satisfied at any stationary state, when (θ, w_0) belongs to a neighbourhood of $(n, \bar{w}(r))$. Hence, such a stationary state is asymptotically stable.

4 External constraint, oil shock and economic policy

This chapter develops an open economy version of the disequilibrium model introduced in chapter 2. We will contemplate an economy where domestic and foreign goods are imperfect substitutes and where prices are fixed at home and abroad in the short run. This open economy framework will allow us to consider a broader range of economic policy instruments, including the exchange rate or trade policy variables like tariffs and export subsidies. We will also emphasize some of the macroeconomic consequences of an oil shock by distinguishing the short-run effects with nominal rigidities and the long-run effects in an economy with real wage rigidities only.[1]

In the first two sections we will present the model and characterize its fix-price equilibria and, in section 3, we will study the short-run macroeconomic policies. In section 4, we will consider a more specific version of the model where energy (oil) is individualized as a special imported good. We will first evaluate the short-run consequences of an increase in the price of oil. As we shall see, an oil shock may lead to a classical or Keynesian depression and thus it may entail inflationary or deflationary effects, depending on the relative values of the elasticities of the demand and supply of goods with respect to the price of energy. Lastly, we will contemplate the long-run consequences of an oil shock when real wage rigidities prevail in the economy.

1 General framework

The model we are contemplating includes two commodities: good 1 is produced in the domestic economy and its price p_1 is set in the domestic currency. Good 2 is imported and its price $\bar{p}_2$ is set in a foreign representative currency; the corresponding price in the domestic currency is $p_2 = e\bar{p}_2$, e being the nominal exchange rate, the price of the foreign currency in terms of the domestic currency. We let

$$q = \frac{tp_2}{p_1} = \frac{te\bar{p}_2}{p_1}$$

where $t-1$ is a unit customs tariff. Therefore, q is the relative price of domestic and foreign goods, including the tariff.

1.1 Households

We will write:

x_i = consumption of good i ($i = 1$ or 2)

M_0 = households' money holdings at the beginning of the current period

M = households' money holdings at the end of the current period

l = employment level

s = money wage rate

We let $m_0 = M_0/p_1$, $m = M/p_1$ and $w = s/p_1$. Here again, we assume that current profits are distributed in the following period. The representative household's budget constraint is

$$x_1 + q x_2 + m = wl + m_0 \tag{4.1}$$

Preferences are represented by a strictly quasi-concave, twice continuously differentiable utility function U, whose arguments are the quantities consumed x_1 and x_2, leisure time $l_0 - l$ and final money balances M/p, deflated by a price index p

$$U = U\left(x_1, x_2, l_0 - l, \frac{M}{p}\right)$$

The price index p is defined by

$$p = \phi(p_1, t p_2)$$

where ϕ is homogeneous of degree 1, such that $\phi_1' > 0, \phi_2' > 0$.
Thus we may write

$$p = p_1 \phi(1, q) \equiv p_1 \varphi(q) \tag{4.2}$$

where φ is an increasing function. This gives

$$U = U\left[x_1, x_2, l_0 - l, \frac{m}{\varphi(q)}\right] \tag{4.3}$$

In what follows, the foreign supply of good 2 is taken to be infinitely elastic. We will also assume that domestic agents (households and firms) have priority in case of excess demand on good 1 market. Consequently, domestic demand is never rationed.

As the representative household does not perceive any rationing constraint on the goods markets his effective supply of labour coincides with his notional supply l_s^*. The notional demand for good i will be denoted by x_i^*, with $i=1,2$; x_1^*, x_2^* and l_s^* are solutions of the following problem

P_0 Maximize $U\left[x_1,x_2,l_0-l,\dfrac{m}{\varphi(q)}\right]$ with respect to $x_1\geq 0$, $x_2\geq 0$,
$m\geq 0$ and $0\leq l\leq l_0$ subject to:
$x_1+qx_2+m=wl+m_0$

l_s^*,x_1^*,x_2^* and the corresponding demand for money m^* are functions of q, w, and m_0

$$l_s^*=l_s^*(q,w,m_0)$$
$$x_1^*=x_1^*(q,w,m_0)$$
$$x_2^*=x_2^*(q,w,m_0)$$
$$m^*=m^*(q,w,m_0)$$

These functions are differentiable (in the interior of their definition set) and we assume

$$\frac{\partial l_s^*}{\partial q}<0,\ \frac{\partial l_s^*}{\partial w}>0,\ \frac{\partial l_s^*}{\partial m_0}<0$$

$$\frac{\partial x_1^*}{\partial q}>0,\ \frac{\partial x_1^*}{\partial w}>0,\ \frac{\partial x_1^*}{\partial m_0}>0$$

$$\frac{\partial x_2^*}{\partial q}<0,\ \frac{\partial x_2^*}{\partial w}>0,\ \frac{\partial x_2^*}{\partial m_0}>0$$

Thus goods 1 and 2 as well as leisure are normal goods: demand for these goods increases along with initial money holdings m_0. Labour supply is an increasing function of the wage rate w: if w increases, the substitution effect which makes consumption increase at the expense of leisure time, dominates the income effect which makes demand for leisure increase. Both effects cumulate in case of a demand for goods 1 or 2, which is thus an increasing function of the real wage. Finally, we assume gross substitutability between leisure and consumption goods.

Let l_d be the effective demand for labour of the production sector. The effective demands for goods, written x_{1d} and x_{2d}, are defined by:

P_1 Maximize $U\left[x_1,x_2,l_0-l,\dfrac{m}{\varphi(q)}\right]$ with respect to $x_1\geq 0$, $x_2\geq 0$,
$m\geq 0$ and $0\leq l\leq l_0$ subject to:
$x_1+qx_2+m=wl+m_0$
$l\leq l_d$

Let us consider problem $P_2(l)$, where l is fixed, defined by:

$P_2(l)$

Maximize $U\left[x_1 x_2, l_0 - l, \dfrac{m}{\varphi(q)}\right]$ with respect to $x_1 \geq 0,\ x_2 \geq 0$ and

$m \geq 0$ subject to:

$x_1 + qx_2 + m = wl + m_0$

The optimal solution of $P_2(l)$ is denoted by $(\tilde{x}_1, \tilde{x}_2, \tilde{m})$ and depends upon q, w, l and m_0

$$\tilde{x}_i = \tilde{x}_i(q, w, l, m_0) \qquad i = 1, 2$$
$$\tilde{m} = \tilde{m}(q, w, l, m_0)$$

Note that the optimal solution of $P_2(l)$ coincides with the solution of P_0 when $l = l_s^*$, that is to say

$$\tilde{x}_i(q, w, l_s^*(q, w, m_0), m_0) = x_i^*(q, w, m_0) \qquad i = 1, 2$$

Functions $\tilde{x}_1$, $\tilde{x}_2$ and $\tilde{m}$ are differentiable and we assume

$$\frac{\partial \tilde{x}_1}{\partial l} > 0, \quad \frac{\partial \tilde{x}_1}{\partial q} > 0, \quad \frac{\partial \tilde{x}_1}{\partial m_0} > 0, \quad \frac{\partial \tilde{x}_1}{\partial w} > 0$$

$$\frac{\partial \tilde{x}_2}{\partial l} > 0, \quad \frac{\partial \tilde{x}_2}{\partial q} < 0, \quad \frac{\partial \tilde{x}_2}{\partial m_0} > 0, \quad \frac{\partial \tilde{x}_2}{\partial w} > 0$$

In particular, the constrained consumption demand for both goods increases with the employment level. This allows us to write

$$x_{id} = \text{Min}\{x_i^*(q, w, m_0), \tilde{x}_i(q, w, l_d, m_0)\} \qquad i = 1, 2 \tag{4.4}$$

Thus, the effective demand for good i is the minimum of the notional demand x_i^* and the demand constrained by the rationing prevailing on the labour market, that is to say $\tilde{x}_i$.

1.2 The production sector

The representative domestic firm produces good 1 and for that purpose uses labour services, as well as good 2, as inputs. Both resources are assumed to be complements: we will write $a(y)$ the quantity of labour services necessary to produce y units of good 1, and $b(y)$ the volume of input of good 2 used for the production. Functions $a(.)$ and $b(.)$ are assumed to be twice differentiable with $a' > 0, a'' > 0, b' > 0, b'' > 0$ and $a(0) = b(0) = 0$. Returns to scale are thus decreasing.

The firm perceives quantity constraints that determine the exchanges that can be made on the different markets. On the labour market, the household supply l_s^* determines the maximum quantity the firm may purchase. In good 1 market, the firm perceives an effective demand constraint y_d equal to the sum of domestic and foreign demands. Finally, the firm is never rationed on the market for good 2 owing to the hypothesis of perfect elasticity of foreign supply. The perceived constraints l_s^* and y_d allow us to define the effective demand for labour l_d, the effective demand for good 2, written z_d, and the effective supply of good 1, written y_s.

The notional domestic supply y_s^* is obtained by maximizing profit $y - wa(y) - qb(y)$ with respect to $y \geq 0$. The effective demand for labour l_d maximizes the firm's profit under the sales constraint; therefore, it is the solution of the following problem:

Maximize $a^{-1}(l) - wl - qb(a^{-1}(l))$ with respect to $l \geq 0$ subject to: $a^{-1}(l) \leq y_d$

which implies

$$l_d = \mathrm{Min}\{a(y_s^*(q,w)), a(y_d)\}$$

that is

$$l_d = \mathrm{Min}\{l_d^*(q,w), a(y_d)\} \tag{4.5}$$

where l_d^*, equal to $a(y_s^*)$, is the notional demand for labour. Similarly, the effective demand for good 2 is defined by

$$z_d = \mathrm{Min}\{b(y_s^*(q,w)), b(y_d)\}$$

that is

$$z_d = \mathrm{Min}\{z_d^*(q,w), b(y_d)\} \tag{4.6}$$

with $z_d^* = b(y_s^*)$.

Finally, effective domestic goods supply y_s is defined by the profit-maximizing problem under the labour supply constraint, that is:

Maximize $y - wa(y) - qb(y)$ with respect to $y \geq 0$ subject to: $a(y) \leq l_s^*$

which implies

$$y_s = \mathrm{Min}\{y_s^*(q,w), a^{-1}(l_s^*)\} \tag{4.7}$$

1.3 *Foreign sector*

The rest of the world supplies good 2 in a perfectly elastic way and its demand for good 1 will be denoted by D. It depends on the relative prices of goods 1 and 2, including a possible export subsidy. This leads us to write

$$D = D\left[\frac{p_2}{(1-v)p_1}\right] \quad \text{with } D' > 0 \tag{4.8}$$

where v is the export subsidy rate $(0 < v < 1)$.

1.4 The government

The government directly intervenes on:
    public expenditures in goods 1 and 2, denoted by g_1 and g_2,
    money holdings m_0,
    the exchange rate e,
    customs tariff t,
    the export subsidy rate v.
It may also influence the wage rate w through an incomes policy. Public expenditures are either financed by taxes (the initial money holdings m_0 are evaluated after tax deduction) or by money creation.

2 Fix-price equilibrium

The previous section led to the following relations

$$l_s = l_s^*(q, w, m_0) \tag{4.9}$$

$$l_d = \text{Min}\{l_d^*(q, w), a(y_d)\} \tag{4.10}$$

$$y_s = \text{Min}\{y_s^*(q, w), a^{-1}(l_s)\} \tag{4.11}$$

It remains to define the effective demand for good 1, denoted by y_d. It is the sum of the consumer's effective demand x_{1d}, public consumption demand g_1 and foreign demand D. By using the definition of x_{1d}, given in (4.4), we deduce

$$y_d = \text{Min}\left\{x_1^*(q, w, m_0) + g_1 + D\left[\frac{q}{t(1-v)}\right], \right.$$
$$\left. \tilde{x}_1(q, w, l_d, m_0) + g_1 + D\left[\frac{q}{t(1-v)}\right]\right\} \tag{4.12}$$

Finally, the transactions are set at the minimum of effective demand and supply. The volume of domestic production y and the employment level l are thus determined by

$$y = \text{Min}\{y_d, y_s\} \tag{4.13}$$

$$l = \text{Min}\{l_d, l_s\} \tag{4.14}$$

For a fixed value of parameters w, m_0, q, t, v and g_1 a solution $(y_d, y_s, l_d, l_s, y, l)$ of the system of equations (4.9) to (4.14) is a fix-price

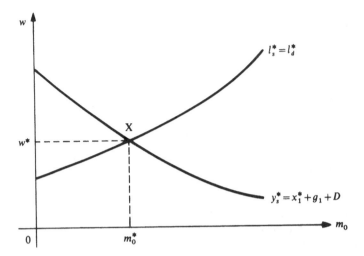

Figure 4.1 Determination of the Walrasian equilibrium

equilibrium. This system is solved as in the case of a closed economy (see chapter 2). However, there is here a simplification, owing to the fact that the domestic demand for goods is not rationed. According to the equation (4.9), the effective supply of labour l_s is defined exogeneously (for given values of q, w and m_0) and is equal to the notional supply l_s^*. Then, equation (4.11) directly defines the effective supply of goods and equations (4.10) and (4.12) simultaneously define the effective demand for labour l_d and the effective demand for the domestic good y_d.

Since the system of equations (4.10) and (4.12) is a priori likely to allow several solutions (l_d, y_d) the analysis will be confined to a local reasoning, in the neighbourhood of the Walrasian equilibrium, defined by

$$l_s^*(q,w,m_0) = l_d^*(q,w) \tag{4.15}$$

$$y_s^*(q,w) = x_1^*(q,w,m_0) + g_1 + D\left[\frac{q}{t(1-v)}\right] \tag{4.16}$$

For a given real exchange rate q and for fixed values of the policy parameters t, v and g_1, equations (4.15) and (4.16) can be represented in the (m_0, w) plane by respectively increasing and decreasing curves. These curves cross each other at the Walrasian equilibrium X whose coordinates are m_0^* and w^*.

The volumes of employment and production at the equilibrium are denoted by (l^*, y^*) and defined by

$$l^* = l_s^*(q,w^*,m_0^*) = l_d^*(q,w^*) \tag{4.17}$$

$$y^* = y_s^*(q,w^*) = x_1^*(q,w^*,m_0^*) + g_1 + D\left[\frac{q}{t(1-v)}\right] \tag{4.18}$$

Let α^* be the marginal propensity to consume wage incomes in good 1 at the Walrasian equilibrium; α is defined by

$$\alpha^* = \frac{1}{w^*}\frac{\partial \tilde{x}_1}{\partial l}(q,w^*,l^*,m_0^*)$$

We assume $0 < \alpha^* < 1$ which implies

$$a'(y^*)\frac{\partial \tilde{x}_1}{\partial l}(q,w^*,l^*,m_0^*) < 1$$

This ensures the local uniqueness of the fix-price equilibrium. In more explicit words, under this assumption, equations (4.10) and (4.12) determine a unique value of the pair (l_d,y_d) when (m_0,w) is in a certain neighbourhood of X, if we only take into account the solution located in the neighbourhood of the Walrasian transactions (l^*,y^*).

The nature of the disequilibrium prevailing on the labour and good 1 markets will determine the kind of disequilibrium obtained: Keynesian unemployment (if $y_d < y_s$ and $l_d < l_s$), classical unemployment (if $y_d > y_s$ and $l_d < l_s$) and repressed inflation (if $y_d > y_s$ and $l_d > l_s$). Here also, the firm may not be simultaneously constrained on both markets, hence the impossibility of the case $l_d > l_s, y_d < y_s$.

Let us now define the conditions of validity of the three disequilibrium regimes.

1   Under Keynesian unemployment, we have

$$y = \tilde{x}_1(q,w,a(y),m_0) + g_1 + D\left[\frac{q}{t(1-v)}\right] \tag{4.19}$$

and the conditions of validity of this regime ($y_d < y_s$ and $l_d < l_s$) are expressed similarly with production y being less than notional supply y_s^* and full-employment production $a^{-1}(l_s^*)$

$$y < y_s^*(q,w) \tag{4.20}$$

$$y < a^{-1}(l_s^*(q,w,m_0)) \tag{4.21}$$

Under the condition $\alpha^* < 1$, inequalities (4.20) and (4.21) are established in the neighbourhood of X if

$$y_s^*(q,w) > \tilde{x}_1(q,w,l_d^*(q,w),m_0) + g_1 + D\left[\frac{q}{t(1-v)}\right] \tag{4.22}$$

$$a^{-1}(l_s^*(q,w,m_0)) > x_1^*(q,w,m_0) + g_1 + D\left[\frac{q}{t(1-v)}\right] \tag{4.23}$$

2   In the classical unemployment regime, production is equal to notional domestic supply y_s^*, and employment is equal to the notional demand for labour l_d^*. Classical unemployment corresponds to an excess demand for good 1 and an excess supply of labour, that is to say

$$y_s^*(q,w) < \tilde{x}_1(q,w,l_d^*(q,w),m_0) + g_1 + D\left[\frac{q}{t(1-v)}\right] \tag{4.24}$$

$$l_d^*(q,w) < l_s^*(q,w,m_0) \tag{4.25}$$

3   In a repressed inflation context, full employment is reached. Thus we have $l = l_s^*$. There is an excess demand in the labour and domestic good markets, that is to say

$$a^{-1}(l_s^*(q,w,m_0)) < x_1^*(q,w,m_0) + g_1 + D\left[\frac{q}{t(1-v)}\right] \tag{4.26}$$

$$l_s^*(q,w,m_0) < l_d^*(q,w) \tag{4.27}$$

Requirements (4.22) to (4.27) define the conditions of validity of the three disequilibrium regimes. For fixed values of parameters q, t, v and g_1, they can be represented in the (m_0,w) plane. For that purpose, let us consider the following relations

$$l_s^*(q,w,m_0) = l_d^*(q,w) \tag{4.28}$$

$$y_s^*(q,w) = \tilde{x}_1(q,w,l_d^*(q,w),m_0) + g_1 + D\left[\frac{q}{t(1-v)}\right] \tag{4.29}$$

$$a^{-1}(l_s^*(q,w,m_0)) = x_1^*(q,w,m_0) + g_1 + D\left[\frac{q}{t(1-v)}\right] \tag{4.30}$$

Relation (4.28) expresses the equality between notional demand and notional supply on the labour market. For a fixed value of q, it defines an increasing curve C_1 represented in the (m_0,w) plane, with a slope

$$\frac{dw}{dm_0}\bigg|C_1 = \frac{\dfrac{\partial l_s^*}{\partial m_0}}{\dfrac{\partial l_d^*}{\partial w} - \dfrac{\partial l_s^*}{\partial w}} > 0$$

With regard to (4.29), it expresses the equality of production and demand on the domestic goods market when the production level is equal to notional supply. It is represented by a curve C_2, whose slope is defined by

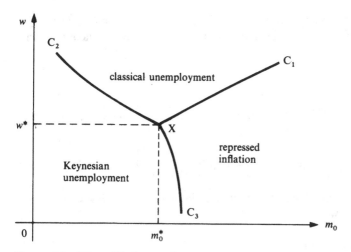

Figure 4.2   Disequilibrium regimes

$$\frac{dw}{dm_0}\bigg|C_2 = \frac{\dfrac{\partial \tilde{x}_1}{\partial m_0}}{\dfrac{\partial y_s^*}{\partial w}\left(1 - a'\dfrac{\partial \tilde{x}_1}{\partial l}\right) - \dfrac{\partial \tilde{x}_1}{\partial w}} < 0$$

Finally, (4.30) means that production and demand are equal when full employment is achieved. The slope of curve C_3, which represents (4.30) in the (m_0, w) plane is defined by

$$\frac{dw}{dm_0}\bigg|C_3 = \frac{\dfrac{\partial x_1^*}{\partial m_0} - \dfrac{1}{a'}\dfrac{\partial l_s^*}{\partial m_0}}{\dfrac{1}{a'}\dfrac{\partial l_s^*}{\partial w} - \dfrac{\partial x_1^*}{\partial w}}$$

and can be positive or negative.

These three curves cross each other at the Walrasian equilibrium X and define the conditions of validity of the disequilibrium regimes (figure 4.2).

3   Short-run macroeconomic policy

In this section, we assume that nominal prices p_1 and $\bar{p}_2$ are fixed in the short run and we will consider the following instrumental variables: the real wage rate w, the exchange rate e, public expenditures g_1 and g_2, households money holdings m_0, customs tariffs t and the export subsidy v. For simplicity's sake, we will assume that the initial situation is characterized by the absence of customs tariffs and export subsidy: thus, we have $t = 1$ and $v = 0$.

3.1 *Keynesian unemployment*

When Keynesian unemployment prevails, domestic production is equal to the demand

$$y = \tilde{x}_1 \left[\frac{te\bar{p}_2}{p_1}, w, a(y), m_0 \right] + g_1 + D \left[\frac{e\bar{p}_2}{(1-v)p_1} \right] \tag{4.31}$$

The effect on production of a change in economic policy variables, is defined as follows

$$\frac{\partial y}{\partial w} = \sigma \frac{\partial \tilde{x}_1}{\partial w} > 0 \tag{4.32}$$

$$\frac{\partial y}{\partial e} = \sigma \frac{q}{e} \left(\frac{\partial \tilde{x}_1}{\partial q} + D' \right) > 0 \tag{4.33}$$

$$\frac{\partial y}{\partial g_1} = \sigma > 0 \tag{4.34}$$

$$\frac{\partial y}{\partial m_0} = \sigma \frac{\partial \tilde{x}_1}{\partial m_0} > 0 \tag{4.35}$$

$$\frac{\partial y}{\partial t} = \sigma q \frac{\partial \tilde{x}_1}{\partial q} > 0 \tag{4.36}$$

$$\frac{\partial y}{\partial v} = \sigma q D' > 0 \tag{4.37}$$

where we write

$$\sigma = \frac{1}{1 - a' \dfrac{\partial \tilde{x}_1}{\partial l}} > 1 \tag{4.38}$$

Let us briefly comment on these results. Variable σ defined above plays the role of a Keynesian multiplier and is equal to the effect on domestic production of a unit increase in domestic consumption demand. Condition $\alpha^* < 1$ implies that σ is greater than 1 in the neighbourhood of the Walrasian equilibrium.

A rise in the households' wealth, through a rise in real wages – relation (4.32) – or in transferred incomes – relation (4.35) – exerts a positive effect on the level of domestic production and therefore on employment. These are the usual consequences of a demand stimulating policy under Keynesian unemployment. Relation (4.33) shows that a devaluation exerts a positive effect on output. This is partly due to the shift of households' consumption demand towards domestic production and partly to a rise in export demand. Finally, relations (4.36) and (4.37) show that an increase in the tariff or in the export subsidy exerts a favourable effect on economic activity. It is worth noting, however, that if the devaluation of the currency or the rise in tariffs improve output and employment, they do not necessarily increase households' welfare since they also make prices of imported goods rise: the global effect on households satisfaction results from the summing of an income effect and a price effect, which is not necessarily positive.

Let us now contemplate the consequences of the different economic policy measures on the trade balance. In a Keynesian underemployment context, exports EX_1 are equal to foreign demand (since there is an excess supply of good 1), that is to say

$$EX_1 = D\left[\frac{e\bar{p}_2}{(1-v)p_1}\right]$$

Imports IM_2 include households demand $\tilde{x}_2$, domestic firms' intermediate goods demand $b(y)$ and public consumption g_2

$$IM_2 = \tilde{x}_2\left[\frac{te\bar{p}_2}{p_2}, w, a(y), m_0\right] + b(y) + g_2$$

Consequently, the trade balance in domestic currency is

$$B = (1-v)p_1 D\left[\frac{e\bar{p}_2}{(1-v)p_1}\right]$$
$$- e\bar{p}_2\left[\tilde{x}_2\left[\frac{tep_2}{p_1}, w, m_0, a(y)\right] + b(y) + g_2\right] \tag{4.39}$$

and may be considered as a function of w, e, g_1, g_2, m_0, t and v. Let us first analyse the effect on B of a change in the exchange rate. We obtain

$$\frac{1}{\bar{p}_2}\frac{\partial B}{\partial e} = \underbrace{-IM_2}_{\substack{\text{Increase in}\\\text{the price of}\\\text{imported goods}}} \underbrace{-q\left[\frac{\partial \tilde{x}_2}{\partial q} + \frac{\partial y}{\partial e}\left(a'\frac{\partial \tilde{x}_2}{\partial l} + b'\right)\right]}_{\substack{\text{Change in the volume}\\\text{of imports}}} + \underbrace{D'}_{\substack{\text{Increase}\\\text{in exports}}} \tag{4.40}$$

where $\partial y/\partial e$ is defined by (4.33) and thus is positive.

The effect of a devaluation on the foreign trade balance appears as the result of three components. The first is equal to IM_2, and consists in an increase in the cost of imports represented by a unit rise in the exchange rate, the volume being equal. The second term is the change in the volume of imports. It includes, on the one hand, the decrease in households' demand due to the rise in the price of imports represented by the term $\partial \tilde{x}_2 / \partial q$ and, on the other hand, the rise in the demand for imports, due to a rise in domestic production, that is $(\partial y / \partial e)(a' \partial \tilde{x}_2 / \partial l + b')$. Finally, D' measures the effect of the unit increase in the exchange rate on demand for exports.

Equation (4.40) differs from Marshall–Lerner's traditional formula, which applies when devaluation does not generate any income effect, its impact on the foreign trade balance consisting in price-effects only. Such a formula can be easily obtained if we assume that the government sets public domestic consumption, so as to stabilize production at a given level $\bar{y}$. In this case, the change in imports is limited to the price-effect on households consumption, that is to say $\partial \tilde{x}_2 / \partial q$. Thus we have

$$\frac{1}{\bar{p}_2} \frac{\partial B}{\partial e} = -IM_2 - q \frac{\partial \tilde{x}_2}{\partial q} + D'$$

which implies

$$\frac{\partial B}{\partial e} > 0 \Leftrightarrow D' - q \frac{\partial \tilde{x}_2}{\partial q} > IM_2$$

If we assume that trade is balanced in the situation in question, that is

$$D = qIM_2$$

we obtain

$$\frac{\partial B}{\partial e} > 0 \Leftrightarrow \frac{qD'}{D} - \frac{q \dfrac{\partial \tilde{x}_2}{\partial q}}{IM_2} > 1$$

Let

$$\varepsilon_1 = \frac{qD'}{D}$$

$$\varepsilon_2 = - \frac{q \dfrac{\partial \tilde{x}_2}{\partial q}}{IM_2}$$

ε_1 and ε_2 are export and import price elasticities. Thus, we deduce

$$\frac{\partial B}{\partial e} > 0 \Leftrightarrow \varepsilon_1 + \varepsilon_2 > 1$$

That is the Marshall–Lerner condition: a devaluation will exert a positive effect on the trade balance only if the sum of price-elasticities is greater than 1.

The term $-q(\partial y/\partial e)(a'\partial \tilde{x}_2/\partial l + b')$ in equation (4.40) shows that the Marshall–Lerner condition is not sufficient to insure a positive effect of a devaluation on the foreign trade balance, since the increase in output, due to a devaluation, induces additional imports, which downplay the positive effect.

We also have

$$\frac{\partial B}{\partial w} = -p_2 \left[\frac{\partial \tilde{x}_2}{\partial w} + \left(\frac{\partial \tilde{x}_2}{\partial l} a' + b' \right) \frac{\partial y}{\partial w} \right] \tag{4.41}$$

$$\frac{\partial B}{\partial g_1} = -p_2 \left(\frac{\partial \tilde{x}_2}{\partial l} a' + b' \right) \frac{\partial y}{\partial g_1} \tag{4.42}$$

$$\frac{\partial B}{\partial g_2} = -p_2 \tag{4.43}$$

$$\frac{\partial B}{\partial m_0} = -p_2 \left[\frac{\partial \tilde{x}_2}{\partial m_0} + \left(\frac{\partial \tilde{x}_2}{\partial l} a' + b' \right) \frac{\partial y}{\partial m_0} \right] \tag{4.44}$$

$$\frac{\partial B}{\partial t} = -p_2 \left[q \frac{\partial \tilde{x}_2}{\partial q} + \left(\frac{\partial \tilde{x}_2}{\partial l} a' + b' \right) \frac{\partial y}{\partial t} \right] \tag{4.45}$$

$$\frac{\partial B}{\partial v} = -D + qD' - p_2 \left(\frac{\partial \tilde{x}_2}{\partial l} a' + b' \right) \frac{\partial y}{\partial v} \tag{4.46}$$

Since we have $\partial y/\partial w > 0$, $\partial y/\partial g_1 > 0$ and $\partial y/\partial m_0 > 0$, the derivatives $\partial B/\partial w$, $\partial B/\partial g_1$ and $\partial B/\partial m_0$ are negative: an increase in wages, public consumption or in the money stock worsens the balance of trade. In order to evaluate the effect of increasing the customs tariff, let us develop the term $\partial y/\partial t$ in (4.45). We will here further assume $\partial \tilde{m}/\partial q > 0$ (gross substitutability from good 2 to money holdings) and $\partial \tilde{m}/\partial l > 0$.

$$\frac{\partial B}{\partial t} = -p_2 \sigma \left[q \frac{\partial \tilde{x}_2}{\partial q} \left(1 - a' \frac{\partial \tilde{x}_1}{\partial l} \right) + q \frac{\partial \tilde{x}_1}{\partial q} \left(\frac{\partial \tilde{x}_2}{\partial l} a' + b' \right) \right] \tag{4.47}$$

Using

$$\frac{\partial \tilde{x}_1}{\partial q} + q \frac{\partial \tilde{x}_2}{\partial q} = -\tilde{x}_2 - \frac{\partial \tilde{m}}{\partial q} < -\tilde{x}_2 < 0$$

relation (4.47) allows us to write

$$\frac{\partial B}{\partial t} > -q p_2 \sigma \frac{\partial \tilde{x}_2}{\partial q} \left[1 - a' \left(\frac{\partial \tilde{x}_1}{\partial l} + q \frac{\partial \tilde{x}_2}{\partial l} \right) - q b' \right]$$

Table 4.1. *Economic policy under Keynesian unemployment*

	w	e	g_1	g_2	m_0	t	v
y	+	+	+	0	+	+	+
B	−	?	−	−	−	+	?

Moreover, in the Keynesian unemployment regime, we have $wa' + qb' < 1$, since the marginal cost of production is less than the price of output. This gives

$$\frac{\partial B}{\partial t} > -a'qp_2\sigma\frac{\partial \tilde{x}_2}{\partial q}\left[w - \left(\frac{\partial \tilde{x}_1}{\partial l} + q\frac{\partial \tilde{x}_2}{\partial l}\right)\right]$$

Finally, using

$$w - \left(\frac{\partial \tilde{x}_1}{\partial l} + q\frac{\partial \tilde{x}_2}{\partial l}\right) = \frac{\partial \tilde{m}}{\partial l} > 0$$

we obtain

$$\frac{\partial B}{\partial t} > -a'qp_2\sigma\frac{\partial \tilde{x}_2}{\partial q}\frac{\partial \tilde{m}}{\partial l} > 0$$

Therefore, in a Keynesian unemployment context, the rise in tariffs probably exerts a positive effect on the trade balance.

Finally, (4.46) shows that a *necessary* condition for an export subsidy to improve upon the foreign trade balance is $\varepsilon_1 > 1$.

These results are gathered in table 4.1.

3.2   *Classical unemployment*

If unemployment is classical, domestic production y is equal to notional supply y_s^* and thus is defined by the equality of price and marginal cost

$$1 = wa'(y) + \frac{te\bar{p}_2}{p_1}b'(y)$$

By differentiating this relation, we obtain the effect of a change in the wage rate w, the exchange rate e and the customs tariff t on the volume of production y. At a point where $t = 1$, we have

$$\frac{\partial y}{\partial w} = -\frac{a'}{wa'' + qb''} < 0 \tag{4.48}$$

$$\frac{\partial y}{\partial e} = -\frac{qb'}{e(wa'' + qb'')} < 0 \tag{4.49}$$

$$\frac{\partial y}{\partial t} = -\frac{qb'}{wa'' + qb''} < 0 \tag{4.50}$$

Here, a rise in w, e or t exerts a negative effect on the volume of production. The reason is that when employment is classical output is determined by supply and will decrease should costs increase, an increase caused either by a rise in the wage rate or in the price of intermediate imported goods.

It is worth noting that a revaluation of the domestic currency (which causes e to drop) exerts a favourable effect on production and therefore on employment, but also on households' satisfaction since it makes the cost of imported goods decrease. Unlike the Keynesian unemployment case, there is here no contradiction in increasing both the employment level and households' satisfactions. While the other instrumental variable (fiscal expenditures, transfers, export subsidies), have no effect on the volume of production.

Let us now consider the balance of trade. We assumed earlier that any excess demand in good 1 market led to export rationing. Thus, exports EX_1 are equal to the difference between output y_s^* and internal demand $\tilde{x}_1 + g_1$. We can here speak of an exportable surplus, since external demand has no effect on the volume of output. Thus, we have

$$EX_1 = y_s^*(q,w) - \tilde{x}_1(q,w,l_d^*(q,w),m_0) - g_1$$

Moreover, imports are given by

$$IM_2 = \tilde{x}_2(q,w,l_d^*(q,w),m_0) + b(y_s^*(q,w)) + g_2$$

Let us first analyse the effect of a change in the exchange rate on the trade balance B, defined by

$$B = (1-v)p_1 EX_1 - e\bar{p}_2 IM_2$$

We obtain

$$\frac{1}{\bar{p}_2}\frac{\partial B}{\partial e} = \underbrace{-IM_2}_{\substack{\text{Increase in the} \\ \text{price of imported} \\ \text{goods}}} - \underbrace{q\left[\frac{\partial \tilde{x}_2}{\partial q} + \frac{\partial y_s^*}{\partial q}\left(a'\frac{\partial \tilde{x}_2}{\partial l} + b'\right)\right]}_{\text{Decrease in imports}}$$

$$+ \underbrace{\left[\frac{\partial y_s^*}{\partial q}\left(1 - a'\frac{\partial \tilde{x}_1}{\partial l}\right) - \frac{\partial \tilde{x}_1}{\partial q}\right]}_{\substack{\text{Decrease in the} \\ \text{exportable surplus}}} \tag{4.51}$$

As in the Keynesian case, the derivative $\partial B/\partial e$ appears as the sum of three terms. The first term indicates a rise in the cost of imported goods – the volume being equal – due to a unit rise in the exchange rate. The second term indicates the effect on imports of such a rise. Contrary to the results obtained in the Keynesian unemployment context, this effect is no doubt negative: the rise in the exchange rate makes the imported quantity of goods decrease, owing to the price effect (negative term $\partial \tilde{x}_2/\partial q$) and to the drop in the volume of domestic production (since we have $\partial y_s^*/\partial q < 0$). In relation (4.51), the third term indicates the change in the exportable surplus, due to a unit rise in the exchange rate. This variation is negative owing to the decrease in production and the shift of consumers' demand towards domestic production. The global effect of a devaluation on the trade balance is still rather ambiguous. However, as we shall see, the possibility of an adverse effect of a devaluation on the foreign trade balance is more likely here than in the Keynesian unemployment situation.

Indeed, we may rewrite (4.51) as follows

$$\frac{1}{\bar{p}_2}\frac{\partial B}{\partial e} = -\left(\tilde{x}_2 + q\frac{\partial \tilde{x}_2}{\partial q} + \frac{\partial \tilde{x}_1}{\partial q}\right) - b(y_s^*) - g_2$$
$$+ \frac{\partial y_s^*}{\partial q}\left[1 - a'\frac{\partial \tilde{x}_1}{\partial l} - q\left(a'\frac{\partial \tilde{x}_2}{\partial l} + b'\right)\right]$$

By using

$$\tilde{x}_2 + q\frac{\partial \tilde{x}_2}{\partial q} + \frac{\partial \tilde{x}_1}{\partial q} = -\frac{\partial \tilde{m}}{\partial q}$$

and

$$1 - a'\frac{\partial \tilde{x}_1}{\partial l} - q\left(a'\frac{\partial \tilde{x}_2}{\partial l} + b'\right) = a'\left[w - \left(\frac{\partial \tilde{x}_1}{\partial l} + q\frac{\partial \tilde{x}_2}{\partial l}\right)\right] = a'\frac{\partial \tilde{m}}{\partial l}$$

we obtain

$$\frac{1}{\bar{p}_2}\frac{\partial B}{\partial e} = \frac{\partial \tilde{m}}{\partial q} - b(y_s^*) - g_2 + a'\frac{\partial y_s^*}{\partial q}\frac{\partial \tilde{m}}{\partial l}$$

Assume $\partial \tilde{m}/\partial q > 0$ and $\partial \tilde{m}/\partial l > 0$. The above equality does not define for sure the sign of $\partial B/\partial e$. We may, however, believe that the term $\partial \tilde{m}/\partial q$ is dominated by the other terms which are negative. The derivative $\partial B/\partial e$ is thus probably negative. As a matter of fact, it is rather easy to interpret this result: should a devaluation occur, the drop in domestic supply, due to a rise in the cost of intermediate imported goods, will be only partially compensated for by a decrease in households' consumption due to a decrease in their earned incomes. Jointly with the rise in the price of imports, this will lead to a decrease in the trade balance surplus.

We also have

$$\frac{\partial B}{\partial w} = p_1 \frac{\partial y_s^*}{\partial w} \left[1 - a' \left(\frac{\partial \tilde{x}_1}{\partial l} + q \frac{\partial \tilde{x}_2}{\partial l} \right) - qb' \right] - p_1 \left(\frac{\partial \tilde{x}_1}{\partial w} + q \frac{\partial \tilde{x}_2}{\partial w} \right) \quad (4.52)$$

$$\frac{\partial B}{\partial g_1} = -p_1 \quad (4.53)$$

$$\frac{\partial B}{\partial g_2} = -p_2 \quad (4.54)$$

$$\frac{\partial B}{\partial m_0} = -p_1 \left(\frac{\partial \tilde{x}_1}{\partial m_0} + q \frac{\partial \tilde{x}_2}{\partial m_0} \right) \quad (4.55)$$

$$\frac{\partial B}{\partial t} = p_1 \frac{\partial y_s^*}{\partial q} \left[1 - a' \left(\frac{\partial \tilde{x}_1}{\partial l} + q \frac{\partial \tilde{x}_2}{\partial l} \right) - qb' \right] - p_1 \left(\frac{\partial \tilde{x}_1}{\partial q} + q \frac{\partial \tilde{x}_2}{\partial q} \right) \quad (4.56)$$

$$\frac{\partial B}{\partial v} = -p_1 EX_1 \quad (4.57)$$

The derivatives $\partial B / \partial g_1$, $\partial B / \partial g_2$ and $\partial B / \partial m_0$ are negative: a rise in fiscal expenditures or households' money holdings will adversely affect the external balance. Relations (4.52) and (4.56) may be rewritten as follows

$$\frac{\partial B}{\partial w} = p_1 a' \frac{\partial \tilde{m}}{\partial l} \frac{\partial y_s^*}{\partial w} - p_1 \left(\frac{\partial \tilde{x}_1}{\partial w} + q \frac{\partial \tilde{x}_2}{\partial w} \right) < 0$$

$$\frac{\partial B}{\partial t} = p_1 a' \frac{\partial \tilde{m}}{\partial l} \frac{\partial y_s^*}{\partial q} - p_1 \left(\frac{\partial \tilde{x}_1}{\partial q} + q \frac{\partial \tilde{x}_2}{\partial q} \right)$$

Thus, a rise in the wage rate exerts a negative effect on the trade balance. Unlike the Keynesian case, the sign of $\partial B / \partial t$ is here uncertain. Indeed, the increase in tariffs makes the exportable surplus decrease: such a drop is due partly to the decrease in the volume of domestic production caused by a rise in the cost of intermediate imported goods, and partly to the shift of households' demand towards locally produced goods. This rise in tariffs also makes households' demand for imported goods decrease owing to both the drop in earned wages and the reorientation of their choices towards the domestic good. Therefore, the global effect on the foreign trade balance remains ambiguous. Finally, the volume of exports is here independent from the export subsidy rate. Therefore, the establishment of a subsidy only results in diminishing the value of exported goods, the volume being constant. This is what relation (4.57) signifies.

Table 4.2. *Economic policy under classical unemployment*

	w	e	g_1	g_2	m_0	t	v
y	$-$	$-$	0	0	0	$-$	0
B	$-$	$-$	$-$	$-$	$-$	?	$-$

The results we obtained for the classical unemployment regime are gathered in table 4.2.

Tables 4.1 and 4.2 show that the same economic policy will have quite different consequences in a classical or Keynesian unemployment context. If we only consider variables e, t and v which represent the choice of exchange and trade policies, we can see that the effect of a devaluation on the external balance is rather uncertain in the Keynesian context and probably negative in a classical situation. Under Keynesian unemployment, a devaluation stimulates domestic production, while the effect is reversed when classical unemployment prevails. The increase in the tariff is usually beneficial for production and for the trade balance in the Keynesian unemployment regime, while in the classical regime such an increase exerts a negative effect on output and its effect on the trade balance remains uncertain. Finally, under Keynesian unemployment, the establishment of an export subsidy is beneficial for production but its effect on the external balance is uncertain. While under classical unemployment, this subsidy will not affect the level of production and will have a negative effect on the foreign trade balance.

3.3   Repressed inflation

In the repressed inflation regime, full employment is achieved: output is thus equal to $a^{-1}(l_s^*(q,w,m_0))$ which gives

$$\frac{\partial y}{\partial w} = \frac{1}{a'}\frac{\partial l_s^*}{\partial w} > 0 \tag{4.58}$$

$$\frac{\partial y}{\partial e} = \frac{q}{ea'}\frac{\partial l_s^*}{\partial q} < 0 \tag{4.59}$$

$$\frac{\partial y}{\partial m_0} = \frac{1}{a'}\frac{\partial l_s^*}{\partial m_0} < 0 \tag{4.60}$$

$$\frac{\partial y}{\partial t} = \frac{q}{a'}\frac{\partial l_s^*}{\partial q} < 0 \tag{4.61}$$

A rise the wage rate w or a decrease in money holdings stimulates the labour supply and therefore, production as well. However, a rise in the price of imported goods, either due to a devaluation or a rise in the customs tariff, makes the labour supply decrease, since good 2 and leisure are gross substitutes. The other variables have no effect on the quantity produced.

As in the classical unemployment situation, there is here an excess demand for domestic production. Exports of good 1 here again are defined as an exportable surplus, equal to the difference between the quantity produced and domestic demand. Since the consumer's demand is now equal to his notional demand x_1^*, we obtain

$$EX_1 = a^{-1}(l_s^*(q,w,m_0)) - x_1^*(q,w,m_0) - g_1$$

while imports are equal to

$$IM_2 = x_2^*(q,w,m_0) + b[a^{-1}(l_s^*(q,w,m_0))] + g_2$$

and the trade balance B is defined by

$$B = p_1(1-v)EX_1 - e\bar{p}_2 IM_2$$

The effect of a change in the exchange rate is defined by

$$\frac{1}{\bar{p}_2}\frac{\partial B}{\partial e} = \underbrace{-IM_2}_{\substack{\text{Increase in} \\ \text{the price of} \\ \text{imported} \\ \text{goods}}} - \underbrace{q\left(\frac{\partial x_2^*}{\partial q} + \frac{b'}{a'}\frac{\partial l_s^*}{\partial q}\right)}_{\substack{\text{Decrease in} \\ \text{imports}}} + \underbrace{\left(\frac{1}{a'}\frac{\partial l_s^*}{\partial q} - \frac{\partial x_1^*}{\partial q}\right)}_{\substack{\text{Decrease in the} \\ \text{exportable} \\ \text{surplus}}} \tag{4.62}$$

Here again, the derivative $\partial B/\partial e$ may be broken up into three distinct terms: a rise in the price of imported goods (the volume being constant), a decrease in imports and a decrease in exports. A rise in the exchange rate makes the volume of imports decrease, owing to the shift in households' demand and the decrease in domestic production. Similarly, the exportable surplus will decrease owing to the decrease in production and the rise in domestic demand. Then, the sign of $\partial B/\partial e$ remains ambiguous. We also have

$$\frac{\partial B}{\partial w} = \frac{p_1}{a'}\frac{\partial l_s^*}{\partial w}(1 - qb') - p_1\left(\frac{\partial x_1^*}{\partial w} + q\frac{\partial x_2^*}{\partial w}\right) \tag{4.63}$$

$$\frac{\partial B}{\partial g_1} = -p_1 \tag{4.64}$$

$$\frac{\partial B}{\partial g_2} = -p_2 \tag{4.65}$$

Table 4.3. *Economic policy under repressed inflation*

	w	e	g_1	g_2	m_0	t	v
y	+	−	0	0	0	−	0
B	−	?	−	−	−	+	−

$$\frac{\partial B}{\partial m_0}=\frac{p_1}{a'}\frac{\partial l_s^*}{\partial m_0}(1-qb')-p_1\left(\frac{\partial x_1^*}{\partial m_0}+q\frac{\partial x_2^*}{\partial m_0}\right) \qquad (4.66)$$

$$\frac{\partial B}{\partial t}=\frac{p_2}{a'}(1-qb')\frac{\partial l_s^*}{\partial q}-p_1\left(\frac{\partial x_1^*}{\partial q}-q\frac{\partial x_2^*}{\partial q}\right) \qquad (4.67)$$

$$\frac{\partial B}{\partial v}=-p_1 EX_1 \qquad (4.68)$$

A rise in public expenditures, in the form of purchases of goods or transfers to households, exerts a negative effect on the trade balance. The consequences of a rise in real wages are a priori undetermined since the negative effect, caused by an increase in the demand for consumption, can be compensated for by a rise in the exportable surplus, caused by a rise in the labour supply. However, we may think that the elasticity of the labour supply is sufficiently limited to make the compensation only partial and so that the rise in wages tend to worsen the trade surplus. As in the classical situation, the effect of increasing the customs tariff on the trade balance is a priori undetermined, owing to a decrease in the exportable surplus caused by a drop in the labour supply. Nevertheless, this effect is very likely to be dominated by the shift in household demand towards the domestic good and therefore, the derivative $\partial B/\partial t$ is positive. Finally, the export subsidy exerts a negative effect on the foreign exchange balance. All these results are gathered in table 4.3.

4   Some macroeconomic consequences of an oil shock

The analysis of the macroeconomic effects of an oil shock can usefully be developed with the help of fix-price models.[2] Indeed, an oil shock that causes an unexpected sharp rise in the price of energy, exerts adverse effects both on supply and demand in the domestic goods' market and this may lead either to a Keynesian depression or to a classical unemployment situation according to the relative importance of these two effects. Firstly, energy is used as an intermediate good and any increase in its price reduces disposable domestic income and exerts an adverse effect on consumption demand, which is likely to be compensated for only partially by a substitution effect between energy and domestic goods. Secondly, an oil shock lowers domestic firms' profitability and this reduces the notional domestic goods' supply.

The analysis of short-run and long-run consequences of an oil shock deeply differ. In the short run, nominal rigidities may be postulated. Furthermore, the economy may be in position to bear the consequences of a transitory deficit in its current account. In the long run, only real rigidities may prevail (in particular, real wages may not be perfectly flexible) and, moreover, the current-account equilibrium condition limits the set of possible policy choices.

Analysing some macroeconomic effects of an oil shock clearly requires adding a third good to the model: energy. We will simplify matters by assuming that the labour supply is exogenously set and that behavioural relationships are log-linear. The exchange rate and the creation of money are the only instruments of economic policy we will consider.

4.1 The model

Thus, the model includes three commodities. Good 1 is the domestic production, likely to be exported. Good 2 is an imported commodity, and is an imperfect substitute with good 1. Finally, good 3 is energy; it may be produced locally or imported. We will, however, assume that the domestic production of energy is fixed in the short run and that the economy is a net-importing country.

For the sake of simplicity, we will not derive behaviour relations from explicit optimization programmes. More simply, we will consider a log-linear macroeconomic model. In what follows, *all the variables will be represented by their logarithm* but we keep notations unchanged since no ambiguity will occur: p_h stands for the logarithm of good h price, expressed in national currency, s is the logarithm of the money wage rate (in national currency also), y is the logarithm of production, etc. . . . We assume that p_1 is fixed in the short run. Prices p_2 and p_3 are deduced from the corresponding prices, expressed in a representative foreign currency $\bar{p}_2$ and $\bar{p}_3$, now with

$$p_2 = \bar{p}_2 + e$$
$$p_3 = \bar{p}_3 + e$$

where e is the exchange rate (in log) expressing the price of the foreign currency in terms of domestic currency.

We define the following relative prices

$$q = p_2 - p_1$$
$$\pi = p_3 - p_1$$
$$\omega = s - \lambda_1 p_1 - \lambda_2 p_2 - \lambda_3 p_3 \qquad \lambda_i > 0,\ \sum_i \lambda_i = 1,\ i = 1,2,3$$

q and π respectively stand for the relative prices of good 2 and good 3 with respect to the price of good 1 produced locally; ω stands for the real wage rate, with λ_1, λ_2 and λ_3 standing for the weights of the different consumption goods in the consumers price index.

Let

y_0: the full-employment production (exogeneously given)
y_s: the effective supply of good 1
y_s^*: the notional supply of good 1
y_d: the effective demand for good 1
M_0: the initial money holdings (and $m_0 = M_0 - p_1$)
B: the current account, identified here as the balance of trade, in relative terms, i.e. $B = \text{Log}(\text{exports/imports})$

The following four relations define the model

$$y_s = \min\{y_s^*, y_0\} \tag{4.69}$$

$$y_s^* = \alpha_1 - \alpha_2 \omega - \alpha_3 q - \alpha_4 \pi \tag{4.70}$$

$$y_d = \beta_1 + \beta_2 m_0 + \beta_3 q - \beta_4 \pi + \beta_5 y \tag{4.71}$$

$$B = \gamma_1 + \gamma_2 q - \gamma_3 \pi - \gamma_4 y - \gamma_5 m_0 \tag{4.72}$$

where the coefficients affected by the different variables are assumed positive and such that $\beta_5 < 1, \beta_3 > \beta_4$ and $\gamma_2 > \gamma_3$. Let us briefly comment on these relations.

Equation (4.69) defines the effective domestic supply which is the minimum of full-employment production y_0 and notional supply y_s^*. There, we assume that y_0 is fixed, which implies that, on the one hand, the labour supply is exogeneously defined and, on the other hand, that the inputs necessary to produce good 1 (that is, labour and goods 2 and 3) are complements.

The notional supply y_s^* is defined by (4.70) as a function of ω, q and π. Indeed, under decreasing returns to scale, profit maximization leads to expressing the notional supply y_s^* as a function of real factor prices, that is

$$y_s^* = \alpha_1 - \alpha_2(s - p_1) - \alpha_3' q - \alpha_4' \pi$$

with

$$\alpha_2 > 0, \alpha_3' > 0, \alpha_4' > 0,$$

and we let

$$\alpha_3 = \alpha_3' + \alpha_2 \lambda_2$$
$$\alpha_4 = \alpha_4' + \alpha_2 \lambda_3$$

which leads to (4.70).

Equation (4.71) defines the demand for domestic goods as a function of m_0, q, π and y. A rise in the relative price q exerts a positive effect on this demand, owing to the shift of domestic and external demands towards domestic goods, which become more competitive. Conversely, we assume that a rise in the price of energy makes the demand for domestic goods decrease, because the increase in the cost of energy used as an intermediate good reduces households' disposable income, for a given level of domestic production. A similar effect also occurs for the price of good 2, since this good is also used as an intermediate good for domestic production. However, as far as good 2 is concerned, we will assume that such an effect is dominated by the above mentioned substitutability mechanism. Similarly, a rise in the price of energy may, through a substitution effect, make the domestic demand for good 1 increase. Therefore, we will assume that the possibilities of substitution between energy and domestic goods are limited, so that the substitution effect is dominated by the income effect that tends to reduce households real incomes. In a nutshell, the substitution possibilities between good 1 and good 2 are taken to be high, while they are assumed to be low between goods 1 and 3.

Moreover, since we have by definition $q = \bar{p}_2 + e - p_1$ and $\pi = \bar{p}_3 + e - p_1$, the hypothesis $\beta_3 > \beta_4$ comes down to assuming that, for fixed prices $p_1, \bar{p}_2$ and $\bar{p}_3$, a devaluation stimulates the demand for good 1: the additional demand caused by the greater competitiveness of domestic production dominates the negative income effect of a rise in the cost of intermediate imported goods.

Finally, for simplicity's sake, we have assumed that domestic demand does not depend on the distribution of the national income between wages and other incomes.

The current account is defined by (4.72). Note that the hypothesis $\gamma_2 > \gamma_3$ implies that, *ceteris paribus*, a devaluation improves upon the foreign trade balance, which corresponds to a Marshall–Lerner type condition on exports and imports demands.

4.2   *Fix-price equilibrium and an oil shock*

We will assume that domestic production is set at the minimum of supply and demand, that is the hypothesis of a frictionless market. This leads us to write

$$y = \min\{y_d, y_s\}$$

that is

$$y = \min\{y_d, y_s^*, y_0\}$$

Thus, we obtain the three usual types of temporary fix-price equilibria: Keynesian unemployment, classical unemployment and repressed inflation.

In the Keynesian unemployment regime, production y is equal to effective demand y_d, that is to say

$$y = \beta_1 + \beta_2 m_0 + \beta_3 q - \beta_4 \pi + \beta_5 y$$

and

$$y = \frac{\beta_1 + \beta_2 m_0 + \beta_3 q - \beta_4 \pi}{1 - \beta_5} \tag{4.73}$$

In this case, a rise in the relative price q exerts a favourable effect on goods demand and therefore on output and employment, owing to the improved competitiveness of domestic production. Conversely, a rise in the relative price of energy π worsens the external deficit and makes the demand for domestic goods decrease. Consequently, employment and production decrease as well.

Finally, for fixed prices p_1, $\bar{p}_2$ and $\bar{p}_3$ we have

$$\frac{\partial y}{\partial e} = \frac{\beta_3 - \beta_4}{1 - \beta_2} > 0$$

Therefore, when Keynesian unemployment prevails, devaluation exerts a favourable effect on economic activity.

In the classical unemployment regime, output is equal to the notional supply

$$y = \alpha_1 - \alpha_2 \omega - \alpha_3 q - \alpha_4 \pi$$

In this case, if the real wage rate ω is fixed, production decreases when the relative prices of imported goods increase. This is particularly the case when the rise in q and π is caused by devaluation. Indeed, for fixed prices p_1, $\bar{p}_2$ and $\bar{p}_3$, we have

$$\frac{\partial y}{\partial e} = -(\alpha_3 + \alpha_4) < 0$$

Devaluation is thus unfavourable to economic activity. As in the previous model, the distinction between Keynesian and classical unemployment allows us to clearly distinguish two mechanisms which relate the level of the economic activity to the exchange rate: depreciation improves upon the competitiveness of domestic production and therefore the demand for it, but it also makes the price of imported goods increase. When Keynesian unemployment prevails, demand determines the level of production and therefore devaluation exerts a favourable effect. Conversely, in the classical unemployment regime, production is determined by supply and it is an appreciation of the domestic currency that can stimulate the activity.

Note that in both Keynesian and classical contexts, a rise in the price of energy makes the level of production decrease, but the causes are different. In a Keynesian unemployment situation, an oil shock affects production through its deflationary effect on demand. In a classical unemployment regime, its impact on production is linked to a decrease in the profitable supply.

Finally, *in the repressed inflation regime*, production reaches its full-employment level y_0 and therefore is fixed in the short run.

For given values of real wages ω and money balances m_0, the conditions of validity of these three disequilibrium regimes can be represented in the (π, q) plane.

When Keynesian unemployment prevails, production is defined by (4.73) and we have $y < y_0$ and $y < y_s^*$, that is

$$\beta_3 q - \beta_4 \pi < (1 - \beta_5) y_0 - \beta_1 - \beta_2 m_0 \tag{4.74}$$

$$[\alpha_3(1 - \beta_5) + \beta_3] q + [\alpha_4(1 - \beta_5) - \beta_4] \pi$$
$$< (1 - \beta_5)(\alpha_1 - \alpha_2 \omega) - \beta_1 - \beta_2 m_0 \tag{4.75}$$

Under classical unemployment, production is equal to the notional supply y_s^* and satisfies $y_s^* < y_d$ and $y_s^* < y_0$ that is

$$[\alpha_3(1 - \beta_5) + \beta_3] q + [\alpha_4(1 - \beta_5) - \beta_4] \pi$$
$$> (1 - \beta_5)(\alpha_1 - \alpha_2 \omega) - \beta_1 - \beta_2 m_0 \tag{4.76}$$

$$\alpha_3 q + \alpha_4 \pi > \alpha_1 - \alpha_2 \omega - y_0 \tag{4.77}$$

Finally, in the repressed inflation regime, $y_0 < y_d$ and $y_0 < y_s^*$, which leads to

$$\beta_3 q - \beta_4 \pi > (1 - \beta_5) y_0 - \beta_1 - \beta_2 m_0 \tag{4.78}$$

$$\alpha_3 q + \alpha_4 \pi < \alpha_1 - \alpha_2 \omega - y_0 \tag{4.79}$$

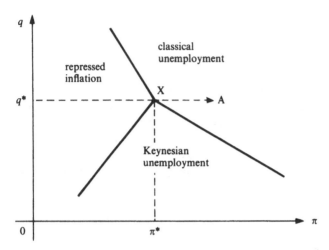

Figure 4.3   Disequilibrium regimes. Case $\beta_4 < \alpha_4(1-\beta_5)$

For given values of ω and m_0, conditions (4.74) to (4.79) allow us to divide the (π,q) plane into three areas, each of them corresponding to a disequilibrium regime. Two cases have to be distinguished, depending on the direction of the inequality $\beta_4 \gtrless \alpha_4(1-\beta_5)$.

Both cases can easily be interpreted by contemplating the consequences of a rise in the price of energy π. Let us assume that the economy is initially at a Walrasian equilibrium X. A rise in π causes a shift from X to A. It is always an underemployment equilibrium, if the real wage rate ω, real money balances m_0 and the exchange rate e are not altered. If we have $\beta_4 > \alpha_4(1-\beta_5)$, the economy is led to the Keynesian unemployment regime and classical unemployment will appear in the reverse situation when $\beta_4 < \alpha_4(1-\beta_5)$. Note that $\beta_4/(1-\beta_5)$ is equal to the effect on domestic goods demand of a unit increase in the price of energy, taking into account the Keynesian multiplier effect, and α_4 stands for the effect on notional supply. Thus, both demand and supply are adversely affected by the increase in the price of energy, and the nature of the disequilibrium regime which prevails after the shock depends on the relative magnitude of these two effects. If the price p_1 tends to increase under excess demand $(y_d > y_s)$ and to decrease under excess supply $(y_s > y_d)$, the oil shock entails short-run inflationary consequences when $\beta_4 < \alpha_4(1-\beta_5)$ and short-run deflationary consequences when $\beta_4 > \alpha_4(1-\beta_5)$.

If the rise in the price of energy has led to the Keynesian unemployment regime, its short-run impact on production can be minimized only by compensating for the deflationary effect of the additional external deficit by a depreciation of the domestic currency or by an expansionary monetary

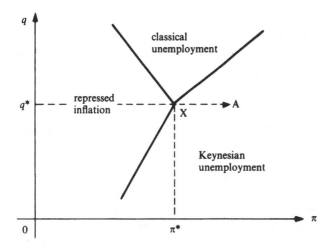

Figure 4.4   Disequilibrium regimes. Case $\beta_4 > \alpha_4(1 - \beta_5)$

policy. Conversely, in a classical unemployment situation, an appreciation of the domestic currency or a decrease in real wages are desirable. If we assume that real wages are fixed in the short run, only the exchange rate e and the money holdings m_0 may be manipulated. Nevertheless, they are sufficient to balance both labour and good 1 markets.

Indeed, a computation shows that the coordinates of the Walrasian equilibrium X are

$$\pi^* = \frac{\beta_3(\alpha_1 - \alpha_2\omega - y_0) - \alpha_3[(1 - \beta_5)y_0 - \beta_1 - \beta_2 m_0]}{\beta_3\alpha_4 + \alpha_3\beta_4}$$

$$q^* = \frac{\beta_4(\alpha_1 - \alpha_2\omega - y_0) + \alpha_4[(1 - \beta_5)y_0 - \beta_1 - \beta_2 m_0]}{\beta_3\alpha_4 + \alpha_3\beta_4}$$

Using $\pi = \bar{p}_3 + e - p_1$ and $q = \bar{p}_2 + e - p_1$, we deduce that for fixed prices p_1 and $\bar{p}_2$, the economy will remain at the Walrasian equilibrium if the change in the price of energy $\Delta\bar{p}_3$ is compensated for by the variations in the exchange rate Δe and money holdings Δm_0, such that

$$\Delta\bar{p}_3 + \Delta e = \frac{\alpha_3\beta_2}{\beta_3\alpha_4 + \alpha_3\beta_4}\Delta m_0$$

$$\Delta e = -\frac{\alpha_4\beta_2}{\beta_3\alpha_4 + \alpha_3\beta_4}\Delta m_0$$

which implies

$$\Delta m_0 = \frac{(\beta_3\alpha_4 + \alpha_3\beta_4)}{\beta_2(\alpha_3 + \alpha_4)}\Delta\bar{p}_3 \text{ and } \Delta e = -\frac{\alpha_4}{\alpha_3 + \alpha_4}\Delta\bar{p}_3$$

If the price of energy increases ($\Delta \bar{p}_3 > 0$), the real wage rate being constant, a Walrasian equilibrium may still prevail only if households benefit from an expansionary monetary policy through transfers, and if, simultaneously, the domestic currency appreciates ($\Delta m_0 > 0, \Delta e < 0$). Consequently, the foreign trade balance deteriorates owing to transfers to households, which stimulate the domestic demand, and to the loss of competitiveness caused by the change in the exchange rate.

Such a policy may be rational in the short run, since a transitory shock can be dampened by allowing a temporary deficit in the current account. In the long run, its cost in terms of greater inflation and worsening of the current account makes it unbearable. Then, a balanced current account becomes a constraint which, if not respected, imposes a readjustment of the exchange rate. Further, the fix-price hypothesis is an extreme modelling of nominal rigidities which makes sense in the short run only. In the long run, only real rigidities may possibly last. We will now contemplate the long-run consequences of an oil crisis from that angle, assuming that domestic nominal prices and the exchange rate are perfectly flexible and that the only rigidity affecting wages is real and not nominal.

4.3   *Oil shock and real wage rigidity*

Let $\bar{p}_1 = p_1 - e$ be the price of the domestic good in foreign currency. At the Walrasian equilibrium, m_0, $\bar{p}_1$ and ω are linked by the following relations

$$y_0 = \alpha_1 - \alpha_2 \omega - \alpha_3(\bar{p}_2 - \bar{p}_1) - \alpha_4(\bar{p}_3 - \bar{p}_1) \qquad (4.80)$$

$$(1 - \beta_5)y_0 = \beta_1 + \beta_2 m_0 + \beta_3(\bar{p}_2 - \bar{p}_1) - \beta_4(\bar{p}_3 - \bar{p}_1) \qquad (4.81)$$

Moreover, the condition $B = 0$ imposes

$$\gamma_1 + \gamma_2(\bar{p}_2 - \bar{p}_1) - \gamma_3(\bar{p}_3 - \bar{p}_1) - \gamma_4 y_0 - \gamma_5 m_0 = 0 \qquad (4.82)$$

Relations (4.80), (4.81) and (4.82) form an equation system where the unknowns are m_0, $\bar{p}_1$ and ω and where $\bar{p}_2$ and $\bar{p}_3$ are parameters. Let $m_0^*, \bar{p}_1^*, \omega^*$ be the solution of this system. Solving (4.81)–(4.82) gives

$$\bar{p}_1^* = \frac{\beta_2 \eta_2 - \gamma_5 \eta_1}{\beta_2 \varepsilon_1 + \gamma_5 \varepsilon_2}$$

$$m_0^* = \frac{\varepsilon_1 \eta_1 + \varepsilon_2 \eta_2}{\beta_2 \varepsilon_1 + \gamma_5 \varepsilon_2}$$

with

$$\eta_1 = (1 - \beta_5)y_0 - \beta_1 - \beta_3 \bar{p}_2 + \beta_4 \bar{p}_3$$
$$\eta_2 = \gamma_1 + \gamma_2 \bar{p}_2 - \gamma_3 \bar{p}_3 - \gamma_4 y_0$$
$$\varepsilon_1 = \gamma_2 - \gamma_3 > 0$$
$$\varepsilon_2 = \beta_3 - \beta_4 > 0$$

Using (4.80) and $p_1^* = M_0 - m_0^*$ and $e^* = p_1 - \bar{p}_1^*$ allows us to evaluate the effect of a variation in the price of energy $\Delta\bar{p}_3$ on the equilibrium values of real wages ω^*, domestic price p_1^* and exchange rate e^*, for a given money stock M_0

$$\Delta\omega^* = -\frac{k_1\alpha_3 + (1+k_1)\alpha_4}{\alpha_2}\Delta\bar{p}_3$$

$$\Delta p_1^* = k_2\Delta\bar{p}_3$$

$$\Delta e^* = (k_1 + k_2)\Delta\bar{p}_3$$

where

$$k_1 = \frac{\beta_2\gamma_3 + \beta_4\gamma_5}{\beta_2\varepsilon_1 + \gamma_5\varepsilon_2} > 0$$

$$k_2 = \frac{\beta_3\gamma_3 - \beta_4\gamma_2}{\beta_2\varepsilon_1 + \gamma_5\varepsilon_2}$$

Assume $\Delta\bar{p}_3 > 0$. We then have $\Delta\omega^* < 0$ and $\Delta\bar{p}_1^* = \Delta p_1^* - \Delta e^* = -k_1\Delta\bar{p}_3 < 0$.

Very simple conclusions emerge from these results. After an oil shock, profitability on domestic production necessarily deteriorates for two cumulative reasons: first, of course, because of the increase in the price of energy used as an intermediate good, and secondly because of the decrease in the price of domestic goods in terms of foreign currency, which is necessary to increase exports to finance the additional cost of energy. Because of these two reasons, a decrease in consumption real wages is unavoidable to maintain the profitability of the production sector at a level compatible with full employment. Equivalently, in a more realistic perspective, during a transitory period, wage increases should be lower than productivity gains for a durable full-employment situation to be recovered.

Indeed, the oil price shock leads to a simple dilemma: either a wage cut is implemented or involuntary unemployment will prevail in the long run. With nominal prices being perfectly flexible, in case of involuntary unemployment, the economy will be at the borderline of Keynesian and classical unemployment regimes. The long-run relation between the decrease in output and real wages Δy, $\Delta\omega$ and the increase in the price of oil $\Delta\bar{p}_3$ can be obtained by differentiating relations (4.80), (4.81) and (4.82) where y is put in place of y_0 (with $y < y_0$). This gives

$$\Delta y = -\alpha_2\Delta\omega + (\alpha_3 + \alpha_4)\Delta\bar{p}_1 - \alpha_4\Delta\bar{p}_3$$

$$(1 - \beta_5)\Delta y = \beta_2\Delta m_0 - \varepsilon_2\Delta\bar{p}_1 - \beta_4\Delta\bar{p}_3$$

$$-\varepsilon_1\Delta\bar{p}_1 - \gamma_3\Delta\bar{p}_3 - \gamma_4\Delta y - \gamma_5\Delta m_0 = 0$$

After some simple calculations, this yields

$$[1+k_3(\alpha_3+\alpha_4)]\Delta y + \alpha_2\Delta\omega = -[k_1\alpha_3+(1+k_1)\alpha_4]\Delta\bar{p}_3$$

where

$$k_3 = \frac{\gamma_4\beta_2+\gamma_3(1-\beta_5)}{\beta_2\varepsilon_1+\gamma_5\varepsilon_2} > 0$$

A 1 percent wage cut thus gives an increase of $\alpha_2/[1+k_3(\alpha_3+\alpha_4)]$ percent in output, an elasticity which incorporates at the same time coefficients drawn from the goods supply and demand functions and from the current account equation. This clearly shows that, in the long run, an oil shock depresses economic activity all the more as wages are insensitive in real terms to business depression and increasing unemployment. Countries where wage rigidity is purely nominal are thus in a better position to react against an oil shock than those where real wages are downward rigid because of indexation procedures, imperfect competition features of the labour market or other reasons.[3]

Finally, coming back to the case where wages are fully flexible, it may be observed that the oil shock may exert a positive or negative long-run effect on domestic prices since the sign of k_2 is ambiguous. Furthermore, this sign does not depend on the nature of the disequilibrium regime induced by the shock in the short run. For instance, the oil shock may lead at the same time to a Keynesian depression in the short run and to higher prices of domestic goods, in terms of domestic currency, in the long run.

Lastly, let us note that the model only determines the equilibrium quantity of *real* money m_0^*: Increasing the stock of money would allow us to reduce the intensity of a Keynesian recession but only at the cost of higher equilibrium prices in the long run and without any long-term effect on economic activity.

5 Implicit contracts and unions

Our main concern in chapters 5 and 6 is to analyse why real wages may be downward rigid, while some degree of involuntary unemployment prevails in the economy. Two possible explanations are explored in this chapter, implicit contracts and unions, while the third, efficiency wages, is the subject of chapter 6.

The theory of implicit contracts is based on the assumption that wages and employment result from long-term agreements between firms and their employees. Such agreements allow them to share out risk that might affect the profitability of the firms. In this framework, firms are able to provide insurance against uncertainty to their employees and this may lead to some degree of real wage rigidity.

We may introduce the notion of long-term implicit contract as follows. Consider two successive periods 0 and 1. Workers who are actually productive in period 1 were hired in period 0 because for instance training on the job was necessary. In period 0, workers and firms sign contracts specifying their respective obligations in different situations that might occur in period 1. If we assume that an individual can provide an indivisible unit of labour, a contract will define a wage, a level of unemployment benefit and the number of individuals actually employed by the firm for every state of nature in period 1. When the state of nature is revealed, each party fulfils its respective obligations.

Thus, the implicit contract theory holds that the operation of the labour market in a given period (period 1) results from the implementation of binding preliminary agreements between workers and firms in order to share-out risk in an *ex ante* optimal way. *Implicit* means that this theory contemplates contracts with clauses that are seldom included in real labour contracts, like for instance clauses indicating the number of individuals a firm will hire as a function of the state of nature which gives the probability for a worker to be dismissed for any state. It is generally assumed that a firm will respect all the clauses of an agreement in order to preserve its reputation, even though such clauses cannot be observed by a third party and therefore cannot lead to a law-suit.

In the models elaborated by Azariadis (1975), Baily (1974) and Gordon (1974), the firms are assumed to be risk-neutral, while employees are risk-averse. This hypothesis can be justified by the assumption that the firms' owners can share out risks by diversifying their investments in the financial markets while employees cannot. Therefore, labour contracts insure workers against income uncertainty and, as we shall see, this explains the stability of real wages. However, the hypothesis holding that firms are risk-neutral is no doubt overrestrictive, since generally risk cannot be totally diversified. Further, if owners are imperfectly informed about managers' efforts, an incentive scheme would make managers' wages depend on the firms' profits, which would ultimately explain why managers are risk-averse *vis-à-vis* profits, even though shareholders are risk-neutral. Thus we will also contemplate the situation when the firms, as much as their employees, are risk-averse.

The simplest models of implicit contracts rest on two main hypotheses. First, firms and workers have the same information: information is symmetrical. More precisely, at period 1, the state of nature is revealed to everybody. Second, firms and workers may commit themselves in respecting the terms of their contracts. As we shall see in section 1, such an elementary version of the implicit contract theory may account for the rigidity of real wages but it explains involuntary unemployment or inefficient fluctuations in the employment level only by imposing rather unconvincing restrictions on the possible contracts (by not providing for an unemployment benefit). Since originally the implicit contract theory sought to put forward some failures of the labour market, it is not surprising that further research has tried to explain what makes contracts inefficient. The emphasis was mainly put on the consequences of asymmetrical information (section 2). Indeed, if at period 1 the state of nature can be observed by the firm only, the latter must announce it honestly. We intuitively understand that an incentive contract, e.g., a contract leading the firm to announce the actual state of nature, includes some restrictions that may affect the terms of the contract eventually selected. For instance, a contract providing for a constant remuneration for each individual whatever the state of nature, and a variable employment level, will obviously lead the firm to choose the state with the highest employment level. Thus, such a contract is not incentive compatible. We will see that the contract that is actually selected under asymmetrical information may include *ex post* inefficiencies (that is, when the state of nature is announced) and may sometimes lead to excess underemployment. Unfortunately, the qualitative results provided by these models depend highly on the modelling options and are very sensitive to modifications in their hypotheses.

In a perfectly competitive economy, the standard implicit contract approach in fact is less in accordance with a non-Walrasian approach than with the principles of market clearing models which explain the instability of economic activity through the variability of the labour supply. Indeed, in the usual microeconomic analysis of consumers' choices, the labour supply is often considered to be rather insensitive to the variations in wages, owing to the income effect which runs counter the substitution effect and this can affect considerably the empirical relevance of macroeconomic market clearing models. In so far as implicit contracts lead to a transfer of wages from good to bad states, in comparison with a spot competitive labour market, implicit contract models may cause a higher instability in the labour supply than traditional neoclassical models. This is shown in the appendix to this chapter.

In the implicit contract theory, a perfectly competitive contract market is supposed to be open at period 0 and, under symmetric information, contracts with private unemployment insurance lead to the same allocation of labour as in a perfectly competitive spot market economy, without any involuntary unemployment. Do the results change if the market for contracts were imperfectly competitive, with a union on one side and one or several firms on the other side? Two models dominate the literature on trade unions: the monopoly union model and the bilateral monopoly model. We will contemplate them both in section 3, still considering the case of contingent contracts signed at period 0, which allows a simple comparison with the implicit contract approach. In each model, the union is supposed to care about its members' wages and the employment level. We will first consider the case of a utilitarian objective function: all individuals are members of the union and the union maximizes the expected utility of its members.

In the monopoly union model, a union is supposed to face a great number of firms so that it is less costly not to bargain individually with all of them. Hence, the union unilaterally chooses the wage rate and each firm determines its employment level, whilst taking as given this wage rate. The model predicts higher wages and lower employment than at the competitive equilibrium and also constant wages in all states whenever the elasticity of labour demand is constant. However, as noticed by Leontieff (1946) and emphasized by McDonald and Solow (1981), the monopoly union model leads to an inefficient outcome: the resulting wage–employment combination does not belong to the bargaining contract curve, that is to the set of tangency points between isoprofit lines and indifference curves. In fact, at the monopoly union equilibrium, each firm has an incentive to directly negotiate with the union in order to obtain lower wages against the promise of a higher employment level.

In the bilateral monopoly model, a firm and a union bargain simultaneously on wages and employment and the resulting contingent contract is *ex post* efficient. Considering the Nash solution to this bargaining problem, the bilateral monopoly model with contingent contracts and no private unemployment benefit predicts involuntary unemployment in bad states, constant wages when the firm is risk-neutral and also a higher employment level than in an equivalent competitive labour market. As in an implicit contract model without private unemployment insurance, such as Azariadis' (1975), overemployment acts here as a substitute for insurance against the risk of unemployment. The results of the bilateral monopoly model are deeply modified when contracts include unemployment benefits. In that case, as in the implicit contract model with private unemployment insurance, there is no involuntary unemployment any more and the employment level coincides with the competitive equilibrium. In short, when the union maximizes the expected utility of identical members, the monopoly model with contingent contracts provides results that are qualitatively similar to those of the symmetric information implicit contract model.

However, many writings on economic theory of trade unions have challenged the assumption of a utilitarian union. In particular, the influence of seniority on the objectives of unions has been frequently emphasized and this opens a new perspective for the analysis of labour contracts. The insiders–outsiders approach is an extreme version of this view. In the simplest insiders–outsiders model, only insiders' interests are represented in wage bargaining. Insiders also have priority in employment and the firm begins to hire outsiders only when all insiders are employed. More generally, empirical observation suggests that lay-offs are not done randomly but often more or less by seniority. Such 'last-in, first out' firing practices may modify the objectives of the trade union. In particular, when senior workers dominate the voting over the firm's offers or when the median voter considers himself as sure not to be fired, the union becomes locally indifferent to the employment level. As we will see, seniority in wage–employment bargaining may explain allocative inefficiencies and involuntary unemployment on the labour market.

1   Contracts with symmetric information

1.1   *The model*

Let us consider an economy with m identical firms and mL identical workers, m and L being integers. All the firms produce the same consumption good with labour. The production function of a firm is $y = \theta f(l)$ with $f' > 0, f'' < 0$ where y is output and l is employment. θ is a productivity parameter[1] and we assume $\theta \in \{\theta_1, \theta_2, \ldots, \theta_n\} \subset R_+$ with $\theta_1 < \theta_2 \ldots < \theta_n$. Each θ_i characterizes a state i.

The model includes two periods labelled 0 and 1. In period 0, θ is unknown but it is common knowledge that

$$\text{Prob}(\theta = \theta_i) = \pi_i \qquad i = 1, \ldots, n$$

with $\pi_i > 0$ for each i and $\sum_{i=1}^{n} \pi_i = 1$. The firm and its workers discover the realized value of θ in period 1.

Each individual is able to provide an indivisible unit of labour. Let R be the individual welfare in terms of money in period 1. All individuals sign their contracts in period 0 but they may be employed or dismissed in period 1. The government does not provide any unemployment benefit. For an employed individual, we have $R = w - k$, where w stands for the wage paid and k represents the labour disutility expressed in monetary terms. For a jobless individual, we have $R = \bar{w}$, where $\bar{w}$ stands for the unemployment benefit exclusively paid by the firm to its workers. Workers are risk-averse. In period 0, they maximize their expected utility $EU(R)$, where $U(.)$ is a von Neumann–Morgenstern utility function which satisfies $U' > 0$, $U'' < 0$ and $U(0) = 0$.

We set the price of the output at 1. If the firm hired N individuals in period 0 and keeps l of them in period 1, its profit writes as

$$\Pi = \theta f(l) - wl - \bar{w}(N - l)$$

In period 0 the firm seeks to maximize the expected utility of profit $EV(\Pi)$, where $V(.)$ satisfies $V' > 0, V'' \leq 0$.

In period 0, the firm signs labour contracts with N individuals. For each state $i = 1, \ldots, n$ a contract will define the wage w_i, the unemployment benefit $\bar{w}_i$, and the employment level l_i, with $l_i \leq N$. The workers bound to be dismissed in period 1 are drawn among the N individuals hired in period 0. Thus, a labour contract C writes as follows

$$C = (w_1, \ldots, w_n, \bar{w}_1, \ldots, \bar{w}_n, l_1, \ldots, l_n)$$

We assume that it is the firm which proposes the labour contracts to the N individuals and workers accept them when their expected utility is at least equal to u_0. For the time being, u_0 and N are given parameters. u_0 stands for the contract value (in terms of expected utility for workers) and we assume that $u_0 > 0$. N stands for the number of labour contracts signed by the firm. We will see that u_0 and N result from the equilibrium prevailing on a market which is open in period 0: the labour contract market.

1.2   *The optimal contract*

The optimal contract maximizes the firm's expected utility under two conditions: on the one hand, the expected utility of the hired N individuals must not be less than their reservation utility u_0 and, on the other hand, the employment level must not exceed N. The optimal contract is thus the solution of the following program:

Maximize $\displaystyle\sum_{i=1}^{n} \pi_i V(\theta_i f(l_i) - w_i l_i - \bar{w}_i(N - l_i))$ with   respect   to
$w_i \geq 0, \bar{w}_i \geq 0$ and $l_i \geq 0$, $i = 1, \ldots, n$ subject to:

$$\sum_{i=1}^{n} \pi_i \left[\frac{l_i}{N} U(w_i - k) + \frac{N - l_i}{N} U(\bar{w}_i) \right] \geq u_0 \tag{5.1}$$

$$l_i \leq N \qquad i = 1, \ldots, n \tag{5.2}$$

A few elementary calculations allow us to characterize the optimal contract.

Let α and β_i, $i = 1, \ldots, n$ be Kuhn–Tucker multipliers, respectively associated with the constraints (5.1) and (5.2). The optimality conditions for each state i are[2]

$$\pi_i V'(i)[\theta_i f'(l_i) - w_i + \bar{w}_i] + \frac{\pi_i \alpha}{N} [U(w_i - k) - U(\bar{w}_i)] - \beta_i = 0 \tag{5.3}$$

$$V'(i) = \frac{\alpha}{N} U'(w_i - k) = \frac{\alpha}{N} U'(\bar{w}_i) \tag{5.4}$$

where

$$V'(i) \equiv V'(\theta_i f(l_i) - w_i l_i - \bar{w}_i(N - l_i))$$

We also have $\alpha > 0$, according to (5.4) and $\beta_i \geq 0, \beta_i = 0$ if $l_i < N$. By using (5.4) and $U'' < 0$, we immediately deduce

$$w_i = \bar{w}_i + k \text{ for all } i \tag{5.5}$$

Thus, in each state, the wage rate is equal to the sum of the redundancy benefit and the labour disutility: an individuals' utility is thus the same despite his being actually employed or dismissed in period 1. This model therefore will not result in involuntary unemployment. We also have

$$\frac{V'(i)}{V'(j)} = \frac{U'(i)}{U'(j)} \qquad \text{if } i \neq j \tag{5.6}$$

where $U'(i) \equiv U'(w_i - k) = U'(\bar{w}_i)$.

For any pair of states, the marginal rate of substitution between state-contingent income claims is the same for the firm and its workers. We

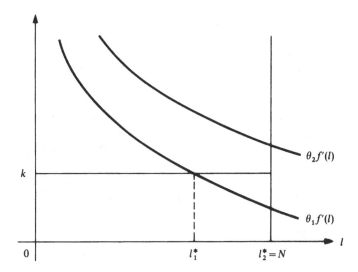

Figure 5.1   Determination of the efficient employment level

find here the Arrow–Borch condition which characterizes an optimal sharing out of risk for a surplus $\pi_i + R_i \equiv \theta_i f(l_i) - kl_i$ to be distributed in state i between the firm and its workers. Condition (5.6) leads to a particularly typical result when the firm is risk-neutral. Then, we have $V'(i) = V'(j)$ *and thus* $U'(w_i - k) = U'(w_j - k)$. By using $U'' < 0$, we deduce $w_i = w_j \equiv w$: *when workers are risk-averse and the firm is risk-neutral, the optimal contract thus provides for a constant level of wages in all states.*

The employment level can be characterized by using (5.3) and (5.5). We have $\theta_i f'(l_i) = k$ if $l_i < N$ and $\theta_i f'(l_i) \geq k$ if $l_i = N$. We deduce from this that l_i maximizes the total surplus $\theta_i f(l_i) - kl_i$ under the condition $l_i \leq N$. In each state, the employment level is thus efficient *ex post*. This is represented in figure 5.1, when $n = 2$. Let l_i^* be the efficient employment level in state i, that is $l_i^* = \text{Arg}_l \text{Max}\{\theta_i f(l) - kl | l \leq N\}$. We assume that $l_1^* < N$ and $l_2^* = N$: in the 'bad state' (state 1) the efficient employment level is less than N, while there is full employment in the 'good state'.

We should also note that this first implicit contract model leads to the very same employment level as when the economy does not include long-term contracts but a simple competitive spot labour market open in period 1. Indeed, in the absence of unemployment benefit paid by the government, workers' reservation wages would be equal to k. When the spot market is at equilibrium, wages would be equal to k and underemployment would be voluntary at state 1 (both employed and unemployed individuals having their welfare levels equal to $u(0) = 0$). At state 2, full employment would prevail and wages would be equal to $\theta_2 f'(N)$.

Eventually, *the implicit contract model under symmetric information leads to the same employment level as in the case of a competitive spot market and this level maximizes the total surplus in each state.*

It remains for us to explain how the number of individuals hired by each firm is determined in period 0 and the workers' reservation utility, that is parameters N and u_0. This will result from the contract market open in period 0. When the firm hires a certain number of individuals, it considers as given their reservation utility (which is determined without ambiguity since individuals are all identical). The firm determines N by maximizing its expected profit, as it results from the optimal contracting problem we have just addressed. Let us write $\phi(N,u_0)$ the firm's expected profit. The firm's demand for labour in period 0 (e.g., its supply of contracts) will be written $N^d(u_0)$ and defined by

$$N^d(u_0) = \text{Arg Max}_N \, \phi(N,u_0)$$

In order to characterize function $N^d(.)$, we will limit ourselves to the situation when the firm is risk-neutral: $V(\Pi) \equiv \Pi$. By using the envelope theorem and the condition $w_i = \bar{w}_i + k$, we obtain

$$\frac{\partial \phi}{\partial N} = -\sum_{i=1} \pi_i \bar{w}_i + \sum_i \beta_i \tag{5.7}$$

When the firm is risk-neutral, we have $\bar{w}_i = w_i - k = U^{-1}(u_0)$ for each i. (5.3) and (5.7) thus imply

$$\frac{\partial \phi}{\partial N} = -U^{-1}(u_0) + \sum_{i=1}^{n} \pi_i [\theta_i f'(l_i^*) - k]$$

Therefore we have

$$\frac{\partial^2 \phi}{\partial N^2} = \sum_{i=1}^{n} \pi_i \theta_i f''(l_i) \frac{dl_i^*}{dN} \leq 0$$

$$\frac{\partial^2 \phi}{\partial N \partial u_0} = -\frac{1}{U'} < 0$$

Function $N \to \phi(N,u_0)$ is thus concave and N^d is defined by $\frac{\partial \phi}{\partial N}(N^d,u_0) = 0$.

We have[3]

$$\frac{\partial N^d}{\partial u_0} = -\frac{\partial^2 \phi / \partial N \partial u_0}{\partial^2 \phi / \partial N^2} < 0$$

Thus function $N^d(u_0)$ is decreasing and satisfies $N^d(0) \geq f'^{-1}(k/\theta_n)$.

Since no spot market is open in period 1, the supply of labour (e.g., workers' demand for labour contracts) is equal to mL when $u_0 > 0$, and it is

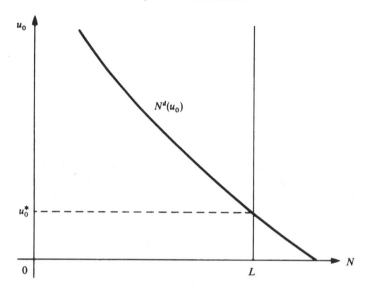

Figure 5.2   Contract market equilibrium

equal to zero when $u_0 < 0$. At the equilibrium of the contract market, we have $u_0 = u_0^*$, with $N^d(u_0^*) = L$ and $u_0^* > 0$ if $\theta_n f'(L) > k$.

If the theory of implicit contract under symmetric information accounts for the rigidity of real wages, it neither explains involuntary unemployment nor the inefficient fluctuations in the employment level. We may then ponder on the consequences of a more restrictive definition of these contracts. We may for instance consider the situation when unemployment benefit does not appear as a clause in these contracts but is set at an exogenous level $\bar{w}$ and paid by the government to all the unemployed workers.[4]

1.3   *Contracts not providing for unemployment benefits*

Now, the contract writes $C = (w_1, \ldots, w_n, l_1, \ldots, l_n)$. The optimal contract is the solution of the following problem:

Maximize $\sum_{i=1}^{n} \pi_i V(\theta_i f(l_i) - w_i l_i)$ with respect to $w_i \geq 0$ and $l_i \geq 0$, $i = 1, \ldots, n$, subject to:

$$\sum_{i=1}^{n} \pi_i \left[\frac{l_i}{N} U(w_i - k) + \frac{N - l_i}{N} U(\bar{w}) \right] \geq u_0 \qquad (5.8)$$

$$l_i \leq N \qquad i = 1, \ldots, n \qquad (5.9)$$

Let α and β_i, $i=1, \ldots, n$ be multipliers, respectively associated with (5.8) and (5.9). The optimality conditions write as

$$\pi_i V'(i)[\theta_i f'(l_i) - w_i] + \frac{\pi_i \alpha}{N}[U(w_i - k) - U(\bar{w})] - \beta_i = 0 \qquad (5.10)$$

$$V'(i) = \frac{\alpha}{N} U'(w_i - k) \qquad (5.11)$$

for all state i.

Obviously, since we exogenously defined dismissed workers' incomes, the utility of those individuals actually hired in period 1 will be strictly higher than that of the dismissed individuals. Consequently, unemployment is involuntary in that case. Assume for instance that the firm is risk-neutral: $V(\Pi) \equiv \Pi$. From (5.11), we have $w_1 = w_2 =, \ldots, = w_n = w$: the real wage is thus constant and, according to the binding constraint (5.8), it is defined by

$$U(w-k) \sum_{i=1}^{n} \frac{\pi_i l_i}{N} + U(\bar{w})\left[1 - \sum_{i=1}^{n} \frac{\pi_i l_i}{N}\right] = u_0 \qquad (5.12)$$

Thus we have $w - k > \bar{w}$ when $u_0 > U(\bar{w})$, that is when it is more profitable to sign a labour contract than remain unemployed. Then involuntary unemployment prevails in every state where $l_i < N$[5]. Further, (5.10) and (5.11) imply

$$\theta_i f'(l_i) - w_i + \frac{U(w_i - k) - U(\bar{w})}{U'(w_i - k)} \geq 0$$

$$= 0 \text{ if } l_i < N$$

This condition allows us to compare the employment l_i with the employment level which would prevail in a competitive spot market.[6] Indeed, owing to the concavity of $U(.)$, we have

$$U(w_i - k) - U(\bar{w}) > U'(w_i - k)(w_i - k - \bar{w})$$

and thus

$$\theta_i f'(l_i) < k + \bar{w} \qquad \text{if } l_i < N \qquad (5.13)$$

while, in a spot market, the reservation wage would be equal to $k + \bar{w}$ and the employment level $\bar{l}_i$ would be given by

$$\theta_i f'(\bar{l}_i) = k + \bar{w} \qquad (5.14)$$

in every state i where the model would lead to unemployment. In view of

(5.13) and (5.14), $l_i > \bar{l}_i$ if $l_i < N$. In other words, the model leads to lower fluctuations in the employment level than in a competitive spot market. In particular, when $\bar{w} = 0$ we have $\bar{l}_i = l_i^*$ and thus $l_i > l_i^*$ if $l_i^* < N$.

In fact, setting the unemployment benefit exogenously comes down to depriving workers from their insurance against income instability. Therefore, risk-averse individuals will naturally compensate this lack of insurance by being more cautious. That is what we observe in the present case since a drop in unemployment is a partial insurance against redundancy. *In the aftermath, when the unemployment benefit is set exogenously, the model simultaneously accounts for involuntary unemployment and inefficient overemployment.* All this is far from being satisfactory. First because nothing can stop firms from including in their labour contracts redundancy benefits higher than the legal benefit and that is often the case in the real world. Second, we do not explain that inefficient underemployment might result: on the contrary, we only show that overemployment may occur. Instead of introducing *ad hoc* constraints on the set of possible contracts, it is certainly more satisfactory to transfer these restrictions on the information firms and workers have. Let us turn to it now.

2 Contracts under asymmetric information

2.1 *General overview of results*

As long as firms and workers do not have at their disposal the same information either *ex ante* or *ex post*, contracts do not allow any optimal risk sharing and some forms of inefficiencies might appear. The implicit contract theory mostly puts the emphasis on the situation when the firm observes the realized state of nature in period 1, while workers cannot. It is the firm which has to announce the realized state of nature and thus the clauses that must be applied. Obviously, since the firm only knows the truth, it will announce the most convenient state, i.e., the profit-maximizing state.

Let us still write a contract as follows

$$C = (w_1, \ldots, w_n, \bar{w}_1, \ldots, \bar{w}_n, l_1, \ldots, l_n)$$

If the firm announces that state i is realized – that is it claims that $\theta = \theta_i$ – the wage, unemployment benefit and employment level will respectively be w_i, $\bar{w}_i$ and l_i.

Let $\Pi(i,j)$ be the profit of the firm if $\theta = \theta_i$ and if the firm announces $\theta = \theta_j$. We have

$$\Pi(i,j) = \theta_i f(l_j) - w_j l_j - \bar{w}_j (N - l_j)$$

Let $\tilde{j}(i)$ be the state announced by the firm when $\theta=\theta_i$.[7] Since the state announced has been chosen in order to maximize profit, we have

$$\Pi(i,\tilde{j}(i))\geq\Pi(i,h) \text{ for all } h=1,\ldots,n$$

Thus we have to take into account such misinformation on the part of the firm in order to determine the employment level and the payments a contract will lead to. Contract C will lead to $w=w_{\tilde{j}(i)}, \bar{w}=\bar{w}_{\tilde{j}(i)}$ and $l=l_{\tilde{j}(i)}$ in state i.

A contract is said to be *incentive compatible* if the firm truthfully announces the actual state, that is if $\tilde{j}(i)=i$ for all i. According to the *Revelation Principle*, for any contract C^0 there is an incentive compatible contract C^1 leading to the same resource allocation, that is, with the same payments and employment level in each state. This principle is really convenient while analysing contracts under asymmetric information, since it shows that it is not restrictive to only consider incentive compatible contracts. We can easily prove it. Let us consider any contract

$$C^0=(w_1^0,\ldots,w_n^0,\bar{w}_1^0,\ldots,\bar{w}_n^0,l_1^0,\ldots,l_n^0)$$

and the corresponding function $\tilde{j}(.)$. We define C^1 by

$$C^1=(w_1^1,\ldots,w_n^1,\bar{w}_1^1,\ldots,\bar{w}_n^1,l_1^1,\ldots,l_n^1)$$

with

$$w_i^1=w_{\tilde{j}(i)}^0,\bar{w}_i^1=\bar{w}_{\tilde{j}(i)}^0,l_i^1=l_{\tilde{j}(i)}^0 \text{ for each state } i$$

In other words, we define C^1 as the contract that specifies the payments and the employment levels that result from the implementation of C^0, taking into account the possible misrepresentation of the states by the firm.

Let $\Pi^0(i,j)$ and $\Pi^1(i,j)$ be the profit functions respectively for contracts C^0 and C^1. We have

$$\Pi^1(i,i)=\Pi^0(i,\tilde{j}(i)) \qquad \text{for all } i$$

and thus

$$\Pi^1(i,i)\geq\Pi^0(i,j) \qquad \text{for all } i,j$$

In particular when $j=\tilde{j}(h)$ with $h\in\{1,\ldots,n\}$, we have

$$\Pi^1(i,i)\geq\Pi^0(i,\tilde{j}(h))=\Pi^1(i,h) \qquad \text{for all } i,h$$

This proves that C^1 is incentive compatible and leads to the same allocation as C^0.

The optimal contract maximizes the firm's expected profit under incentive compatibility and feasibility constraints. Does imposing incentive compatibility alter the results obtained in section 1? It depends on firms' and workers' behaviours towards risk. Indeed, let us consider both following examples with

$$l_i^* = \text{Arg Max}\{\theta_i f(l) - kl | l \le N\}$$

and

$$C^* = (w_1^*, \ldots, w_n^*, \bar{w}_1^*, \ldots, \bar{w}_n^*, l_1^*, \ldots, l_n^*)$$

stands for the optimal contract under symmetric information. Let $\Pi^*(i,j)$ be the corresponding profit function.

Example 1 $U'' < 0$ and $V'' = 0$
Here, workers are risk-averse while firms are risk-neutral

$$\Pi^*(i,i) = \theta_i f(l_i^*) - w_i^* l_i^* - \bar{w}_i^*(N - l_i^*)$$
$$= \theta_i f(l_i^*) - k l_i^* - \bar{w}^* N$$

because $\bar{w}_i^* = w_i^* - k = U^{-1}(u_0) \equiv \bar{w}^*$ for all i if $U'' < 0, V'' = 0$. According to the definition of l_i^*, we have

$$\Pi^*(i,i) \ge \theta_i f(l_j^*) - k l_j^* - \bar{w}^* N \text{ for all } j \ne i$$

that is

$$\Pi^*(i,i) \ge \Pi^*(i,j) \qquad \text{for all } j \ne i$$

Therefore, contract C^* is incentive compatible and optimal under asymmetric information.

Example 2 $U'' = 0$ and $V'' < 0$
Here, workers are risk-neutral while the firms are risk-averse. Under symmetric information, the firms are totally insured against variations in their profits. Using (5.6), it follows that

$$\Pi^*(i,i) = \theta_i f(l_i^*) - w_i^* l_i^* - \bar{w}_i^*(N - l_i^*)$$
$$= \theta_j f(l_j^*) - w_j^* l_j^* - \bar{w}_j^*(N - l_j^*)$$
$$< \theta_i f(l_j^*) - w_j^* l_j^* - \bar{w}_j^*(N - l_j^*) \qquad \text{if } j < i$$

that is

$$\Pi^*(i,i) < \Pi^*(i,j) \qquad \text{if } j < i$$

With contract C^*, it is more profitable for the firm to pretend that the state is worse than it actually is. Thus, this contract is not incentive compatible.

The second example is far from being realistic but it shows the consequences of the firm's risk-aversion. Indeed, if the firm seeks to insure itself against excess variations in its profit, it will agree to pay higher wages and redundancy benefits when the state is good in order to lower wage costs

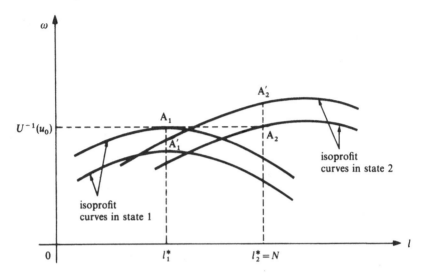

Figure 5.3   Example where the symmetric information optimal contract is not incentive compatible

when the state is bad, the employment level being set at the efficient level l_i^*. With contract C^*, under asymmetric information the firm may find it more profitable to pretend that the state is worse than it actually is in order to enjoy lower wages.

This is shown in figure 5.3, when $n=2$. Let $\omega = \bar{w}N$. Assume $w = \bar{w} + k$ (which is not restrictive); we have

$$\Pi = \theta f(l) - kl - \omega$$

We drew isoprofit curves when $\theta = \theta_1$ and $\theta = \theta_2$. State i isoprofit curves reach a maximum on $[0,N]$ at l_i^*. If $V'' = 0$ and $U'' < 0$, the optimal contract under symmetric information corresponds to points A_1 and A_2 where workers are completely insured against income variations. This shows that the perfect information optimal contract is incentive compatible. For instance, if we choose A_1 in state 2, the profit will be lower than if we choose A_2, and it is the same when we choose A_2 in state 1.

When $V'' < 0$, an optimal sharing-out of risk implies higher wages in state 2 and lower wages in state 1, as shown in figure 5.3, since ω_1 and ω_2 are linked in the relation $\pi_1 U(\omega_1/N) + \pi_2 U(\omega_2/N) = u_0$. If the firm is sufficiently risk-averse, the optimal contract under symmetric information can be (A_1', A_2'). In state 2, A_1' is located on a lower isoprofit curve than A_2': the firm may thus find it more convenient to pretend that the situation is bad while it is good. Therefore, contract C^* is not incentive compatible in the present case.

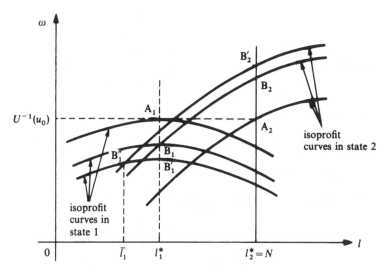

Figure 5.4   If the firm is risk-averse, the inefficient contract (B''_1, B'_2) is preferred to the efficient contract (B_1, B_2)

If the employment level remains equal to l_i^* at state i, it is unlikely that an optimal sharing-out of risk can be reached. Points B_1 and B_2 in figure 5.4 represent the maximum gap between ω_1 and ω_2 that is compatible simultaneously with an efficient employment in each state ($l_i = l_i^*$ for $i = 1,2$) and with incentive compatibility and individual rationality.

Assume that, in order to share out risk, the firm finds it more profitable to establish a larger difference between wages in both states by increasing ω_2 and reducing ω_1, while preserving the equality $\pi_1 U(\omega_1/N) + \pi_2 U(\omega_2/N) = u_0$. Then it is not possible to move from (B_1,B_2) to a contract like (B'_1,B'_2) because the latter is not incentive compatible. While on the contrary, contract (B''_1,B'_2) is incentive compatible: B''_1 has been obtained by simultaneously reducing wages and employment in state 1 so that B''_1 and B'_2 become equivalent for the firm in state 2. If we contemplate small shifts (B'_2 close to B_2 and B''_1 to B_1), $\bar{l}_1$ is close to l_1^*. Since we are in the neighbourhood of the efficient employment level, moving from l_1^* to $\bar{l}_1$ has only a second-order effect on profit at state 1, while reducing employment has a first-order negative effect on the firm's profit in state 2 if the firm announces state 1. Thus, a small drop in employment in state 1 has little effect on profit in state 1, but it allows a wider difference between both states' wages since state 1 allocation becomes less attractive to the firm when the real state is state 2. It may ultimately increase the expected utility of the risk-averse firm.

2.2 *Inefficiency results*

A more rigorous characterization of the optimal contract will confirm our intuitive argument. For simplicity's sake, we will confine ourselves to the case when $n=2$. We assume that $U''<0$ and $V''<0$. The optimal contract is the solution of the following problem where the incentive compatibility constraints $\Pi(i,i)\geq\Pi(i,j),i\neq j$ have been introduced:[8]

Maximize $\sum\limits_{i=1}^{2} \pi_i V(\theta_i f(l_i)-w_i l_i-\bar{w}_i(N-l_i))$ with respect to $w_i\geq 0$, $\bar{w}_i\geq 0$ and $l_i\geq 0$ for $i=1,2$, subject to:

$$\sum_{i=1}^{2} \pi_i\left[\frac{l_i}{N} U(w_i-k)+\frac{N-l_i}{N} U(\bar{w}_i)\right]\geq u_0$$

$$\theta_1 f(l_1)-w_1 l_1-\bar{w}_1(N-l_1)\geq\theta_1 f(l_2)-w_2 l_2-\bar{w}_2(N-l_2)$$

$$\theta_2 f(l_2)-w_2 l_2-\bar{w}_2(N-l_2)\geq\theta_2 f(l_1)-w_1 l_1-\bar{w}_1(N-l_1)$$

$$l_i\leq N \qquad i=1,2$$

The concavity of $U(.)$ implies $w_i=\bar{w}_i+k$: here again individual welfare will be the same whether the individual is employed or made redundant: thus there will be no involuntary unemployment. This leads to writing $\omega_i=\bar{w}_i N=(w_i-k)N$. The problem may then be rewritten with only the variables ω_1, ω_2, l_1 and l_2. We obtain:

Maximize $\sum\limits_{i=1}^{2} \pi_i V(\theta_i f(l_i)-kl_i-\omega_i)$ with respect to $\omega_i\geq 0$ and $l_i\geq 0$, for $i=1,2$, subject to:

$$\sum_{i=1}^{2} \pi_i U(\omega_i/N)\geq u_0 \tag{5.15}$$

$$\theta_1 f(l_1)-kl_1-\omega_1\geq\theta_1 f(l_2)-kl_2-\omega_2 \tag{5.16}$$

$$\theta_2 f(l_2)-kl_2-\omega_2\geq\theta_2 f(l_1)-kl_1-\omega_1 \tag{5.17}$$

$$l_1\leq N \tag{5.18}$$

$$l_2\leq N \tag{5.19}$$

The perfect information optimal contract C^* corresponds to $l=l_i^*$ and $\omega=\omega_i^*\equiv\bar{w}_i^* N$. In what follows, we assume that this contract does not meet the incentive compatibility conditions (5.16) and (5.17), otherwise C^* would also be the optimal solution under asymmetric information. We also assume that $l_1^*<N$. Let α, γ_1, γ_2, β_1 and β_2 be Kuhn–Tucker multipliers respectively associated with the constraints (5.15) to (5.19). The first-order optimality conditions are

$$\pi_1 V'(1) - \gamma_2 + \gamma_1 - (\alpha \pi_1 / N) U'(1) = 0 \tag{5.20}$$

$$\pi_2 V'(2) - \gamma_1 + \gamma_2 - (\alpha \pi_2 / N) U'(2) = 0 \tag{5.21}$$

$$[\pi_1 V'(1) + \gamma_1][\theta_2 f'(l_1) - k] - [\theta_2 f'(l_1) - k]\gamma_2 - \beta_1 = 0 \tag{5.22}$$

$$[\pi_2 V'(2) + \gamma_2][\theta_2 f'(l_2) - k] - [\theta_1 f'(l_2) - k]\gamma_1 - \beta_2 = 0 \tag{5.23}$$

where $V'(i) \equiv V'(\theta_i f(l_i) - k l_i - \omega_i)$ and $U'(i) \equiv U'(\omega_i / N)$. The intuitive argument of the previous section suggests that (5.17) should be tight at the optimum while (5.16) shouldn't. This is what we will show in two steps. The characterization of the optimal contract will directly follow.

(i) Let us first show that one of the multipliers γ_1, γ_2 is positive while the other is equal to zero.

We cannot have $\gamma_1 = \gamma_2 = 0$, otherwise the solution would correspond to contract C^* which by hypothesis is not incentive compatible. Let us assume that $\gamma_1 > 0$ and $\gamma_2 > 0$. (5.16) and (5.17) would then both be tight, and we would have

$$\theta_1 [f(l_1) - f(l_2)] - k(l_1 - l_2) = \omega_1 - \omega_2$$
$$= \theta_2 [f(l_1) - f(l_2)] - k(l_1 - l_2)$$

This implies $l_1 = l_2$ (since $\theta_2 > \theta_1$) and thus $\omega_1 = \omega_2$. Using (5.20), (5.21) and $U'(1) = U'(2) \equiv U'$, we have

$$\pi_1 V'(1) + \gamma_1 = \gamma_2 + (\alpha \pi_1 / N) U'$$
$$\pi_2 V'(2) + \gamma_2 = \gamma_1 + (\alpha \pi_2 / N) U'$$

By using (5.22) and (5.23), we deduce

$$[\gamma_2 + (\alpha \pi_1 / N) U'][\theta_1 f'(l) - k] - [\theta_2 f'(l) - k]\gamma_2 - \beta_1 = 0 \tag{5.24}$$

$$[\gamma_1 + (\alpha \pi_2 / N) U'][\theta_2 f'(l) - k] - [\theta_1 f'(l) - k]\gamma_1 - \beta_2 = 0 \tag{5.25}$$

Let $l = l_1 = l_2$. If $l < N$, we have $\beta_1 = \beta_2 = 0$ and (5.24)–(5.25) yield

$$[\gamma_2 + (\alpha \pi_1 / N) U']\delta_1 - \delta_2 \gamma_2 = 0$$
$$[\gamma_1 + (\alpha \pi_2 / N) U']\delta_2 - \delta_1 \gamma_1 = 0$$

with $\delta_i = \theta_i f'(l) - k$ and $\delta_2 > \delta_1$. We deduce from this

$$\gamma_1 = -\frac{\alpha \pi_2 U' \delta_2}{N(\delta_2 - \delta_1)} < 0$$

$$\gamma_2 = \frac{\alpha \pi_1 U' \delta_1}{N(\delta_2 - \delta_1)} > 0$$

which is impossible.

If $l = N$, (5.24) implies

$$[\gamma_2 + (\alpha\pi_1/N)U'][\theta_1 f'(N) - k] \geq [\theta_2 f'(N) - k]\gamma_2 \qquad (5.26)$$

Since $l_1^* < N$, we have $\theta_1 f'(N) - k < 0$. Using $\gamma_2 > 0$ and (5.26) yields

$$(\theta_1 - \theta_2)f'(N)\gamma_2 > 0$$

which is at variance with $\theta_1 < \theta_2$

(ii) Let us show that $\gamma_1 = 0$ and $\gamma_2 > 0$.
In view of (i), the other possibility is $\gamma_1 > 0$ and $\gamma_2 = 0$. In that case, (5.16) would be tight and we would have

$$\theta_2 f(l_2) - kl_2 - \omega_2 > \theta_1 f(l_2) - kl_2 - \omega_2 = \theta_1 f(l_1) - kl_1 - \omega_1$$

This implies $V'(2) < V'(1)$ since $V'' < 0$. Further, (5.20) and (5.21) would imply

$$V'(1) < (\alpha/N)U'(1)$$
$$V'(2) > (\alpha/N)U'(2)$$

and thus

$$\frac{U'(2)}{U'(1)} < \frac{V'(2)}{V'(1)} < 1$$

which yields $\omega_2 > \omega_1$.
Moreover, by using (5.22) and $\gamma_2 = 0$, we obtain

$$\theta_1 f'(l_1) - k \geq 0$$
$$= 0 \text{ if } l_1 < N$$

that is $l_1 = l_1^*$. Since $l_1^* < N$, we have $\theta_1 f'(l_1) - k = 0$. Since (5.16) is tight (because $\gamma_1 > 0$), and owing to concavity of $f(.)$, we have

$$\omega_2 - \omega_1 = \theta_1 [f(l_2) - f(l_1)] - k(l_2 - l_1) \leq [\theta_1 f'(l_1) - k](l_2 - l_1) = 0$$

These results are contradictory. Thus we have $\gamma_1 = 0$ and $\gamma_2 > 0$.
We can now characterize the optimal contract. Since $\gamma_1 = 0$ and $\gamma_2 > 0$, (5.20) and (5.21) imply

$$\frac{V'(2)}{V'(1)} < \frac{U'(2)}{U'(1)}$$

In other words, the marginal rate of income substitution from state 2 to state 1 is lower for the firm than for workers: risk sharing is not optimal. By making ω_1 and ω_2 vary without altering the employment level, it would be possible to improve the firm's and workers' expected utility levels. In practice it would mean increasing profit (by reducing wages) in state 1 and reducing profit (by increasing wages) in state 2. Unfortunately, such a change is unfeasible because it would lead the firm to preferring state 1 to

state 2 on a systematic basis, and the incentive compatibility condition
(5.16) would not be met.

Furthermore, (5.23) and condition $\gamma_1 = 0$ give $l_2 = l_2^*$. Finally, (5.22) and
conditions $\gamma_1 = 0, \gamma_2 > 0, \beta_1 \geq 0$ imply

$$\pi_1 V'(1)[\theta_1 f'(l_1) - k] \geq [\theta_2 f'(l_1) - k]\gamma_2 > [\theta_1 f'(l_1) - k]\gamma_2$$

Using (5.20), we deduce that

$$[\pi_1 V'(1) - \gamma_2][\theta_1 f'(l_1) - k] = \frac{\alpha \pi_1}{N} U'(1)[\theta_1 f'(l_1) - k] > 0$$

which implies $l_1 < l_1^*$.

Therefore, *the optimal contract leads to an efficient employment level in
state 2 and to inefficient underemployment in state 1.*

2.3 Comments

Owing to the incentive constraints, it seems self-evident that labour
contracts under asymmetric information may lead to inefficient employment levels. However, the qualitative results of such models highly depend
on the selected hypotheses. First, unemployment in the previous model is
directly caused by the indivisibility of labour provided by individuals. If the
labour supply were divisible, the model would explain work sharing, not
unemployment. Moreover, the reversal of assumptions about the firm's
risk-aversion is rather striking. The idea behind the implicit contract theory
is that labour contracts are an insurance against income instability offered
by risk-neutral firms to risk-averse workers. But under asymmetric
information, inefficient underemployment is mainly due to the firms'
risk-aversion. Finally, the fact that optimal contracts provide for inefficient
underemployment in a bad state is totally dependent on the workers' utility
function. The latter was written as $U(w - qk)$ where $q \in \{0,1\}$ stands for the
quantity of labour provided. Now assume that this function is separable
between w and q is written as $u(w) - \varphi(q)$ with $u' > 0, u'' < 0, \varphi' > 0, \varphi'' > 0$. w
stands for the individual total wage payment and q for the total quantity of
labour which is assumed to be perfectly divisible.

Owing to these hypotheses, a labour contract simultaneously defines the
wages w and work q in each state i. For the sake of simplicity, let us assume
that the firm is risk-neutral ($V(\Pi) \equiv \Pi$). If N individuals are hired in period
0, the optimal contract under symmetric information is given by:

Maximize $\sum_{i=1}^{n} \pi_i(\theta_i f(Nq_i) - Nw_i)$ with respect to $w_i \geq 0, q_i \geq 0,$
$i = 1, \ldots, n$ subject to:

$$\sum_{i=1}^{n} \pi_i[u(w_i) - \varphi(q_i)] \geq u_0 \tag{5.27}$$

A simple computation gives $w_1 = w_2 = , \ldots, w_n$ and

$$\theta_i f'(Nq_i) - \frac{\varphi'(q_i)}{u'(w_i)} = 0 \text{ for all } i.$$

This last condition implies $q_1 < q_2 <, \ldots, < q_n$. It means that the employment level is efficient in each state. Thus, the symmetric information optimal contract is characterized by a constant wage and an employment level increasing along with θ_i.

Let us now turn to the asymmetric information case: the firm only observes the realized state of nature. Obviously, the optimal contract under symmetric information will not be incentive compatible. Indeed, in so far as the wage w_i is independent of the state, it is always profitable for the firm to announce state n in order for it to profit from the greatest quantity of labour. When $n = 2$, the firm will always announce a good state $(\theta = \theta_2)$ even if it is bad $(\theta = \theta_1)$. This is the symmetrical situation to the one observed in section 2.2.

The incentive compatibility constraints now are

$$\theta_2 f(Nq_2) - w_2 \geq \theta_2 f(Nq_1) - w_1 \tag{5.28}$$

$$\theta_1 f(Nq_1) - w_1 \geq \theta_1 f(Nq_2) - w_2 \tag{5.29}$$

and the optimal contract maximizes the expected profit subject to the constraints (5.27), (5.28) and (5.29).

The optimal contract under symmetric information satisfies (5.28) but not (5.29): intuitively, the problem now consists in defining the best contract which would lead the firm to announcing the true state θ_1. This can be obtained by simultaneously increasing employment and wages in state 2 so that the firm will not lie when $\theta = \theta_1$. We could prove that the optimal contract satisfies $w_2 > w_1$ and

$$\theta_1 f'(Nq_1) - \frac{\varphi'(q_1)}{u'(w_1)} = 0$$

$$\theta_2 f'(Nq_2) - \frac{\varphi'(q_2)}{u'(w_2)} < 0$$

Employment is efficient in state 1, but overemployment prevails in state 2.[9] Results are thus quite symmetrical to those obtained in section 2.2.

Finally, the theory of implicit contracts under asymmetric information is based on hypotheses that one may think little convincing. Essentially, it assumes that workers are informed about the total employment level of the firm but they cannot observe the realized state. For instance, in the model addressed in section 2.2, the firm is lead to telling the truth when the state is good by excessively reducing the level of employment in the bad state. This implies that it is impossible to hire other workers in a competitive spot market in period 1 or conceal an increase in the employment level for instance by keeping the most productive workers and improving the quality of labour. On the other hand, the theory also implies that workers do not observe the profitability of firms, while in the real world sales levels, stocks, registered profits and macroeconomic circumstances may inform them about the firm's performances.

3 Labour contracts and unions

3.1 *The monopoly union model*

Assume now that all the individuals are members of a union and contracts are signed by the union and the firms. In trade union literature, the monopoly model assumes that the union faces a large number of firms. The union chooses the wage w_i that will be paid in each state $i = 1, \ldots, n$, with firms being free to choose employment *ex post*. This assumption may be justified by transaction cost arguments and it also fits well with the empirical observation that more often firms set employment unilaterally.[10]

Assume that each unemployed worker receives unemployment benefit $\bar{w}$ paid by the government. Workers are supposed to be risk-averse ($U'' < 0$) and the union maximizes the expected utility of its members

$$\sum_{i=1}^{n} \pi_i \left[\frac{l_i}{L} U(w_i - k) + \frac{L - l_i}{L} U(\bar{w}) \right]$$

where l_i is the employment level of a firm. Recall that the economy includes m identical firms and mL individuals who are all members of the union. In state i, the aggregate employment level is thus ml_i and there are $m(L - l_i)$ individuals who are unemployed.

The firms do not commit themselves to reach any employment level. In state i each firm chooses the employment level l_i by maximizing profit, considering w_i as given. We thus have $l_i = l^d(\theta_i, w_i)$, where

$$l^d(\theta, w) \equiv \operatorname*{Arg\,Max}_{l} \{ \theta f(l) - wl \}$$

Taking into account the labour supply constraint, the optimal wage profile $(w_1, \ldots, w_n)$ is thus obtained as the solution to:

Maximize $\displaystyle\sum_{i=1}^{n} \pi_i \left[\frac{l^d(\theta_i, w_i)}{L} [U(w_i - k) - U(\bar{w})] + U(\bar{w}) \right]$ with respect to $w_i \geq 0$, $i = 1, \ldots, n$ subject to:

$$l^d(\theta_i, w_i) \leq L \qquad i = 1, \ldots, n$$

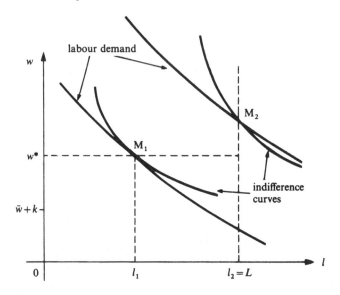

Figure 5.5 The monopoly model: involuntary unemployment in bad states and full employment in good states

Hence w_i maximizes the member's expected utility in state i, that is

$$\frac{l^d(\theta_i,w_i)}{L}[U(w_i-k)-U(\bar{w})]+U(\bar{w})$$

subject to

$$l^d(\theta_i,w_i)\leq L$$

The optimal wage profile is characterized in figures 5.5 and 5.6. In bad states, the optimal wage and the corresponding employment level are obtained at a tangency point between the labour demand curve and an indifference curve of the union (point M_1 in figure 5.5). Involuntary unemployment then prevails since $w_1>\bar{w}+k$. In good states, a corner solution with full employment may prevail (such as point M_2).

At an interior optimum, then

$$\frac{\partial l^d}{\partial w}(\theta_i,w_i)[U(w_i-k)-U(\bar{w})]+l^d(\theta_i,w_i)U'(w_i-k)=0$$

Assume that the elasticity of the demand for labour is constant and equal to ρ, that is

$$-\frac{\partial l^d}{\partial w}(\theta,w)w\equiv\rho l^d(\theta,w)$$

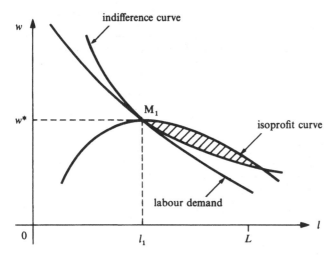

Figure 5.6   The equilibrium in the monopoly model is inefficient

We then have $w_i = w^*$ where w^* is defined by

$$-\rho\left[\frac{U(w^* - k) - U(\bar{w})}{w^*}\right] + U'(w^* - k) = 0$$

Hence, a decrease in the productivity parameter θ has no effect on the union's desired wage rate whenever the elasticity of the demand for labour is constant. Using $\partial l^d/\partial\theta > 0$ then yields a precise characterization of the equilibrium

$$w_i = w^* \text{ and } l_i = l^d(\theta_i, w^*) < L \text{ if } \theta_i < \theta^*$$
$$w_i > w^* \text{ and } l_i = l^d(\theta_i, w_i) = L \text{ if } \theta_i \geq \theta^*$$

where $l^d(\theta^*, w^*) = L$.

The monopoly union model thus accounts for involuntary unemployment and rigidity of real wages. Its main drawback is that it leads to an inefficient equilibrium. This can be easily seen in figure 5.6 where the equilibrium isoprofit line and indifference curve have been drawn. All allocations in the shaded area are preferred both by the union and by firms: thus each firm has an incentive to negotiate with the union so as to obtain lower wages against a higher employment level.

3.2   The bilateral monopoly model

In the bilateral monopoly model, a union and a single firm $(m = 1)$ bargain about wages and employment. We still consider the contingent contract $(w_1, \ldots, w_n, l_1, \ldots, l_n)$ signed at date 0.

We will characterize the Nash solution to this bargaining problem. If no contract is signed, all workers are unemployed (they receive $\bar{w}$ paid by the government) and the firm has zero profit. The Nash solution is obtained from the following problem:

Maximize $[EU - U(\bar{w})][EV - V(0)]^\gamma$ with respect to $w_i \geq 0$, $l_i \geq 0$, $i = 1, \ldots, n$, subject to:

$$w_i - k \geq \bar{w} \qquad i = 1, \ldots, n \qquad (\alpha_i)$$
$$l_i \leq L \qquad i = 1, \ldots, n \qquad (\beta_i)$$

where γ is a strictly positive parameter and

$$EU = \sum_{i=1}^{n} \pi_i \left[\frac{l_i}{L} U(w_i - k) + \frac{L - l_i}{L} U(\bar{w}) \right]$$

$$EV = \sum_{i=1}^{n} \pi_i V(\theta_i f(l_i) - w_i l_i)$$

Let $V'(i) \equiv V'(\theta_i f(l_i) - w_i l_i)$. First-order optimality conditions are

$$\frac{\pi_i l_i U'(w_i - k)}{L} [EV - V(0)]^\gamma$$

$$- \gamma \pi_i l_i V'(i) [EV - V(0)]^{\gamma - 1} [EU - U(\bar{w})] + \alpha_i = 0 \qquad (5.30)$$

$$\frac{\pi_i [U(w_i - k) - U(\bar{w})]}{L} [EV - V(0)]^\gamma$$

$$+ \gamma \pi_i [\theta_i f'(l_i) - w_i] V'(i) [EV - V(0)]^{\gamma - 1} [EU - U(\bar{w})] - \beta_i = 0 \ (5.31)$$

and

$$\alpha_i = 0 \qquad \text{if } w_i - k > \bar{w}$$
$$\beta_i = 0 \qquad \text{if } l_i < L$$

Using (5.30) and (5.31) gives

$$\theta_i f'(l_i) - w_i + \frac{U(w_i - k) - U(\bar{w})}{U'(w_i - k)} = 0$$

for all states i where $l_i < L$ and $w_i - k > \bar{w}$. This is the equation of the contract curve in state i, that is the set of tangency points between the isoprofit lines and indifference curves.

This means that the equilibrium in the bilateral monopoly model is *ex post* efficient. This is not a surprising result since any mutually advantageous move concerning wages and employment in state i could be incorporated in the equilibrium contingent contract, without modifying

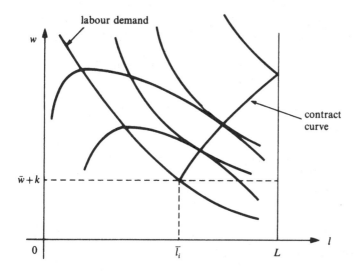

Figure 5.7   The contract curve in state i

anything for other states. Clearly, this change would be mutually beneficial *ex ante*.

Furthermore, using (5.30) for states i and j gives

$$\frac{U'(w_i - k)}{U'(w_j - k)} = \frac{V'(i)}{V'(j)}$$

When the firm is risk-neutral (e.g. $V'' = 0$), this implies

$$U'(w_i - k) = U'(w_j - k)$$

and thus $w_i = w_j$ since $U'' < 0$. The model thus predicts a constant wage rate when the firm is risk-neutral and workers are risk-averse.

Lastly figure 5.7 shows that overemployment prevails (e.g., $l_i > \bar{l}_i$) at any interior solution.[11] The reason is exactly the same as in the implicit contract model without unemployment benefit developed in section 1.3. In the absence of insurance against income uncertainty, workers achieve some additional insurance indirectly by reducing the risk of being laid off and this is obtained by setting employment above the level that would prevail in a competitive spot market economy.

3.3   *Bargaining with contractual unemployment benefit*

We now assume that the firm and the union bargain about complete contracts that specify the wage paid w_i, the unemployment benefit $\bar{w}_i$ and the employment level l_i in all states $i = 1, \ldots, n$. The government does not pay any unemployment benefit. The Nash solution is obtained from:

> Maximize $[EU - U(0)][EV - V(0)]^\gamma$ with respect to $w_i \geq 0$, $\bar{w}_i \geq 0, l_i \geq 0$, $i = 1, \ldots, n$, subject to:
>
> $l_i \leq L$ $i = 1, \ldots, n$ (β_i)

where

$$EU = \sum_{i=1}^n \pi_i \left[\frac{l_i}{L} U(w_i - k) + \frac{L - l_i}{L} U(\bar{w}_i) \right]$$

$$EV = \sum_{i=1}^n \pi_i V(\theta_i f(l_i) - w_i l_i - \bar{w}_i (L - l_i))$$

We assume $U'(0) = +\infty$ so as to have an interior solution: $w_i > k$, and $\bar{w}_i > 0$. Optimality conditions write as

$$\frac{\pi_i l_i U'(w_i - k)}{L} [EV - V(0)]^\gamma$$

$$- \gamma \pi_i l_i V'(i) [EV - V(0)]^{\gamma - 1} [EU - U(0)] = 0 \qquad (5.32)$$

$$\frac{\pi_i (L - l_i) U'(\bar{w}_i)}{L} [EV - V(0)]^\gamma$$

$$- \gamma \pi_i (L - l_i) V'(i) [EV - V(0)]^{\gamma - 1} [EU - U(0)] = 0 \qquad (5.33)$$

$$\frac{\pi_i [U(w_i - k) - U(\bar{w}_i)]}{L} [EV - V(0)]^\gamma$$

$$+ \gamma \pi_i [\theta_i f'(l_i) - w_i + \bar{w}_i] V'(i) [EV - V(0)]^{\gamma - 1} [EU - U(0)]$$

$$- \beta_i = 0 \qquad (5.34)$$

where

$$V'(i) \equiv V'(\theta_i f(l_i) - w_i l_i - \bar{w}_i (L - l_i))$$

Using (5.32) and (5.33) gives $U'(w_i - k) = U'(\bar{w}_i)$ and thus $w_i - k = \bar{w}_i$. Hence, at the equilibrium, workers obtain perfect insurance against the risk of unemployment. Furthermore, one can easily check that wages are equal in all states when the firm is risk-neutral. Lastly, (5.34) gives

$$\theta_i f'(l_i) = k \qquad \text{if } l_i < L$$
$$\theta_i f'(l_i) \geq k \qquad \text{if } l_i = L$$

which means that the employment level l_i is equal to the efficient level $l_i^* = \text{Arg Max}\{\theta_i f(l) - kl \,|\, l \leq L\}$. Hence, bargaining over employment, wages and unemployment benefits leads to an efficient allocation of labour (the same as in a competitive spot market economy) without any involuntary unemployment.

As observed by Oswald (1985), in the usual bilateral monopoly model without contractual unemployment compensation, the firm has an incentive, once the wage w_i fixed, to renege on its commitment l_i by shifting back to the labour demand curve (since $l_i > l^d(\theta_i, w_i)$ on the contract curve). This is not the case here, since l_i^* maximizes the firm's profit once $\bar{w}_i$ and $w_i = \bar{w}_i + k$ are fixed. In that sense, the equilibrium is stable.

The conclusion that emerges is that the bilateral monopoly model with a utilitarian union explains macroeconomic inefficiencies only by arbitrarily restricting the set of feasible contracts. As soon as the bargaining also deals with severance payments (and this is certainly realistic), the employment level coincides with the competitive allocation l_i^*. This allocation is stable once wages and severance payments are fixed, and lastly, there is no involuntary unemployment at the equilibrium.

3.4 Seniority, insiders and unemployment persistence

The conventional view that all workers are considered as identical by unions has been challenged in many writings on trade unions including the insiders–outsiders literature and theoretical models with seniority.[12] The basic idea is that the population of workers is heterogeneous, the distinction being made between insiders or incumbents whose interests are represented in bargaining and outsiders whose preferences do not count or between senior and junior workers when lay-offs are done on a seniority basis within the firm and senior workers dominate the voting over the firm's proposals. In such cases, the outcome of the bargaining may differ from the predictions of the utilitarian union model. For instance, in case of lay-offs by seniority, a union dominated by seniors has a strong incentive to accept a reduction in the workforce in exchange for an increase in wages, although this decision might reduce the expected utility of a worker drawn randomly among employees.

To capture the effects of seniority in the bilateral monopoly model consider a two-group workforce including seniors and juniors and assume that the union maximizes the expected utility of seniors. In each state i, seniors will be employed with probability $\psi(x)$ whenever the employment rate is $x \equiv l_i/L$. Assume $\psi(x) > x$ for all x in $(0,1)$ which means that seniors are less likely to be laid off than juniors. $\psi(.)$ is supposed to be increasing and differentiable with $\psi(0) = 0$ and $\psi(1) = 1$.[13]

Seniors' expected utility is

$$EU = \sum_{i=1}^{n} \pi_i \left[\psi\left(\frac{l_i}{L}\right) U(w_i - k) + \left(1 - \psi\left(\frac{l_i}{L}\right)\right) U(\bar{w}_i) \right]$$

and optimality conditions now are

$$\pi_i \, \psi\left(\frac{l_i}{L}\right) U'(w_i - k)[EV - V(0)]^\gamma$$

$$-\gamma\pi_i l_i V'(i)[EV - V(0)]^{\gamma-1}[EU - U(0)] = 0 \tag{5.35}$$

$$\pi_i \left[1 - \psi\left(\frac{l_i}{L}\right)\right] U'(\bar{w}_i)[EV - V(0)]^\gamma$$

$$-\gamma\pi_i(L - l_i)V'(i)[EV - V(0)]^{\gamma-1}[EU - U(0)] = 0 \tag{5.36}$$

$$\frac{\pi_i \, \psi'\left(\frac{l_i}{L}\right)[U(w_i - k) - U(\bar{w}_i)]}{L} [EV - V(0)]^\gamma$$

$$+ \gamma\pi_i[\theta_i f'(l_i) - w_i + \bar{w}_i]V'(i)[EV - V(0)]^{\gamma-1}[EU - U(0)]$$

$$- \beta_i = 0 \tag{5.37}$$

Assume $0 < \psi\left(\dfrac{l_i}{L}\right) < 1$. Then (5.35) and (5.36) yield

$$\frac{U'(w_i - k)}{U'(\bar{w}_i)} = \frac{\left[1 - \psi\left(\dfrac{l_i}{L}\right)\right]l_i}{(L - l_i)\psi\left(\dfrac{l_i}{L}\right)} < 1$$

which implies $w_i - k > \bar{w}_i$. When $\psi(l_i/L) = 1$, we obviously have $\bar{w}_i = 0$ since seniors are sure not to be dismissed. Furthermore $U'(0) = +\infty$ gives $w_i - k > 0$ at the optimum. *Hence, when unemployment prevails in some states (e.g., $l_i < L$), it is involuntary: employed workers are now strictly better off than those who have been dismissed.* Finally, it is easy to check that the model may lead to socially inefficient underemployment in some states. Let us assume $l_i^* < L$ and $\psi(l_i^*/L) = 1$ for some state i. Suppose $l_i \geq l_i^*$ for the equilibrium contract. This implies $\psi(l_i/L) = 1$ and thus $\bar{w}_i = 0, w_i > k$. We also have $\psi'(l_i/L) = 0$ since $\psi(x) = 1$ for all x in $[l_i^*/L, 1]$. Then, (5.37) gives

$$\theta_i f'(l_i) \geq w_i - \bar{w}_i > k$$

which is at variance with $l_i > l_i^*$. Hence, in that case, *the equilibrium contract will specify too low an employment level in state i.*

However this result may not hold for all states of nature and, in fact, the model may lead to underemployment in some states but to overemployment in others. To show it, let us consider a simple specification of the previous model in which there are $\hat{l}$ seniors (or insiders) already employed during the previous period and $L - \hat{l}$ juniors (or entrants) previously unemployed or employed elsewhere. We assume that seniors have a priority employment right. This gives

$$\psi(x) = \begin{cases} \dfrac{xL}{\hat{l}} & \text{if } x < \dfrac{\hat{l}}{L} \\ \\ 1 & \text{otherwise} \end{cases}$$

Consider a state i. Assume first that $\hat{l} < l_i^*$. Then $\psi(x) = 1$ for all x in $[l_i^*/L, 1]$ and as above we have $l_i < l_i^*$. Now assume $\hat{l} > l_i^*$. Suppose that $l_i \leq l_i^*$. Then $l_i < \hat{l}$ and in the neighbourhood of the optimal solutions, we have $\psi(x) = xL/\hat{l}$ for state i. Using (5.35), (5.37) and $\beta_i = 0$ gives

$$U(w_i - k) - U(\bar{w}_i) + U'(w_i - k)[\theta_i f'(l_i) - w_i + \bar{w}_i] = 0$$

Furthermore $l_i \leq l_i^* < L$ gives $\theta_i f'(l_i) > k$ and we have

$$U(w_i - k) - U(\bar{w}_i) + U'(w_i - k)(k - w_i + \bar{w}_i) < 0$$

which is at variance with the concavity of U. We thus have $l_i > l_i^*$ in that case.

In a nutshell, we have $l_i < l_i^*$ if $\hat{l} < l_i^*$ and $l_i > l_i^*$ if $\hat{l} > l_i^*$. In words, the model predicts inefficient underemployment when efficiency would require hiring new employees and it predicts inefficient overemployment when efficiency would require cutting down the workforce.

Optimal contracting in an insider–outsider setting may thus lead to overemployment as well as to underemployment. More interestingly, for a given state of nature, the direction of the deviation from the efficient employment level depends on past employment. In particular, the model predicts that inefficient underemployment is all the more likely as employment was low in the previous period and also that large adverse shocks on employment usually leads to inefficient underemployment in the next period even if productivity disturbances are independently distributed. In that sense, it explains underemployment persistence.[14]

Matters are less simple once the intertemporal effects of wage–employment bargaining on workers' welfare are taken into account in a non-myopic way. This can be shown by means of a simple three-period model. Assume that, in period 0, a newly created firm and a union bargain over contingent contracts to be enforced in period 1. In period 0, all workers have equal weights in the union's preferences. The firm is supposed to be myopic (at period $t = 0,1$, it maximizes the expected profit of period $t + 1$) and cannot precommit on multiperiod long-term contracts. Thus, a new contingent contract, to be enforced in period 2, is negotiated in period 1. In period 1, workers who have been retained become seniors and, for reorganization reasons, other workers may be hired by the firm. The workers who have been made redundant may be hired (as juniors) by other firms. It is assumed that at period 1 seniors dominate the votings of the union and, lay-offs being made by seniority, seniors enjoy a differential rent Δ, in expected utility terms. Thus, up to a constant, at period 0, the expected utility of a worker of the new firm is

$$EU = \sum_{i=1}^{n} \pi_i \left[\frac{l_i}{L} (U(w_i - k) + \delta\Delta) + \frac{L - l_i}{L} U(\bar{w}_i) \right]$$

where δ is a discount factor, with $0 < \delta < 1$.

At period 0, the union aims at maximizing EU, while the firm maximizes the expected profit of period 1. One easily checks that the optimal contract specifies for period 1: $w_i - k = \bar{w}_i$ for all i and $l_i > l_i^*$ if $l_i^* < L$.

Thus, there is overemployment in the new firm in period 1 (and possibly underemployment in period 2). The intuition of this result is very simple: Since becoming a senior allows workers to enjoy a welfare supplement the union puts more emphasis on the employment level in period 1, and this leads to overemployment. Clearly, assuming that firms are myopic while unions are not is not very satisfactory. Nevertheless, the previous result suggests that seniority rules may exacerbate aggregate employment fluctuations: when macroeconomic perspectives are favourable, new firms are created where all workers have equal weights in unions' preferences, and bargaining in these firms should lead to overemployment, while, in a depression, few new job positions are created and emphasis is more likely to be put on wages than on employment in so far as seniors dominate unions' behaviour.

Appendix   Implicit contracts and labour supply

The theory of implicit contracts under symmetric information initially aimed at explaining macroeconomic inefficiencies and more particularly involuntary unemployment in a non-Walrasian perspective, but, as seen in section 1, it is far from reaching its goal. Strangely enough, it may in fact reinforce the neoclassical market clearing models, holding that the variations in the labour supply are the direct cause of variations in economic activity. Indeed, the main empirical problem of the market clearing approach is the fact that the elasticity of the labour supply is considered to be too low to be a valid explanation of the variations in the employment level. In the traditional problem of allocation of time between work and leisure, a rise in the wage rate tends to favour an increase in the labour supply through the substitution effect, but the income effect has a reverse impact and makes the labour supply not greatly sensitive to variations in the wage rate. On the contrary, if labour contracts provide an insurance, at least partially, against wage instability, the income effect is weaker and labour instability would increase.

To illustrate this property, let us consider an economy where workers are risk-averse while firms are risk-neutral. For simplicity's sake, we will consider an economy with a single worker and a single firm, but the model assumes perfect competition in the labour contract market.[15]

The worker can provide one unit of labour at the most. His utility function writes as $U(w, 1-q)$, where w and q respectively stand for consumption (equal to wages) and employment. $U(.)$ is strictly concave and such that $U'_1 > 0, U'_2 > 0$. To simplify matters, we assume that returns to scale are constant and we write the production function as $y = \theta l$. Here, it is more convenient to assume that θ is continuously distributed according to a distribution function $G(\theta)$ on an interval $[\theta_0, \theta_1]$. The worker has no other income but his wage. His contract thus defines the consumption (e.g., wages) $w(\theta)$ and the employment level $q(\theta)$ in each state $\theta \in [\theta_0, \theta_1]$. The firm's expected profit is

$$E\Pi = \int_{\theta_0}^{\theta_1} [\theta q(\theta) - w(\theta)] dG(\theta)$$

We assume that perfect competition prevails in the labour contract market. Therefore, the equilibrium contract maximizes the worker's expected utility under the condition $E\Pi = 0$, that is

$$\{w(.), q(.)\} \text{maximize} \int_{\theta_0}^{\theta_1} U(w(\theta), 1 - q(\theta)) dG(\theta) \text{ subject to}$$

$$\int_{\theta_0}^{\theta_1} [\theta q(\theta) - w(\theta)] dG(\theta) = 0 \qquad (5.38)$$

Let α be a multiplier associated to (5.38). The first-order optimality conditions are

$$U'_1(w(\theta), 1 - q(\theta)) = \alpha \qquad \text{for all } \theta \qquad (5.39)$$

$$U'_2(w(\theta), 1 - q(\theta)) = \theta \alpha \qquad \text{for all } \theta \qquad (5.40)$$

Differentiation with respect to θ gives

$$U''_{11} w'(\theta) - U''_{12} q'(\theta) = 0$$

$$U''_{21} w'(\theta) - U''_{22} q'(\theta) = \alpha$$

This yields

$$q'(\theta) = -\alpha U''_{11}/\Delta \qquad (5.41)$$

$$w'(\theta) = -\alpha U''_{12}/\Delta \qquad (5.42)$$

where, owing to the concavity of U, $\Delta = [U''_{11} U''_{22} - (U''_{12})^2] > 0$. From (5.41), $q'(\theta) > 0$ since $U''_{11} < 0$ and $\alpha > 0$, owing respectively to the concavity of U and (5.39). *Therefore, the optimal contract always specifies more hours*

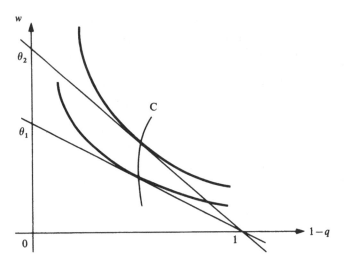

Figure 5.8   Low variations in employment on a spot market

of work when the state is good and less hours when the state is bad. Moreover, in view of (5.42), the wage is constant only when preferences are strongly separable in consumption and leisure (because $U''_{12}=0$ in that case).

Let $s(\theta)=w(\theta)-\theta q(\theta)$ be the worker's net debit position with the firm that is the difference between wage payments and output in state θ. By using (5.41) and (5.42), we obtain

$$s'(\theta) = -q(\theta) + (q'(\theta)/U''_{11})[U''_{12} - (U'_2/U'_1)U''_{11}] \qquad (5.43)$$

In (5.43), the term within brackets is positive if leisure is not an inferior good. Then we have $s'(\theta)<0$. Since

$$\int_{\theta_0}^{\theta_1} s(\theta)\mathrm{d}G(\theta)=0$$

$s(\theta)$ is negative in the good states (θ large) and positive for bad states (θ small).

From (5.39) and (5.40), we deduce that $(w(\theta),q(\theta))$ maximizes $U(w,1-q)$ subject to the constraint

$$w=\theta q+s(\theta)$$

In other words, the worker chooses his income and the number of hours he will work on the basis of a two-part tariff rate providing for a fixed allowance $s(\theta)$ and a variable payment equal to θ for each hour of work.

Figures 5.8 and 5.9 allow us to compare the worker's choices in a competitive spot market and in a long-term contract market. In the spot

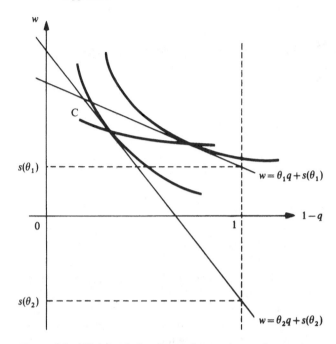

Figure 5.9   High variation in employment on a long-term contract market

market, the individual budget constraint is $w = \theta q$, since the hourly wage rate is θ. The labour supply may increase or decrease along with θ, depending on whether the substitution or income effect dominates. Generally, this will cause a more or less constant number of hours of work. This is shown in figure 5.8, with $\theta_2 > \theta_1$. The C curve represents the relationship between employment and total wages.

Figure 5.9 shows the two-part tariff interpretation of contracts with a highly variable employment level due to adjustments in the lump-sum portion of the two-part tariff which lessens the income effect of productivity variations on the labour supply.

To illustrate this result assume that $U(w, 1-q) = a \operatorname{Log} w + (1-a) \operatorname{Log}(1-q)$, with $0 < a < 1$ and that θ is uniformly distributed over $[0,1]$. Then, in a spot market, we have $w(\theta) = a\theta$ and $q(\theta) = a$ for all θ, that is to say a variable wage and a constant employment level, while in a long-term contract market we have $w(\theta) = a/2$ and $q(\theta) = 1 - (1-a)/2\theta$, that is to say, a constant wage and a variable employment level.

6   Introduction to efficiency wage models

What is it that makes a profit-maximizing firm refuse to reduce wages while the jobless are willing to work for less? Answering this question is vital to understanding why long-term involuntary unemployment may exist in a competitive economy. The efficiency wage models, holding that the quality of labour depends on the wage received, are helpful in this matter. Indeed, the efficiency wage theory argue that real wages do not decrease because any drop in wages causes a drop in the quality of labour, owing to the hiring of less competent individuals, or to the reduced willingness of these individuals to provide effort. Thus, a decrease in wages is unprofitable when the drop in quality is greater than the drop in costs. Accordingly, the optimal wage (minimizing the cost of one unit of 'efficient labour') may be larger than the equilibrium wage in the labour market: then involuntary unemployment appears, but the firms are not willing to reduce wages.

Initially, the relationship between quality of labour and wages has been developed in analyses on developing countries which emphasized the link between nutrition and productivity (Leibenstein, 1963). In the less developed economies, wages directly affect individuals' health, physical welfare and therefore their productivity. This is why firms in the industrial sector find it more profitable to provide their workers with higher standards of living than just the subsistence level prevailing in the traditional sector. This does not apply to developed countries, however, and, as we shall see, this relationship can be justified in a more subtle way. The basic principles of efficiency wage theory can be illustrated by a very simple model due to Solow (1979). Let us consider an economy with N individuals, each supplying one unit of labour with a reservation wage k and a representative firm whose production function writes as

$$y = f(e(w)l)$$

where y is the output, l the number of employed workers and e the effort

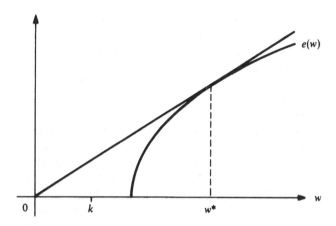

Figure 6.1 The optimal wage

made as a function of the wage w: thus, the output depends on workers' total effort. We assume

$$e(w)=0 \text{ if } w \leq \bar{k}$$

and

$$e'(w)>0, e''(w)<0 \text{ if } w>\bar{k}$$

with $\bar{k}>k$. We also assume $f'(.)>0, f''(.)<0$. The price of the output is equal to 1.

The firm chooses l and w in order to maximize its profit $f(e(w)l)-wl$. Let w^* and l^* be the firm's optimal choice. The first-order optimality conditions are

$$\frac{e'(w^*)w^*}{e(w^*)}=1 \tag{6.1}$$

$$e(w^*)f'(e(w^*)l^*)=w^* \tag{6.2}$$

Given our hypotheses these conditions are sufficient for optimality. According to (6.1), the wage rate is defined by the condition that the effort function's elasticity is equal to 1. We have $w^*>k$, as shown in figure 6.1.

According to (6.2), the marginal productivity of labour and the real wage rate are equal. Here, we assume that $l^*<N$. Thus there are $N-l^*$ individuals who are involuntarily unemployed. Further, productivity shocks modifying function $f(.)$ are likely to alter the employment level but they have no effect on wages, since the latter are fully determined by the effort function. In this very simple version of efficiency wage theory, employment and

output fluctuate with productivity but technological shocks do not affect wages. Moreover unemployment is involuntary.

The heart of efficiency wage theory is thus the relationship existing between the wage rate and workers' individual productivities measured in effort or efficient labour. In most models, this relationship results from an imperfect information context: the firm is assumed to be either imperfectly informed about its employees' capabilities (adverse selection models) or unable to perfectly monitor the provided effort (moral hazard models). We will address adverse selection models in section 1. If individuals have different abilities (measured by the more or less high quantity of efficient labour they are able to provide), several labour markets with different wages should be organized. On a given market, the firm would exchange a given wage for a certain quality of labour. Unfortunately, since the firm cannot distinguish competent individuals from the less competent when hiring them, it can only give them the same wage. When underemployment prevails, not decreasing wages allows firms to attract the most productive individuals in so far as their reservation wages are the highest. This can explain involuntary unemployment in adverse selection models.

In the moral hazard models, contemplated in section 2, the firm is imperfectly informed about the effort provided by its employees since observing workers' actions on the job is costly. For example, in such a context, we may assume that there is a certain probability for a shirker to be caught. More generally, the firm perceives a signal corresponding to the effort made by each individual. If individuals are hired for one period only, labour contracts should include a performance compensation scheme encouraging them to work harder, and specifying the wage paid as a function of the individual productivity signal. When individuals are hired for several periods, dismissal may be a credible threat for shirkers if finding a new job takes time, i.e., when the number of involuntary jobless is large enough. This will occur when wages are high. In such a case, the threat of unemployment acts as a discipline device to prevent shirking.

Section 3 presents two other justifications for the relationship between productivity and wage: the turnover model and sociological explanations. In the turnover model, the firms bear hiring and training costs. They pay higher wages than the market equilibrium wage in order to keep their employees and reduce turnover costs. As for sociological explanations, they refer to the feeling of equity a group of workers may have while comparing their wages with other socially equivalent workers': the standard effort collectively appraised by the group will directly depend on this feeling of equity. Eventually, the firm may be led to increasing wages in order to reinforce cohesion within the group, to give its employees the feeling that they are treated with fairness and to obtain in return higher productivity.

1 Adverse selection

1.1 *The model*[1]

Let us consider a labour market (industrial sector) with m identical firms and N individuals. These individuals differ from each other by their endowments of efficient labour. The production function of the firms in the industrial sector is $y = \theta f(Q)$, where Q stands for the total quantity of efficient labour provided by workers, and θ is a technological parameter. We make the usual hypotheses: $f' > 0, f'' < 0$.

Firms do not observe individual labour endowments and consequently workers are indistinguishable. Furthermore, we assume that individuals' reservation wages are positively correlated with their endowments of efficient labour, for instance because reservation wages correspond to the payments workers might receive for other professional activities where their capabilities could be checked, thanks to outcome-depending wages or simply because they are self-employed. For the sake of simplicity, we simply assume that each individual has an endowment of efficient labour q which is a strictly increasing function of his reservation wage v, so that

$$q = q(v) \text{ with } q'(v) > 0$$

We assume that v is distributed over $[0, +\infty)$ according to a cumulated distribution function $G(v)$ and a density function $g(v)$. Let w be the wage in the industrial sector (per employee) and $\bar{q}(w)$ the average quantity of efficient labour per worker. The individuals hired are randomly chosen among those individuals whose reservation wages are less than w. Thus we have[2]

$$\bar{q}(w) = \frac{\displaystyle\int_0^w q(v)\, dG(v)}{G(w)} \tag{6.3}$$

which implies

$$\frac{d\bar{q}}{dw} = \frac{g(w)}{G(w)^2} \int_0^w (q(w) - q(v))\, dG(v) > 0$$

The average endowment in efficient labour is thus an increasing function of the wage received and this can be easily interpreted: when wages decrease, the most productive individuals decide not to apply for a job in the industrial sector since their reservation wages are the highest and this results in a pool of applicants of worse average quality. Consequently, $\bar{q}(w)$ decreases.

We have $Q = l\bar{q}(w)$, where l stands for the number of employed workers. We assume that the price of industrial output is equal to 1, and profit π may be written as a function of the two choice variables w and l:

$$\pi(w,l) = \theta f(l\bar{q}(w)) - wl$$

Each firm determines l and w so as to maximize its profit. In order to characterize the optimal choice, we assume that the function $w/\bar{q}(w)$ has a unique global minimum at $w = w^*$. When the firm pays its employees at the rate w^*, it minimizes the average cost of efficient labour.

Let us first show that the firm actually chooses w^*. Assume *a contrario* that the firm chooses $w = \hat{w} \neq w^*$ and $l = \hat{l}$. Let $l^0 = \hat{w}\hat{l}/w^*$. Thus we have

$$\pi(w^*,l^0) = \theta f(l^0\bar{q}(w^*)) - w^*l^0$$

$$= \theta f\left(\frac{\hat{w}\hat{l}}{w^*}\bar{q}(w^*)\right) - \hat{w}\hat{l}$$

and thus

$$\pi(w^*,l^0) > \theta f(\hat{l}\bar{q}(\hat{w})) - \hat{w}\hat{l} = \pi(\hat{w},\hat{l})$$

since $\bar{q}(w^*)/w^* > \bar{q}(\hat{w})/\hat{w}$. Therefore, hiring l^0 individuals at wage w^* is more profitable than hiring $\hat{l}$ individuals at wage $\hat{w}$.

Firms will thus choose the wage rate that minimizes the average cost of efficient labour. Then, the optimal employment level l^* is defined by

$$\frac{\partial \pi}{\partial l}(w^*,l^*) = 0$$

that is to say

$$\theta f'(l^*\bar{q}(w^*)) = \frac{w^*}{\bar{q}(w^*)} \tag{6.4}$$

Marginal productivity is thus equal to the average cost of efficient labour. The total demand for labour will be equal to ml^*. The equilibrium thus defined will be feasible if the supply of labour at a rate w^* is larger than the demand, that is to say when

$$NG(w^*) > ml^*$$

The equilibrium is characterized as follows: first, the industrial wage rate is equal to w^* and is independent from the variations that might affect the production function and more particularly the technological parameter θ. Variations in θ only cause variations in the number of employed workers l^*. Further, involuntary unemployment prevails: $NG(w^*) - ml^*$ individuals would like to be employed in the industrial sector but they cannot. Their reservation wages are less than w^*. Thus they would accept work for a lower wage. Though they have the opportunity to hire individuals for less, the firms do not cut down wages because this would affect the most productive workers and ultimately increase the average cost of efficient labour.

Note also that no individual can increase his probability of being hired by directly announcing to a firm that he would accept work at a wage below w^*. In fact, by acknowledging a willingness to work at $\tilde{w} < w^*$, an individual reveals that his reservation wage is less than $\tilde{w}$ and consequently that his expected labour endowment is $\bar{q}(\tilde{w})$. However $\tilde{w}/\bar{q}(\tilde{w}) > w^*/\bar{q}(w^*)$, so that hiring this individual at $\tilde{w}$ would result in increasing the average cost of efficient labour.

When $NG(w^*) < ml^*$, the wage rate minimizing the average cost of efficient labour causes an excess demand for labour. Competition on the labour market would then result in a wage rate larger than w^* which equates supply and demand. For such a full-employment equilibrium we have [3] $w > w^*$ and

$$\theta f'(G(w)\bar{q}(w)N/m) = w/\bar{q}(w)$$

1.2 Equilibrium with discrimination

We now consider the more general case in which workers also differ according to observed characteristics. Differences in observed attributes enable firms to distinguish different groups of individuals. The model explains wage discrimination between the groups and also that chronic involuntary unemployment may prevail in some groups.

Let us assume that there are r groups of workers labelled $k = 1, \ldots, r$. For each group k, $\bar{q}_k(w_k)$ is the average endowment in efficient labour when the wage payment is w_k. Let w_k^* be the optimal wage for group k, that is the one that minimizes $w_k/\bar{q}_k(w_k)$. The groups are ranked in order of increasing average cost of efficient labour:

$$\frac{w_1^*}{\bar{q}_1(w_1^*)} < \frac{w_2^*}{\bar{q}_2(w_2^*)} < \ldots < \frac{w_r^*}{\bar{q}_r(w_r^*)}$$

Here, firms wish to hire type-1 individuals as priority and pay them at a rate w_1^*, the other groups being excluded from the industrial sector. However, if the demand for type-1 individuals at a rate w_1^* exceeds the supply, the wage paid will increase up to w_{12} defined by $w_{12}/\bar{q}_1(w_{12}) = w_2^*/\bar{q}_2(w_2^*)$: then, the firm will be quite indifferent between hiring type-1 individuals at the rate w_{12} or type-2 individuals at the rate w_2^*. If the number of type 1 and type 2 individuals willing to work in these conditions is larger than the demand for labour, some of them will suffer from involuntary unemployment, type $3, \ldots, r$ being excluded from the industrial sector. Otherwise type-1 and

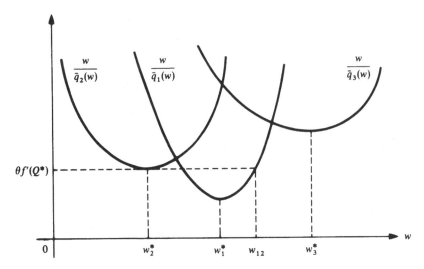

Figure 6.2 Equilibrium with discrimination

type-2 individuals' wage would increase, competition among the firms always resulting in the equality $w_1/\bar{q}_1(w_1)=w_2/\bar{q}_2(w_2)$. We may reach wages $w_1=w_{13}$ and $w_2=w_{23}$ such that $w_1/\bar{q}_1(w_{13})=w_{23}/\bar{q}_2(w_{23})=w_3^*/\bar{q}_3(w_3^*)$, which will lead to hiring type-1, type-2 and type-3 (etc. . . .) individuals. As the wages of the different groups increase and the employed individuals become less efficient, the average cost of efficient labour increases and the demand for efficient labour decreases. At equilibrium, individuals of group $k=1,\ldots,k_0$ receive a wage larger than their optimal wage w_k^*, and individuals of group $k_0+1,\ldots,r$ are excluded from the industrial sector.

Figure 6.2 shows that kind of equilibrium with $r=3$ and $k_0=2$. The firms hire type 1 and type 2 individuals and pay them $w_1=w_{12}>w_1^*$ and $w_2=w_2^*$. Each firm uses a total quantity of efficient labour Q^* such that

$$\theta f'(Q^*)=\frac{w_{12}}{\bar{q}_1(w_{12})}=\frac{w_2^*}{\bar{q}_2(w_2^*)}$$

In this case, each firm hires l_1 type-1 individuals and l_2 type-2 individuals with $l_1\bar{q}_1+l_2\bar{q}_2=Q^*$ and the firm is indifferent to the number of each.

Let N_k be the number of type k individuals and $G_k(.)$ the distribution function of their reservation wages. The feasibility condition writes as

$$N_1G_1(w_{12})\bar{q}_1(w_{12})+N_2G(w_2^*)\bar{q}_2(w_2^*)>mQ^*$$

No individual of group 3 is employed in the industrial sector.

2 Moral hazard

Let us assume now that the firm can observe all the characteristics of individuals, but it cannot monitor the effort provided. At the most, it may perceive a productivity signal corresponding to the effort made. In such a context, labour contracts must encourage individuals to make the required effort. There are several ways to reach that goal. First, the wage can be dependent on the signal perceived: if a good signal means a higher remuneration, and if the signal is correlated with the effort made, a worker may be encouraged to provide more effort in order to obtain higher wages. Further, in a model with several periods where individuals and firms sign long-term implicit contracts, the workers may be dismissed at the end of any period in case of a bad signal. If loosing one's job means reduced welfare because long-term involuntary unemployment prevails, individuals will be encouraged to make all the necessary effort to keep their jobs. Thus, the general feature of contracts depends as much on the feasibility of contingent contracts linking wages to effort signals as on the length of the relationship between employers and employees.

In what follows, we will contemplate two opposite situations. First, we will address the case where firms and workers reach short-term agreements with wages depending on the signals perceived. Later, we will address the situation where firms and workers reach long-term agreements in which the threat of dismissal acts as a discipline device.

2.1 *Short-run contracts and contingent wages*

Let us consider an economy including N identical workers and m identical firms. Workers are risk-averse and their utility function is

$$U = u(r) - ke$$

with $k > 0, u' > 0, u'' < 0, u(0) = 0$; r stands for the individual income (the wage w or the unemployment benefit $\bar{w}$ paid by the government) and e stands for the effort made at work. For the sake of simplicity, we will contemplate only two situations: workers either make the required effort or they don't and, in such a case, they are said to be shirking. For a non-shirker we have $e = 1$ and for a shirker we have $e = 0$. The jobless make no effort and in that case we also have $e = 0$. A non-shirker provides the firm with one unit of efficient labour while the shirker is supposed to be totally useless.

The firm cannot observe the effort provided by each employee, it can only perceive a signal correlated with that effort. Let σ be this signal and we assume that $\sigma \in \{\sigma_G, \sigma_B\}$: σ_G is a good signal and σ_B is a bad signal. We let

$$\pi_1 = \text{Prob}(\sigma = \sigma_G / e = 1)$$
$$\pi_2 = \text{Prob}(\sigma = \sigma_G / e = 0)$$

and we assume $0 < \pi_2 < \pi_1 < 1$ which means that the probability of a good signal is higher for a non-shirker than for a shirker.

A labour contract specifies the wage received as a function of the signal perceived. We have $w = w_1$ if $\sigma = \sigma_G$ and $w = w_2$ if $\sigma = \sigma_B$. The firm offers labour contracts that are incentive compatible and individually rational. A contract (w_1, w_2) is said to be *incentive compatible* if it leads a worker not to shirk, that is if

$$\pi_1 u(w_1) + (1 - \pi_1) u(w_2) - k \geq \pi_2 u(w_1) + (1 - \pi_2) u(w_2) \qquad (6.5)$$

In (6.5), the left-hand side and the right-hand side terms stand for the expected utility levels respectively for a non-shirker and for a shirker. This yields

$$(\pi_1 - \pi_2)[u(w_1) - u(w_2)] \geq k \qquad (6.6)$$

A contract is said to be *individually rational* if it provides a worker with an expected utility at least equal to his reservation utility $u(\bar{w})$, that is

$$\pi_1 u(w_1) + (1 - \pi_1) u(w_2) - k \geq u(\bar{w}) \qquad (6.7)$$

Incentive compatibility and individual rationality constraints are represented in figure 6.3. The incentive compatibility condition defines the increasing curve (IC), with $u(w_1) = k/(\pi_1 - \pi_2)$ if $w_2 = 0$, which corresponds to point A. The individual rationality condition is represented by a decreasing convex curve (IR) on which we have $u(w_1) = [u(\bar{w}) + k]/\pi_1$ if $w_2 = 0$. This is point B. If $\pi_2 k > (\pi_1 - \pi_2) u(\bar{w})$, A is to the right of B.

Let output y be a function of the number of non-shirkers l according to the production function $y = \theta f(l)$. When all workers are non-shirkers, the firm's expected profit is given by

$$E\Pi = \theta f(l) - [\pi_1 w_1 + (1 - \pi_1) w_2] l$$

The firm chooses the contract (w_1, w_2) so as to maximize $E\Pi$ among the set of feasible contracts represented by the shaded area in figure 6.3. The optimal contract minimizes $\pi_1 w_1 + (1 - \pi_1) w_2$ and is located at point C: the incentive compatibility and individual rationality constraints are then both tight. When the signal is good the worker receives a positive wage w_1^*. If the signal is bad, the wage received w_2^* is negative, which comes down to saying that the worker pays for a penalty.

As for the desired employment level l^*, it is defined by

$$\theta f'(l^*) - [\pi_1 w_1^* + (1 - \pi_1) w_2^*] = 0.$$

The equilibrium will be feasible if $ml^* < N$. Then we have ml^* employed workers and $N - ml^*$ unemployed individuals but they all have the same expected utility $u(\bar{w})$ since the individual rationality constraint is tight for

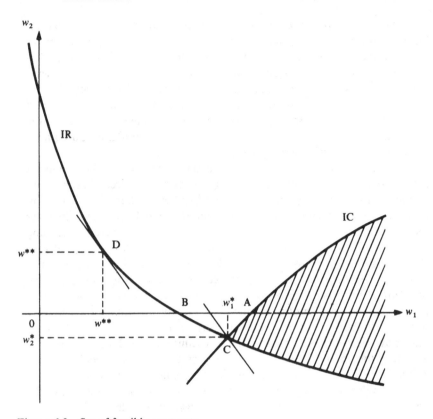

Figure 6.3   Set of feasible contracts

the optimal contract. Thus, there is no involuntary unemployment. However, the level of employment is less than the one which would prevail if the effort could be observed. Indeed, in such a case, labour contracts would totally insure workers against variations in their wages, and they would receive a constant wage w^{**} such that

$$u(w^{**}) = u(\bar{w}) + k$$

and each firm would hire l^{**} individuals, with $\theta f'(l^{**}) = w^{**}$. We have

$$u(w^{**}) = \pi_1 u(w_1^*) + (1 - \pi_1)u(w_2^*) < u(\pi_1 w_1^* + (1 - \pi_1)w_2^*)$$

owing to the concavity of $u(.)$. We obtain

$$w^{**} < \pi_1 w_1^* + (1 - \pi_1)w_2^*$$

and thus $l^* < l^{**}$.

Therefore, the incentive compatibility constraint alone cannot account for involuntary unemployment, but it causes inefficient underemployment. This can be easily interpreted: the incentive compatibility condition implies that the gap between the good signal wage and the bad signal wage is wide enough. A constant wage, which would be optimal under perfect information, is now impossible. In order to be individually rational, the contract offered by the firm must provide for a higher expected wage than in the perfect information case (owing to worker's risk-aversion) and consequently, the profit-maximizing employment level is lower.

As we saw it, the optimal wage can be negative if $\sigma = \sigma_B$.[4] This suggests that the possibilities of making workers provide the required effort without paying them a rent (e.g., an expected utility higher than the reservation level) are totally dependent on the possibilities of penalizing them whenever the signal is bad: if the individual rationality constraint were not binding and arbitrarily severe punishments were feasible, the firm would always choose to reduce w_2. This would not affect incentives and would still induce workers to participate. However, this scenario seems rather unlikely in the real world. First because of the 'money had and received' rule, a basic principle in the law of contracts which excludes the possibility that a private person pays the firm which hired her. Further, the firm may be obliged by law or owing to social standards to pay a minimum wage. Employees may also deny their commitments *ex post* and refuse to pay the penalty. This is all the more likely that they perceive it to be unfair, if they made effort. In order to oblige them to respect their commitments, the firm may ask the new hired to deposit a guarantee equal to $-w_2^*$, retrievable only if the signal is good. This remark goes along with a criticism often put forward about shirking models and we can summarize it as follows:[5] if firms could make their employees pay for their jobs by asking for an employment fee or by making them subscribe to bonds whose reimbursement was conditional, the incentive problem would be solved at zero cost, since employed workers would be deterred from shirking because of the risk of having to pay another fee to find another job if they were dismissed, or of not being reimbursed for the bonds they had already subscribed to. Thus these models would explain involuntary unemployment but only thanks to restrictions imposed on the contracts that may be signed between firms and workers. However, this argument assumes that workers have the required resources to pay the guarantee deposit or the subscription to the bonds, or at least that they are able to borrow the money. This hypothesis may remain unestablished if credit is rationed, because of an asymmetric information context for instance.[6] Moreover, employment fees or performance bonds lead to an additional moral hazard problem since firms may be tempted to pretend that a worker has cheated in order to keep the deposit.

Finally, making an employee pay for his job may simply be forbidden by law, in accordance with the 'money had and received' principle. Besides, in the real world, firms seldom resort to these practices. More often they adopt a stepwise remuneration scheme, gradually increasing a worker's wage owing to his seniority. We will address this question in the next section.

Thus, we may naturally assume that the firms cannot impose any penalty on workers and for instance that wages must not be negative. If we impose that $w_1 \geq 0, w_2 \geq 0$, and take figure 6.3, the optimal contract is now at point A; thus, we have $w_1 = \tilde{w}_1$ and $w_2 = 0$ and this leads to an employment level $\bar{l}$ defined by $\theta f'(\bar{l}) = \pi_1 \tilde{w}_1$. From $\pi_1 \tilde{w}_1 > \pi_1 w_1^* + (1 - \pi_1) w_2^*$, it follows that $\bar{l} < l^*$. The positive wage constraint leads to a lower employment level, but, above all, it explains involuntary unemployment since at point A employed workers' individual rationality constraint is not binding: their expected utility is thus strictly larger than that of the jobless. Hence, when only limited punishments can be imposed on workers and because of the necessity of a wage differential $w_1 - w_2$ to induce effort, employed workers will enjoy a rent relative to unemployed ones.

2.2 Unemployment as a discipline device

We now step into the case where firms and workers sign long-term contracts and where it is the threat of being made redundant that urges workers not to shirk. The model we will address is due to Shapiro and Stiglitz (1984).

Here is the main idea: if there is no reputation at stake, the fear of redundancy can be a good means to prevent shirking only if the wage received is strictly larger than workers opportunity cost (the equilibrium wage if a full-employment equilibrium prevails). Each firm thus would rather increase its workers' wage to encourage them to provide effort. All the firms react the same way, and this leads to a general increase in wages and a drop in the employment level. For a given turn-over rate, the higher the unemployment level, the longer the length of redundancy and the higher the penalty. The fear of redundancy may thus act as a discipline device when involuntary unemployment prevails.

Here again the economy includes N workers and m firms. Time is divided into periods indexed by $t = 0, 1, 2, \ldots$ and we assume that each individual lives over an infinite number of periods. For the sake of simplicity, we assume that workers are risk-neutral. In period t, a worker's utility writes as

$$U_t = r_t - k e_t \qquad k > 0$$

where r_t is the income received and e_t is the level of effort on the job.

The interest rate is equal to i. Each individual maximizes his lifetime utility which is the discount sum of his utility in every period. Let W_τ be the lifetime utility at period τ

$$W_\tau = \sum_{t=\tau}^{+\infty} \frac{U_t}{(1+i)^{t-\tau}} = \sum_{t=\tau}^{+\infty} \frac{r_t - k e_t}{(1+i)^{t-\tau}} \tag{6.8}$$

As in the previous section, we assume that e_t can take on only two values: e_t is equal to 0 for a shirker or a jobless and to 1 for a non-shirker.

At the beginning of period t, each worker receives the same wage w_t and the jobless receive unemployment benefit $\bar{w}$ provided by the government. In that period, a shirker is spotted with probability q. Then he is fired at the end of period t and enters the unemployment pool in period $t+1$. Further, a fraction b of workers is made redundant at the end of each period on reorganization grounds. We ignore the fact that an individual may be fired simultaneously for disciplinary and reorganization reasons, and we assume that $b + q < 1$. Therefore, a worker is made redundant at the end of each period with a probability b if he is a non-shirker and $b + q$ if he is a shirker.

Each firm has a production function $y_t = \theta f(l_t)$ where y_t and l_t respectively stand for the output and the number of non-shirkers in period t.

In each period t, workers must choose whether they want to be shirkers or non-shirkers and the firms must set the wage w_t and the employment level l_t: their decisions are thus respectively e_t and w_t, l_t. However in what follows, we limit ourselves to stationary equilibria: each firm determines a wage rate w and an employment level l for all t and each individual chooses once and for all to be a non-shirker ($e = 1$ for all t) or a shirker ($e_t = 0$ for all t).

Let $V_u^{ns}(\tau)$ and $V_e^{ns}(\tau)$ be a non-shirker's expected lifetime utility at period τ respectively when he is unemployed and employed. Likewise, $V_u^s(\tau)$ and $V_e^s(\tau)$ stand for a shirker's expected lifetime utility respectively when he is unemployed and employed. For any stationary equilibrium, $V_u^{ns}(\tau)$, $V_e^{ns}(\tau)$, $V_u^s(\tau)$ and $V_e^s(\tau)$ do not depend on τ. For such an equilibrium, we will simply write $V_u^{ns} = V_u^{ns}(\tau), V_e^{ns} = V_e^{ns}(\tau) \ldots$ for all τ.

A non-shirker employed in period τ will be unemployed in period $\tau + 1$ with a probability b, and will be employed again in period $\tau + 1$ with a probability $1 - b$. Thus, we have

$$V_e^{ns}(\tau) = w - k + \frac{1}{1+i}[b V_u^{ns}(\tau+1) + (1-b)V_e^{ns}(\tau+1)]$$

and, at a stationary equilibrium, we obtain

$$i V_e^{ns} = (1+i)(w-k) + b(V_u^{ns} - V_e^{ns}) \tag{6.9}$$

Likewise for a shirker, we have

$$V_e^s(\tau) = w + \frac{1}{1+i}[(b+q)V_u^s(\tau+1) + (1-b-q)V_e^s(\tau+1)]$$

and thus

$$iV_e^s = (1+i)w + (b+q)(V_u^s - V_e^s) \tag{6.10}$$

Given (6.9) and (6.10), we obtain

$$V_e^{ns} = \frac{(1+i)(w-k) + bV_u^{ns}}{i+b} \tag{6.11}$$

and

$$V_e^s = \frac{(1+i)w + (b+q)V_u^s}{i+b+q} \tag{6.12}$$

Workers are non-shirkers when $V_e^{ns} \geq V_e^s$. Given (6.11) and (6.12), this implies

$$w \geq \frac{k(i+b+q)}{q} + \frac{(i+b)(b+q)V_u^s - (i+b+q)bV_u^{ns}}{q(1+i)} \tag{6.13}$$

It is optimal for the firms to set the wage rate at a minimal level which ensures that employees do not shirk. This optimal wage is equal to the right-hand side term in (6.13). Thus, at the equilibrium we have $V_e^s = V_e^{ns} \equiv V_e$ which implies $V_u^s = V_u^{ns} \equiv V_u$. Using (6.13) we obtain

$$w = \frac{k(i+b+q)}{q} + \frac{i}{1+i}V_u \tag{6.14}$$

Furthermore, an individual who is unemployed in period τ, finds a job in period $\tau+1$ with a probability π and remains jobless with a probability $1-\pi$. Considering π as a parameter, we have

$$V_u(\tau+1) = \bar{w} + \frac{1}{1+i}[\pi V_e(\tau+1) + (1-\pi)V_u(\tau+1)]$$

and we obtain the stationary equilibrium condition

$$iV_u = (1+i)\bar{w} + \pi(V_e - V_u) \tag{6.15}$$

We now solve (6.11) and (6.15) simultaneously for V_u and V_e to obtain

$$V_u = \frac{\bar{w}(i+b) + \pi(w-k)}{i(i+b+\pi)}(1+i) \tag{6.16}$$

$$V_e = \frac{\bar{w}b + (i+\pi)(w-k)}{i(i+b+\pi)}(1+i) \tag{6.17}$$

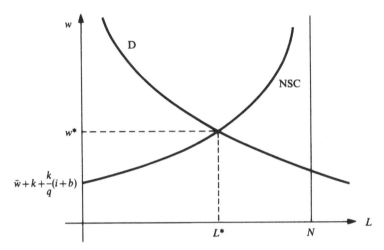

Figure 6.4   No-shirking condition and equilibrium unemployment

Equations (6.14) and (6.16) allow to calculate the optimal wage as a function of the parameters (especially π)

$$w = \bar{w} + k + \frac{k}{q}(i + b + \pi) \tag{6.18}$$

Equation (6.18) shows that the optimal wage rate (e.g., the lowest wage rate encouraging workers not to shirk), is an increasing function of the probability of finding a job. Indeed, in order to encourage workers not to shirk, the threat of redundancy must be efficient, meaning that shirkers must actually loose their jobs. For a given value of the probability π of finding a job again (e.g., for an expected duration of redundancy $1/\pi$), the utility loss due to redundancy $w - k - \bar{w}$ has to be sufficiently high to make workers unwilling to shirk.

Now, we should explain how π is determined. Let us consider a stationary equilibrium where L individuals are employed. In each period, bL individuals are made redundant and bL workers are hired. The new hires are drawn randomly among the $N - L$ jobless individuals of the previous period. Thus we have[7] $\pi = bL/(N - L)$ and, by using (6.18), we obtain

$$w = \bar{w} + k + \frac{k}{q}\left(i + \frac{bN}{N - L}\right) \tag{6.19}$$

Equation (6.19) determines a relation between w and L which characterizes any stationary equilibrium where workers do not shirk. This no-shirking condition is represented by the NSC curve in figure 6.4. It appears

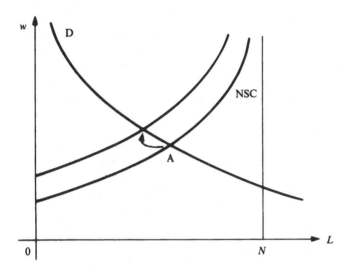

Figure 6.5   Comparative statics in the Shapiro–Stiglitz model

that the no-shirking condition is incompatible with full employment. Indeed, should full employment prevail, redundant individuals would immediately find a new job, and, knowing it, they would choose to shirk.

The equilibrium aggregate employment level L is defined by the profit maximizing condition which can be written

$$\theta f'(L/m) = w \tag{6.20}$$

This defines a labour demand curve D. The equilibrium is reached at the intersection of NSC and D: then, the wage is w^* and the employment level L^*. This is an equilibrium with involuntary unemployment since the $N - L^*$ jobless individuals would accept to work for a wage slightly inferior to w^*. However, they could not commit themselves in not shirking with such a salary and that's why firms prefer not to decrease wages.

We notice that NSC shifts upward when the unemployment benefit $\bar{w}$ or the interest rate i increases and when the probability of detecting a shirker q decreases (figure 6.5). In such a situation, the real wage rate and the unemployment level increase. This can be easily interpreted: when the unemployment benefit is high, a jobless expected utility is high and thus redundancy has little effect on workers. It is thus necessary to increase wages in order to increase the penalty due to the loss of one's job and encourage workers not to shirk. Moreover, when the interest rate increases, the discounted value of the income loss due to redundancy decreases. In order to maintain the incentive effect of the threat of losing one's job, the firms must here again increase wages.

The Shapiro–Stiglitz model also suggests that certain wage differentials, that cannot be explained in terms of differences in human capital, may in fact reflect more or less serious incentive problems. More particularly, for a given human capital, wages should be higher for jobs requiring a certain autonomy, that is when spotting the shirkers is more difficult. Wages should be lower for jobs where effort can be easily monitored and where the direct evaluation of a worker's performance determines his remuneration. This notably rationalizes the dual labour market hypothesis due to Doeringer and Piore (1971). According to this hypothesis the labour market includes a primary sector with high wages, long-term labour contracts and internal markets, and a secondary sector with precarious and low-paying jobs and little chance of promotion. The dual labour market theory presents some empiric bases, but it should explain why firms do not reduce primary sector wages down to the level where workers would be indifferent about being employed in the primary or secondary sectors. The shirking model provides a possible answer. Generally, primary-sector jobs give more responsibility and autonomy to the workers, and monitoring their efforts is difficult and costly. In order to encourage workers not to shirk, the loss of one's job must actually be penalizing, and this accounts for the wage differentials existing between the primary and secondary sectors, which aims at more than simply compensating for the additional amount of effort.[8]

2.3 *Deferred payments as an incentive mechanism*

As we saw in the previous section, the main objection to shirking models is that they exclude some contract agreements that are possible a priori: if the firm could ask for entry fees, the total benefit provided by a job could equal its opportunity cost (this does not interfere with the no-shirking condition since the entry fee is a sunk cost for workers) and only voluntary unemployment would remain. Likewise, if workers subscribe to perform-ance bonds, the fear of not being reimbursed would be sufficient to prevent them from shirking, while their wage would be equal to the opportunity cost of other occupations. These solutions are theoretically satisfactory but in practice they are unrealistic. They stick so little to the real operation of labour markets that they seem fanciful. We may however object to this, that long-term contracts replace entry fees or performance bonds, owing to the stepwise increase in the remunerations they provide. They might urge workers to make an effort, simultaneously maintaining the equality between the amount of discounted wages and the discounted opportunity costs. If the firm has the same rate of discount as workers', contracts should provide for deferred payments which would make redundancy more penalizing and would eliminate involuntary unemployment as a worker discipline device.

This issue is related to Lazear's works (1979, 1981), in which he analysed the shape of the worker's age earnings profile within a shirking model. He has notably shown that an upward sloping age earnings profile indicates a better incentive for effort.[9] This accounts for the kind of long-term implicit contracts often used in the real world: wages increase along with the worker's seniority and sometimes they provide for benefit into retirement, the latter being an incentive to work at full effort until the end of one's career.

However, are these deferred payments a sufficiently efficient alternative to entry fees or performance bonds to make involuntary unemployment a useless discipline device? Akerlof and Katz (1989) have shown that they are not. Their argument is simple and reads as follows: a new employee who is paid his opportunity cost in the form of deferred payments, will certainly shirk if he can because he has nothing to loose. Indeed, let us assume for instance that the job begins at $t = 0$ and ends at $t = T$ and payment is due at time T. Shirking gives an expected loss per unit of time equal to zero if $t = 0$ (and close to 0 when t is close to 0), since a layed-off individual receives the same cumulated wages from 0 to T, but provides a strictly positive instant profit since the worker does not make any effort. The worker will thus shirk if he is a new employee and if he can only expect the deferred payment of his reservation wage. Therefore, in order to encourage a worker to make effort he must be offered the deferred payment of his reservation wage plus a bonus: his welfare will be strictly larger than a jobless' and involuntary unemployment will occur.

We can prove this more rigorously under the following simple hypotheses. Assume that time is continuous and a worker's career has a finite length (from 0 to T). At each instant of his career a worker chooses to shirk or provide effort in order to maximize his expected lifetime utility. The money value of shirking in a short time interval dt is $k\,dt$. During that period a shirker is detected by the firm with a probability $q\,dt$ and is immediately fired. We also assume that a worker has outside opportunities (in the secondary sector for instance) which pay a constant wage w^* per time unit. We finally assume that firms and workers are risk-neutral and, to make things simple, that the rate of discount is equal to zero.

The firm wishes to minimize the average cost of efficient labour. Here, it would be better for the firm to pay the whole remuneration at the worker's retirement date: this does not alter the worker's welfare and provides for the best incentives. Let $w^*T + x$ be a worker's retirement date remuneration, where x stands for a possible bonus added to the acceptance wage; the worker receives this payment only if he was never caught shirking.

At time t, a worker who was never caught shirking before, faces the following alternatives. If he decides to shirk over the interval t to $t+dt$, he earns $k\,dt$ for the effort he did not provide, but he is detected with a probability $q\,dt$. In this case, his total remuneration including future gains in the secondary market will be $w^*(T-t)$ instead of the w^*T+x he should receive when he retires if he was never caught shirking. Thus, shirkers should expect a loss

$$q[w^*T+x-w^*(T-t)]\,dt$$

that is

$$q(x+w^*t)\,dt$$

A worker will not shirk from t to $t+dt$ if

$$k\,dt < q(x+w^*t)\,dt \tag{6.21}$$

This shows that a worker will certainly shirk at the beginning of his career (t close to 0) if his remuneration equals his opportunity cost only (e.g., if $x=0$). Furthermore, later in his career, not shirking may be an optimal strategy for the worker even if $x=0$. If he receives a bonus x, a worker will stop shirking at a date t_x, defined by

$$k=q(x+w^*t_x)\ \text{if}\ t_x>0$$

Therefore, we have

$$t_x=\text{Max}\{(k/q-x)/w^*,0\} \tag{6.22}$$

The firm chooses x in the interval $[0,k/q]$ in order to minimize the average cost of efficient labour which can be written as

$$\frac{w^*T+x}{(T-t_x)}=\frac{w^*T+x}{T-(k/q-x)/w^*} \tag{6.23}$$

This yields $x=k/q$ and thus $t_x=0$: the optimal strategy adopted by the firm consists in paying a bonus x from the beginning of a worker's career thus encouraging him not to shirk. In the aftermath, it appears that the deferred payment formula is not a substitute to employment fees or performance bonds: it is a better incentive only if it provides for a bonus in addition to the opportunity cost.

3   Other efficiency wage models

3.1   *Turnover model*

The firms may find it more profitable to pay high salaries in order to make employment more attractive when hiring and on-the-job training costs make labour turnover costly: then workers will hesitate to quit and additional wage labour costs will be more than compensated for by the gains due to the drop in the quitting rate. As shown by Salop (1979) and Stiglitz (1974), an equilibrium with wages in excess of the market clearing level and involuntary unemployment may result. We can formalize this as follows.[10] Assume that at the beginning of a period a firm hires l workers, promising to pay them a wage w. For each new hire, the firm bears hiring and training costs c. A worker's welfare is equal to $w + s$ where s stands for the monetary equivalent of a worker's job satisfaction. Job satisfaction is a random variable revealed to a worker after he has been hired and trained in the firm. We assume that s is distributed on $(-\infty, a)$ according to a cumulated distribution function $\phi(s)$. The parameter a may be positive, if a positive utility is associated to certain jobs, on social status grounds for instance.

A worker may quit just after the initial training period if his job does not satisfy him. He then receives unemployment benefit $\delta\bar{w}$ paid by the government (with $\delta < 1$), where $\bar{w}$ stands for the benefit paid to workers who remained unemployed the whole period. $\bar{w}$ may also be interpreted as the wage paid in a perfectly competitive secondary market where the firm does not bear any hiring or training costs, and where workers can be hired if they are willing.[11]

A worker will quit if $w + s < \delta\bar{w}$, that is, when his job satisfaction is so low that he would rather remain unemployed or employed in the secondary market for the remainder of the period than accept the job proposed to him. The probability of a worker choosing to quit is thus $\pi(w) = \phi(\delta\bar{w} - w)$ and realized output is $\theta f((1 - \pi(w))l)$.

The firm determines w and l in order to maximize its expected profit, which can be written as

$$\theta f((1-\pi))l) - cl - w(1-\pi)l \tag{6.24}$$

with $\pi = \pi(w)$.

We can easily check that the optimal wage rate w^* minimizes the average labour cost C_M defined by

$$C_M(w) = w + \frac{c}{1 - \pi(w)} \tag{6.25}$$

which corresponds to the sum of wages w and average turnover costs $c/(1 - \pi)$. When w goes to $\delta\bar{w} - a$, the average labour cost becomes very high because the quitting rate $\pi(w)$ goes to unity (figure 6.6). Conversely, for high wages, the quitting rate is very low and the average labour cost is approximately $w + c$.

The optimal level of employment l^* is obtained when the marginal productivity of labour and the average labour cost are equal, that is

$$\theta f'((1 - \pi(w^*))l^*) = C_M(w^*) \tag{6.26}$$

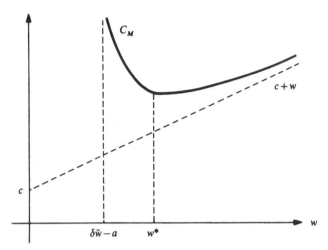

Figure 6.6 Average labour cost minimization in the turnover model

This solution holds if the number of workers N is larger than the total demand for labour of the m firms, e.g., $N > ml^*$. Also, workers must actually be willing to work. If we assume that they are risk-neutral, this participation constraint writes as

$$[1 - \pi(w^*)][w^* + E(s \,|\, s > \delta\bar{w} - w^*)] + \pi(w^*)\delta\bar{w} \geq \bar{w} \qquad (6.27)$$

The latter inequality will not be tight if δ is close to one. In such a case, all individuals are willing to be hired at a rate w^* and involuntary unemployment $N - ml^*$ will prevail. The firms do not find it profitable to decrease wages under w^*, because more workers would choose to quit after their training period, which ultimately would increase the average labour cost and decrease profits.

3.2 *Sociological explanations*

It is generally believed that an individual's willingness to make effort is dependent on how fairly he thinks his employer treats him. This feeling of equity is mostly assessed according to historically and socially well-defined social standards. Basing his analysis on different sociological studies, Akerlof (1982) has tried to explain the effort–wage relationship along that line. He considers labour contracts as 'gift exchanges' between workers and employers. A worker's gift is the effort he makes which is higher than the minimum social standard. The firm's gift consists in paying a wage larger than the opportunity cost. The idea behind this theory is that labour contracts do not result from individual negotiations with each worker but that the group determines some productivity standards that it considers as fair in exchange for a wage higher than the group reference wage. That reference wage can be defined as the average wage of individuals who have similar abilities and who can be employed in other firms or remain redundant. It can also depend on the historical evolution of wages, roughly like in the peak income hypothesis of Duesenberry and Modigliani.

In such a situation, the profit-maximizing firm has to determine the wage w, the number of employees l and the group effort standard e, taking into account the relationship between e, w and the reference wage w_r. Here, we will confine ourselves to an example showing how an underemployment equilibrium may result from these hypotheses.[12]

Assume that the output y is a function of the effort e and labour l according to the production function

$$y = (el)^\alpha \qquad 0 < \alpha < 1 \tag{6.28}$$

and each individual respects the same effort standard which is defined by

$$e = -a + b(w/w_r)^\gamma \tag{6.29}$$

with $0 < \gamma < 1$ and $a > b(1-\gamma) > 0$.[13]

Finally, the reference wage w_r is the geometric mean

$$w_r = w_0^{1-u} \bar{w}^u \tag{6.30}$$

where u is the unemployment rate, w_0 is the wage paid by other firms and $\bar{w}$ is the unemployment benefit.

There are m identical firms and N identical individuals in the economy, which yields

$$ml = (1-u)N \tag{6.31}$$

The firm considers w_r as given and chooses l and w in order to maximize its profits $(el)^\alpha - wl$ subject to the following constraint

$$e = -a + b(w/w_r)^\gamma$$

This yields

$$w/w_r = [a/b(1-\gamma)]^{1/\gamma} \tag{6.32}$$

$$\alpha[a\gamma/(1-\gamma)]^\alpha l^{\alpha-1} = w \tag{6.33}$$

We are looking for an equilibrium in which all the firms pay the same salary. Thus we have $w_0 = w$ and

$$w_r = w^{1-u} \bar{w}^u \tag{6.34}$$

(6.32), (6.33) and (6.34) allow us to calculate the demand for labour associated with such a symmetric equilibrium, as a function of the unemployment rate

$$l = \left[\frac{\bar{w}}{\alpha} \left(\frac{a\gamma}{1-\gamma} \right)^{-\alpha} \left(\frac{a}{b(1-\gamma)} \right)^{1/\gamma u} \right]^{1/(\alpha - 1)} \tag{6.35}$$

Given (6.31), we obtain

$$N(1-u) = m \left[\frac{\bar{w}}{\alpha} \left(\frac{a\gamma}{1-\gamma} \right)^{-\alpha} \left(\frac{a}{b(1-\gamma)} \right)^{1/\gamma u} \right]^{1/(\alpha - 1)} \tag{6.36}$$

Equation (6.36) defines an equilibrium unemployment rate u with $0 < u < 1$. We may not actually say that this model leads to an involuntary unemployment equilibrium owing to the absence of individual utility functions for employed and redundant individuals, allowing a comparison of their respective welfare. We may at the most note that an individual utility function that is compatible with (6.29) should include the reference wage w_r. Then we would have an economy with consumption external effects where the competitive market equilibrium would not be Pareto optimal.

As a conclusion, we may note that this sociological approach provides another possible explanation of the hypothesis of a dual labour market. Indeed primary sector jobs may favour a certain cohesion among the group and the feeling of being treated with equity. Primary sector workers freely accept higher effort standards, considering them as normal counterparts of fair treatment as a work group, while it is a purely individually based relationship that determines the rules of the secondary sector.

7 Efficiency wages, employment fluctuations and fiscal policy

The basic idea underlying efficiency wage theory is that there is a link between workers' productivity and the wages they receive. As seen in the previous chapter, the relationship mainly lies in a situation of asymmetric information. In adverse selection models, the firm cannot distinguish the most efficient workers from the less efficient and a worker's ability is assumed to be correlated with his reservation wage. Then in a situation of involuntary unemployment, the firm may choose not to decrease wages so that the most productive individuals do not give up applying for the jobs. In moral hazard models, individuals' performances depend on their behaviour which cannot be perfectly monitored by employers. Offering higher wages makes the cost of losing one's job higher and thus urges workers to make every effort required to keep their jobs. In other models, a wage policy is a means of stabilizing the labour force when turnover is costly. Finally, in analyses of sociological inspiration, the wage policy is the product of social conventions determining work rules and collective productivity standards.

All these models show that real wage rigidity within an involuntary unemployment context is perfectly compatible with a competitive labour market. However, if the efficiency wage theory explains the existence of involuntary unemployment, using it as an element of macroeconomic analysis aiming at explaining the fluctuations in output and employment is not self-evident. Conventional efficiency wage models usually include only two commodities: labour and one consumption good. They lead to real wages and output levels which are totally independent of the disturbances that might affect aggregate demand, that is to a vertical aggregate supply curve.

Assuming nominal rigidities allow us to reconcile the existence of involuntary unemployment using the efficiency wage theory and the fact that shifts in aggregate demand affect output in the short run. Akerlof and Yellen (1985) did so by using a near-rationality argument. Their model assumes monopolistic competition in the goods market and fixed real wages due to efficiency wage considerations. The firms choose the price that maximizes their profits, but should a disturbance affect demand, the losses due to a sticky price strategy are low (second order) in relation to the disturbances. Keeping rigid prices and wages is thus almost costless and may be considered as near-rational. If the firms behave accordingly, the variations in aggregate demand, including those caused by monetary shocks, will have real effects on production and employment.[1]

In this chapter, we will explore an alternative approach to output fluctuations in efficiency wage models. It depends on the following observation: the length of a labour contract is usually shorter than an individual life span. Many contracts are of limited length, and, even when their lengths are unlimited, an individual may be dismissed on reorganization grounds for instance. In this case, firms and workers will not use the same price system to define real wages: when the goods produced are unstockable, production real wages are determined by the prices prevailing during the duration of the contract, while consumption real wages should be calculated by deflating money wages by an intertemporal price index. If expected future prices are not linked to current prices (which is likely in the case of transitory disturbances affecting the goods market), the consumption real wages rigidity allows a certain flexibility in production real wages and therefore in employment.[2]

The framework in which we will reason is that of a very simple overlapping generations model where individuals live and consume for two periods, but work only for the first and hold savings in the form of money balances. We assume that workers' performances cannot be perfectly monitored but, for each worker, the firms perceive a signal correlated with effort. These signals will determine wage payments as specified in labour contracts. The other incomes consist of profits and possibly unemployment benefits. In this model, we have two types of unemployment equilibria which depend on the values of public consumption and unemployment benefit: a regime with involuntary unemployment and a regime where unemployment is purely voluntary.

An important feature of the model is that the fluctuations in employment are directly linked to the real disturbances affecting the aggregate demand. In particular, equilibrium unemployment is affected by shifts in public consumption. Of course, in market clearing neoclassical models, the employment level is also connected to the real disturbances affecting the aggregate demand. Since the long-run elasticity of the labour supply is too low to provide a worthwhile explanation of the employment fluctuations, it is generally assumed that this relationship goes through an intertemporal substitution phenomenon consisting of a choice between working now and working later, similar to the one initially described by Lucas and Rapping (1969). However, most econometric studies question the empirical validity of the explanation of economic fluctuations based on intertemporal substitution in labour supply, in particular because the elasticity of substitution between leisure in different periods is too low to be consistent with empirical evidence on employment fluctuations.[3] On the contrary, we shall see that, in an intertemporal efficiency wage model, changes in real aggregate demand may have significant repercussions on the employment level, with unemployment being involuntary and the labour supply being possibly totally rigid. In the model developed in this chapter, small variations in the real wage may in fact go along with large variations in the employment level, a phenomenon frequently observed in the real world and that can be explained by conventional neoclassical analysis only with unconvincing hypotheses concerning the labour supply.

In what follows, we will put the emphasis on the macroeconomic effects of variations in government expenditure. As we shall see, the relationship between the employment level and public consumption strictly depends on the transitory or permanent characteristics of the variations in public expenditures, at least when we assume that agents perfectly expect future prices, since the efficiency of a policy requires a change in the expected price/current price ratio. In fact this change generates an intertemporal substitution in consumption which affects incentive compatibility conditions and determines equilibrium wage and employment levels.[4] Hence, as in neoclassical market-clearing models, the effect of real demand shocks on economic activity would be through an intertemporal substitution, but here it would concern consumption and it might be compatible with an inelastic labour supply. Finally, we will also emphasize the fact that this positive externality on employment generated by transitory demand shocks may explain a tendency to choose a level of public consumption which is higher than the optimal stationary level.

The first section of this chapter presents the model and section 2 characterizes the labour contracts offered by the firms. The third section proves the existence and uniqueness of an equilibrium and analyses its properties. Section 4 is devoted to the perfect foresight case. It emphasizes the difference between the effects of transitory and permanent demand shocks and the tendancy for public overspending. In section 5, we contemplate the situation where workers' effort disutility cannot be observed by the employers so that the labour contracts have to take into account moral hazard and adverse selection as well.

1　General framework

We consider an economy with only one consumption good, labour as a factor of production, money which is the sole store of value, and three types of agents: consumers, firms and the government. The context is a simple overlapping generations model where each consumer lives for only two periods and leaves no bequest: a younger and an older generation constantly coexist. In this model, individuals buy consumption goods at each period of life, but they work, make profits, pay taxes and derive a utility from public consumption only when they are young. Thus, older consumers only spend the savings they made when they were younger. Individuals derive utility

$$U_1\left(x,\frac{z}{p^e}\right)+U_2(g)-ea \qquad a>0 \tag{7.1}$$

x and z respectively stand for the first period consumption and final money holdings; p^e stands for the price of the consumer good expected for the next period. Since consumers receive all their incomes when they are young, z/p^e represents expected future consumption. $U_1(x,z/p^e)$ is thus a conventional intertemporal utility function which arguments are the consumption of both lifetime periods. Public consumption is g and $U_2(g)$ stands for the corresponding additional welfare. Disutility of effort is represented by ea with $e=0$ or 1. By hypothesis, each young consumer may provide an indivisible unit of labour but can decide either to work or to shirk on the job. We have $e=1$ for an employed non-shirker and $e=0$ for a shirker or an unemployed individual.

By hypothesis, consumers do not support the same disutility for the efforts they provide at work. Therefore, parameter a is different for each individual owing to psychological or objective reasons. However, we will assume that each firm wanting to hire an individual is able to identify the value of parameter a for this applicant. In other words, we make the hypothesis that the firm observes some of the applicant's characteristics allowing the firm to evaluate the value of his parameter a. The firm may for instance investigate his previous occupations, or base its evaluation on objective criteria like his age or his marital status, or even directly assess the applicant's motivation through an interview. Assuming that a cannot be evaluated by the employer would come down to mixing adverse selection phenomena with the problem of pure moral hazard which we intend to emphasize here. However, as we shall see in section 5, the results will not be fundamentally altered in that case. We will assume that parameter a is distributed in the interval $[a_0,a_1]$, according to a cumulative distribution function $G(a)$. The size of each generation is equal to N: thus, at each period, there are $G(a)N$ young individuals whose disutility to effort is less than a.

At a given date, the 'current period', the total stock of money is M_0 and it is held by the old generation. Since there is no legacy, old individuals consume all their wealth.

Let r be the total resources available to a young individual and p the price of the consumption good. The budget constraint can be written as

$$px + z = r \tag{7.2}$$

Since young people do not have initial money holdings, r is the sum of distributed profits $\bar{r}$ and either wages or possible unemployment benefit whose value is defined below.

By maximizing $U(x,z/p^e)$ under the constraint (7.2), we define young individuals' demand functions for the consumption good and real final money holdings $x = \xi_x(p^e/p, r/p)$ and $z/p^e = \xi_z(p^e/p, r/p)$ as well as the indirect utility function

$$V(p^e/p, r/p) = U_1(\xi_x(p^e/p, r/p), \xi_z(p^e/p, r/p)) \tag{7.3}$$

We assume that $U_1(x, z/p^e)$ is continuously differentiable, strictly quasi-concave, increasing with respect to x and z/p^e, and homogeneous of degree 1. Functions ξ_x and V may then be written as

$$\xi_x = K(p^e/p)\frac{r}{p} \tag{7.4}$$

$$V = r/I(p,p^e) \tag{7.5}$$

where $K(p^e/p)$ is a differentiable function, such that $0 < K(p^e/p) < 1$ and $I(p,p^e)$ is homogeneous of degree 1, differentiable and increasing with respect to p and p^e. Assuming that $I(p,p) = p$ is not restrictive, provided the cardinalization of preferences is adequate. Thus function $I(p,p^e)$ can be interpreted as an intertemporal price index and, according to (7.5), the indirect utility is nothing else but the money income deflated by the intertemporal price index. We assume: $I(p,p^e) \to 0$ when $p^e \to 0$ and $I(p,p^e) \to +\infty$ when $p^e \to +\infty$ for any value of p. We also assume that the expected future price p^e depends on the current price p and the money supply M_1 available at the beginning of the following period, and we write

$$p^e = \psi(p, M_1) \tag{7.6}$$

with $M_1 = (1 + \pi)M_0$, π being the money supply growth rate. The formula (7.6) is relatively general. It may correspond to a subjective expectation-making scheme resulting from some learning process like the one described in section 3.4 of chapter 2. As we shall see below, it is also compatible with a perfect foresight assumption.

Function $\psi(.)$ is supposed to be homogeneous of degree 1, which corresponds to the hypothesis of the absence of money illusion, and such that $\psi(p, M_1)/p$ is decreasing with respect to p, which means that price forecasts display some degree of insensitivity to variations of current prices.

We also make the following technical assumptions

$$\exists\, \varepsilon > 0 \text{ such that } \psi(p,M_1) > \varepsilon\, \forall p > 0 \tag{7.7}$$

$$\psi(p,M_1)/p \to 0 \text{ when } p \to +\infty, \forall M_1 > 0 \tag{7.8}$$

Finally, we let

$$\Gamma(p,M_1) = I(p,\psi(p,M_1)) \tag{7.9}$$

The economy includes J identical firms with a production function $y = f(l)$ where y and l respectively stand for the output and the quantity of efficient labour. We make the usual hypotheses about function $f(.)$, which is assumed to be twice continuously differentiable such that $f' > 0$, $f'' < 0, f(0) = 0, f'(l) \to 0$ when $l \to +\infty, f'(l) \to +\infty$ when $l \to 0$.

Let s be the money wage rate and $w = s/p$ the real wage rate. Maximizing the profit $f(l) - wl$ leads to the demand for labour $l_d^*(w)$ and the supply of goods $y_s^*(w) = f(l_d^*(w))$ of each firm. Under the above hypotheses, $l_d^*(w)$ and $y_s^*(w)$ are decreasing differentiable functions.

Public expenditures include public consumption g and the payment of unemployment benefits equal to $\bar{w}$ in real terms. We let $\bar{s} = \bar{w}p$. Therefore, public expenditures are equal to $p[g + \bar{w}(N - L)]$, where L stands for the employment level (with $L \leq N$).

These expenditures are financed by taxes and by the creation of money. If the money value of taxes is written T and the creation of money necessary to finance the deficit ΔM, the government budget constraint is

$$\Delta M + T = p[g + \bar{w}(N - L)] \tag{7.10}$$

We have

$$\Delta M = M_1 - M_0 = \pi M_0 \tag{7.11}$$

And therefore, according to (7.10) and (7.11)

$$T = p[g + \bar{w}(N - L)] - \pi M_0 \tag{7.12}$$

In what follows, g, $\bar{w}$ and π are considered to be instruments of economic policy and (7.12) defines the taxation resulting from these choices.

Let R be the aggregate wealth of young consumers. We assume that taxes are exclusively paid by the younger generation. If the J firms produce the same quantity y and realized profits are entirely distributed during the current period, we have

$$R = p[Jy + \bar{w}(N - L)] - T$$

that is

$$R = \pi M_0 + p(Jy - g) \tag{7.13}$$

2 Incentive contracts and involuntary unemployment

As far as the labour market is concerned, the model's main hypotheses concern the nature of the information available to the firms to encourage their employees not to shirk. We assume that they do not directly observe the quality of their work; therefore, they cannot distinguish for sure conscientious employees from shirkers. However, the firms perceive signals which partially inform them about the efforts made by each worker. The signals (one for each employee) can be observed by both the firm and its employees. For simplicity's sake, we assume that these signals can have only two values: 'good' or 'bad'. For a conscientious worker, the corresponding signal is good with a probability of θ_1 and bad with a probability of $1-\theta_1$. On the other hand, for a shirker, the signal is good with a probability of θ_2 and bad with a probability of $1-\theta_2$. We assume $0<\theta_2<\theta_1\leq 1$. In other words, the signal perceived by the firm provides partial information about the employee's behaviour since the probability that a good signal appears is higher for a conscientious worker than for a shirker.[5]

In such conditions for each type of worker, (i.e., for a given value of the parameter a), the contracts offered by the firms in the current period specify the wage paid according to the signal perceived. We will formally define a contract as a pair of functions $s_1(.):[a_0,a_1]\to R_+$ and $s_2(.):[a_0,a_1]\to R_+$ which define the wage received depending on the type of the worker and on the perceived signal: $s_1(a)$ represents the wage received by a worker whose type is a, if the signal is good, and $s_2(a)$ stands for the wage when the signal is bad. Here, we limit functions $s_1(.)$ and $s_2(.)$ to taking their values in R_+: whatever the signal, the wage cannot be negative. This hypothesis is important because it limits the magnitude of the penalty applied should a bad signal appear.[6]

Shirkers are supposed to be totally useless: they provide no efficient work. Hence, the firms will sign contracts that encourage workers not to shirk. For an individual of type a, this incentive constraint is

$$\frac{\theta_1 s_1(a)+(1-\theta_1)s_2(a)+\bar{r}}{I(p,p^e)}-a\geq\frac{\theta_2 s_1(a)+(1-\theta_2)s_2(a)+\bar{r}}{I(p,p^e)} \quad (7.14)$$

We assume that consumers maximize their expected utility. The left-hand and right-hand side terms of equation (7.14) respectively represent non-shirkers' and shirkers' expected utility levels. According to (7.14) it is more profitable for a worker not to shirk. Taking (7.6) and (7.9) into account, this gives

$$(\theta_1-\theta_2)[s_1(a)-s_2(a)]\geq a\Gamma(p,M_1) \quad (7.15)$$

When (7.15) is satisfied, the contract $\{s_1(.),s_2(.)\}$ is said to be *incentive compatible* for type-a workers. Moreover, workers will only sign contracts that insure a satisfaction level at least as high as the satisfaction level they have when unemployed and receiving unemployment benefit. For a type-a individual who signs an incentive compatible contract, this gives

$$\frac{\theta_1 s_1(a) + (1 - \theta_1)s_2(a) + \bar{r}}{I(p,p^e)} - a \geq \frac{p\bar{w} + \bar{r}}{I(p,p^e)} \tag{7.16}$$

In view of (7.6) and (7.9), the inequality (7.16) becomes

$$\theta_1 s_1(a) + (1 - \theta_1)s_2(a) \geq p\bar{w} + a\Gamma(p,M_1) \tag{7.17}$$

When (7.17) holds, the contract $\{s_1(.),s_2(.)\}$ is said to be *individually rational* for type-a workers.

Let $S(a,p)$ be the set of contracts which are simultaneously incentive compatible and individually rational for type-a individuals when the current price is p.

In order to complete the description of the labour market, let us introduce a function $\lambda(.):[a_0,a_1] \rightarrow \{0,1\}$ which means that type-a individuals are actually employed if $\lambda(a) = 1$ and that they are unemployed if $\lambda(a) = 0$. Since the efficient works of different types are perfect substitutes, at the labour market equilibrium, the expected wage rate must be the same whatever the type of the employee (otherwise, the firms would replace the high wage rate employees by low wage rate employees). Therefore, for any labour market equilibrium there corresponds a unique expected wage rate s and a function $\lambda(.)$. However, in order to obtain an actual equilibrium, three conditions must be met: first, for any employee, there exists an incentive compatible, individually rational contract leading to a wage rate equal to s. Secondly, for any unemployed individual, any incentive compatible individually rational contract leads to a wage rate greater than s. And thirdly, the number of employees is equal to the demand for labour. These conditions characterize a labour market equilibrium compatible with the existence of involuntary unemployment: firms can obtain the desired quantity of efficient labour for the same price s whatever the type of the individual employed. Moreover, no unemployed may be offered a contract that would simultaneously be more profitable for the firm than the existing contract and acceptable and incentive compatible for the individual. When such an equilibrium prevails on the labour market, contracts mutually profitable to the firms and some unemployed individuals might exist if the effort could be monitored, that is to say if we could do without the incentive compatibility condition. Therefore, the equilibrium is not a Pareto optimum. However, these contracts are not signed, since the unemployed individuals' promises not to shirk are not credible. In that sense, the above defined equilibrium may coexist with involuntary unemployment. Such an equilibrium on the labour market may be formally defined by introducing the following definition:

Definition 7.1 Condition E_1 holds for $s,p,\lambda(.)$ when we have:
If $\lambda(a)=1$: there exists $\{s_1(.),s_2(.)\}$ in $S(a,p)$ such that
$\theta_1 s_1(a)+(1-\theta_1)s_2(a)=s$
If $\lambda(a)=0$: $\theta_1 s_1(a)+(1-\theta_1)s_2(a)>s$ for all $\{s_1(.),s_2(.)\}$ in $S(a,p)$

In confirmity with the above-mentioned definition, a labour market equilibrium is obtained when employment is equal to the demand for labour expressed by the firms, and condition E_1 holds. We will assume that the goods market is perfectly competitive with price p adjusting supply to demand. This leads to definition 7.2, where an equilibrium corresponds to a wage rate s, a price p and a function $\lambda(.)$.

Definition 7.2 $\{s,p,\lambda(.)\}$ is an equilibrium if

(i) condition E_1 holds

(ii) $Jl_d^*\left(\dfrac{s}{p}\right)=N\displaystyle\int_{a_0}^{a_1}\lambda(a)\,dG(a)$

(iii) $Jy_s^*\left(\dfrac{s}{p}\right)=K\left(\psi\left(1,(1+\pi)\dfrac{M_0}{p}\right)\right)\left[\pi\dfrac{M_0}{p}+Jy_s^*\left(\dfrac{s}{p}\right)-g\right]$
$\qquad\qquad +\dfrac{M_0}{p}+g$

Conditions (i)–(ii) mean that there is an equilibrium on the labour market and condition (iii) characterizes the equilibrium on the goods market.

Proposition 7.1 allows a better interpretation of the equilibrium on the labour market. In this proposition and in the remainder of the chapter, the real wage rate and the initial real money holdings are respectively represented by $w=s/p$ and $m_0=M_0/p$, and we write $\gamma(m_0)\equiv\Gamma(1,(1+\pi)m_0)$.

Proposition 7.1 For any equilibrium $\{s,p,\lambda(.)\}$, we have $\lambda(a)=1$ if $a_0\leq a\leq\hat{a}$ and $\lambda(a)=0$ if $\hat{a}<a\leq a_1$, where

$$\hat{a}=\text{Min}\left\{a_1,\dfrac{w-\bar{w}}{\gamma(m_0)},\dfrac{(\theta_1-\theta_2)w}{\theta_1\gamma(m_0)}\right\}$$

Proof
Let $\{s,p,\lambda(.)\}$ be an equilibrium. Let $a\in[a_0,a_1]$ be such that $\lambda(a)=1$.

According to (i) and definition 7.1, there exist $\{s_1(.),s_2(.)\}$ such that (7.15), and (7.17) hold and

$$s=\theta_1 s_1(a)+(1-\theta_1)s_2(a) \tag{7.18}$$

From (7.15) and (7.18), we have

$$\frac{(\theta_1-\theta_2)s}{\theta_1} \geq (\theta_1-\theta_2)[s_1(a)-s_2(a)] \geq a\Gamma(p,M_1)$$

which implies

$$a \leq \frac{(\theta_1-\theta_2)w}{\theta_1\gamma(m_0)}$$

Similarly, from (7.17) and (7.18), we have

$$a \leq \frac{w-\bar{w}}{\gamma(m_0)}$$

These two last inequalities imply $a \leq \hat{a}$. Conversely, if $\lambda(a)=0$, we have

$$(\theta_1-\theta_2)[s_1(a)-s_2(a)] < a\Gamma(p,M_1) \tag{7.19}$$

or

$$\theta_1 s_1(a)+(1-\theta_1)s_2(a)) < p\bar{w}+a\Gamma(p,M_1) \tag{7.20}$$

for any contract $\{s_1(.),s_2(.)\}$ which satisfies

$$\theta_1 s_1(a)+(1-\theta_1)s_2(a) \leq s \tag{7.21}$$

This is particularly true if $s_1(a)=s/\theta_1$ and $s_2(a)=0$. Hence

$$a > \text{Min}\left\{\frac{w-\bar{w}}{\gamma(m_0)}, \frac{(\theta_1-\theta_2)w}{\theta_1\gamma(m_0)}\right\} \geq \hat{a}$$

According to proposition 7.1, only individuals whose types are lower than a threshold $\hat{a}$ will be employed at the equilibrium. Since $\hat{a}$ varies with the real wage rate w (for a given value of m_0), we are lead to define a labour quasi-supply function $L_s(w)$ by the relation

$$L_s(w)=N\int_{a_0}^{a_1}\lambda(a)\,dG(a)=NG(\hat{a}(w))$$

and the equilibrium prevails on the labour market when $L_s(w)=Jl_d^*(w)$. We may also write

$$L_s(w)=\text{Min}\{L_s^*(w),L_s^{**}(w)\}$$

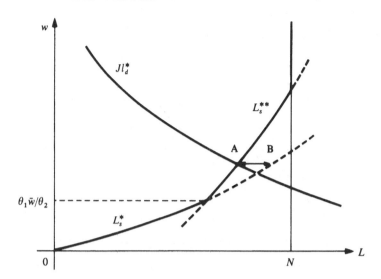

Figure 7.1 Equilibrium with involuntary unemployment

where

$$L_s^*(w) = NG\left[\text{Min} \left\{ a_1, \frac{w - \bar{w}}{\gamma(m_0)} \right\} \right]$$

and

$$L_s^{**}(w) = NG\left[\frac{(\theta_1 - \theta_2)w}{\theta_1 \gamma(m_0)} \right]$$

$L_s^*(w)$ stands for the labour supply function which would prevail if the effort were perfectly monitored, since the individuals willing to work at a rate w (by providing an effort) are those whose type is lower than $(w - \bar{w})/\gamma(m_0)$. However, the incentive compatibility condition requires a to be less than $(\theta_1 - \theta_2)w/\theta_1 \gamma(m_0)$. This leads to defining function $L_s^{**}(w)$ which represents the number of individuals likely to be hired at a rate w, in view of the incentive compatibility constraint. The quasi-supply function L_s is thus the minimum of L_s^* and L_s^{**}.

For $L_s^*(w) < L_s^{**}(w)$ we have $w < \theta_1 \bar{w}/\theta_2$. In figure 7.1 we have assumed that the curves L_s^* and L_s^{**} cross each other within $[0,N]$. This figure represents an involuntary unemployment situation whose magnitude is measured by AB.

It is important to note that the position of the curves L_s depends on real money holdings. As we shall see, a change in fiscal policy may generate a

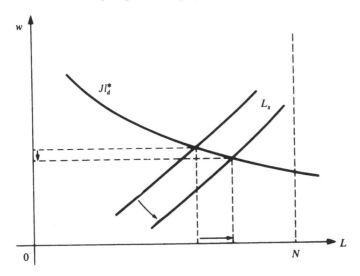

Figure 7.2   Large employment fluctuations

change in the equilibrium price p and therefore helps reduce involuntary unemployment. This is shown in figure 7.2. The rise in the equilibrium price makes the curve L_s shift downward and causes a drop in the real wage rate and a rise in the employment level. If the labour-demand curve is flat enough, large variations in the employment level occur along with low variations in the real wage rate, even though the observed supply of labour is perfectly inelastic: indeed, everybody wants to be hired whatever the wage rate, since they have the opportunity to shirk.

The same phenomenon may occur in the case of technological shocks which would make the labour demand curve shift: if the labour quasi-supply curve were flat enough, we would observe large employment fluctuations along with an inelastic supply of labour.[7]

Two other situations are a priori possible, one being full employment, the other a purely voluntary unemployment. In the next section, we will show that, under certain hypotheses, there exists a unique equilibrium whose characteristics we will study.

3   Equilibrium analysis

Let us first give a precise definition of the notion of involuntary unemployment which is considered here. At an equilibrium $\{s,p,\lambda(.)\}$, a type-a individual such that $\lambda(a)=0$ is said to be in a situation of involuntary unemployment if his welfare would strictly increase if he were employed without shirking, and paid at a wage rate s like employed individuals. Otherwise, unemployment is voluntary.

The threshold $\hat{a}$ defined in proposition 7.1 implies the existence of three types of equilibrium. The case $\hat{a} = (\theta_1 - \theta_2)w/\theta_1\gamma(m_0)$ has been represented in figure 7.1 and corresponds to an involuntary unemployment, while the situation where $\hat{a} = (w - \bar{w})/\gamma(m_0)$ is a case of voluntary unemployment. Finally, full employment occurs when $\hat{a} = a_1$.

In this model, involuntary unemployment equilibria are characterized as follows. First of all, a transitory rise in public consumption is likely to reduce the extent of the involuntary unemployment, with a variation in the real wage rate which may be low and a supply of labour totally inelastic. Second, we will show that the criterion for a transitory increase in public consumption financed by taxes to be socially desirable is different from the usual proposition of welfare economics, meaning that the total willingness to pay for this increase must be larger than the additional fiscal expenditures. This criterion will be valid for a full-employment or voluntary unemployment situation but not in the case of involuntary unemployment. Thirdly, we will see that the consequences of a rise in unemployment benefits depend on the nature of the prevailing unemployment. In a situation of voluntary unemployment, any rise in $\bar{w}$ reduces the social surplus while it is totally neutral when unemployment is involuntary. The immediate consequence is that the concern for equity (which can justify a rise in $\bar{w}$) runs counter to the objective of macroeconomic efficiency in a situation of voluntary unemployment, while it is not the case when unemployment is involuntary.

Let $ED(p,Y,g)$ be the excess demand for goods when the price, the aggregate output and public consumption are respectively p, Y and g, that is

$$ED(p,Y,g) \equiv K\left(\psi\left(1,(1+\pi)\frac{M_0}{p}\right)\right)\left(\pi\frac{M_0}{p} + Y - g\right) + \frac{M_0}{p} + g - Y$$

In order to ensure the existence and uniqueness of an equilibrium, we will assume that the demand for goods is a decreasing function of the price, when production is equal to the full-employment output and public demand is equal to zero (i.e., private income as high as possible in real terms). Function $p \to ED(p,Jf(N/J),0)$ is thus supposed to be decreasing. We then have:

Proposition 7.2 If $Y \le Jf(N/J)$ and $Y > g \ge 0$, function $p \to ED(p,Y,g)$ is decreasing and $ED(p,Y,g) < 0$ (>0) when $p \to +\infty (p \to 0)$.

Proof
Let $p' > p$. First, assume that

$$K(\psi(1,(1+\pi)M_0/p')) < K(\psi(1,(1+\pi)M_0/p))$$

Then we have

$$ED(p',Y,g) - ED(p,Y,g) < K(\psi(1,(1+\pi)M_0/p))\pi\left(\frac{M_0}{p'} - \frac{M_0}{p}\right) < 0$$

When

$$K(\psi(1,(1+\pi)M_0/p')) \geq K(\psi(1,(1+\pi)M_0/p))$$

we have

$$ED(p',Y,g) - ED(p,Y,g) < ED(p',Jf(N/J),0) - ED(p,Jf(N/J),0) < 0$$

which proves the first part of the proposition. Furthermore, when p goes to infinity, we have

$$ED(p,Y,g) \to K(\psi(1,0))(Y-g) + g - Y < 0$$

since $K(\psi(1,0)) < 1$. Lastly $ED(p,Y,g)$ goes to infinity when p goes to 0.

We will now analyse the characteristics and the conditions of existence of the three types of equilibrium. Let $w^* = f'(N/J)$ be the marginal productivity of labour under full employment.

3.1 *Involuntary unemployment*

In an involuntary unemployment equilibrium, we have

$$\hat{a} = \frac{(\theta_1 - \theta_2)w}{\theta_1 \gamma(m_0)} < \text{Min}\left\{a_1, \frac{w - \bar{w}}{\gamma(m_0)}\right\} \tag{7.22}$$

$$Jy_s^*(w) = K(\psi(1,(1+\pi)m_0))[\pi m_0 + Jy_s^*(w) - g] + m_0 + g \tag{7.23}$$

$$Jl_d^*(w) = NG\left[\frac{(\theta_1 - \theta_2)w}{\theta_1 \gamma(m_0)}\right] \tag{7.24}$$

According to proposition 7.2, the equation (7.23) can be represented by a decreasing curve C_1 in the (m_0,w) plane. Furthermore, the hypotheses made about functions $I(.)$ and $\psi(.)$ imply that the function $\gamma(m_0)$ is increasing and $\gamma(m_0) \to 0$ when $m_0 \to 0$ and $\gamma(m_0) \to +\infty$ when $m_0 \to +\infty$. Consequently, there exists $\bar{m}_0 > 0$ such that

$$\gamma(\bar{m}_0) = \frac{(\theta_1 - \theta_2)w^*}{\theta_1 a_1}$$

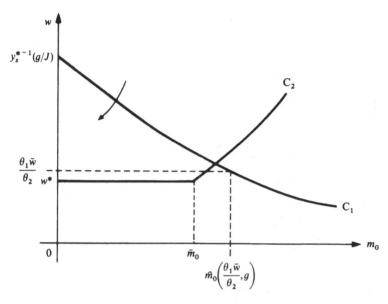

Figure 7.3   Involuntary unemployment equilibrium

The condition (7.24) thus holds if $w = w^*, m_0 \leq \bar{m}_0$. If $w > w^*$, (7.24) defines an increasing curve C_2 in the (m_0, w) plane.

The equilibrium is reached at the intersection of C_1 and C_2. A unique intersection point exists if

$$g \leq Jf(N/J) \tag{7.25}$$

It is actually an involuntary unemployment equilibrium if (7.22) holds. Let us first examine condition $\hat{a} < a_1$, which is equivalent to $w > w^*$. It will be met if and only if

$$Jf(N/J) > K(\psi(1,(1+\pi)\bar{m}_0))[\pi\bar{m}_0 + Jf(N/J) - g] + \bar{m}_0 + g$$

that is to say

$$g < g^* \tag{7.26}$$

with

$$g^* = \frac{Jf(N/J)[1 - K(\psi(1,(1+\pi)\bar{m}_0))] - K(\psi(1,(1+\pi)\bar{m}_0))\pi\bar{m}_0 - \bar{m}_0}{1 - K(\psi(1,(1+\pi)\bar{m}_0))}$$

Note that (7.25) is implied by (7.26).

Regarding condition $\hat{a} < (w - \bar{w})/\gamma(m_0)$, it is equivalent to $w > \theta_1 \bar{w}/\theta_2$. Let $\hat{m}_0(w,g)$ be defined by

$$Jy_s^*(w) = K(\psi(1,(1+\pi)\hat{m}_0))[\pi\hat{m}_0 + Jy_s^*(w) - g] + \hat{m}_0 + g$$

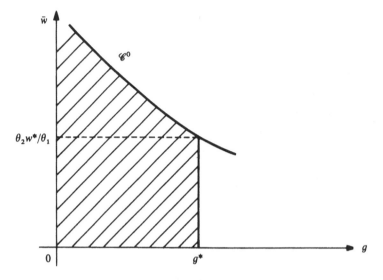

Figure 7.4   The involuntary unemployment regime

According to proposition 7.2, the function $\hat{m}_0(w,g)$ is defined for $w^* \leq w \leq y_s^{*-1}(g/J)$. It is decreasing with respect to w and g. We have $w > \theta_1 \bar{w}/\theta_2$ at the intersection point between C_1 and C_2 if and only if

$$
\begin{aligned}
\text{either} \quad & \theta_1 \bar{w}/\theta_2 \leq w^* \\
\text{or} \quad & w^* < \theta_1 \bar{w}/\theta_2 \leq y_s^{*-1}(g/J) \text{ and} \\
& Jl_d^*(\theta_1 \bar{w}/\theta_2) > NG\left[\frac{(\theta_1 - \theta_2)\bar{w}}{\theta_2 \gamma(\hat{m}_0(\theta_1 \bar{w}/\theta_2, g))}\right]
\end{aligned}
\tag{7.27}
$$

Thus, we have:

> *Proposition 7.3*   An involuntary unemployment equilibrium prevails if and only if (7.26) and (7.27) hold and, in that case, the equilibrium is unique.

In the $(g, \bar{w})$ plane, the equation

$$
Jl_d^*(\theta_1 \bar{w}/\theta_2) = NG\left[\frac{(\theta_1 - \theta_2)\bar{w}}{\theta_2 \gamma(\hat{m}_0(\theta_1 \bar{w}/\theta_2, g))}\right]
\tag{7.28}
$$

defines the curve $\mathscr{C}^0$. Involuntary unemployment occurs when $(g, \bar{w})$ is in the shaded area. As shown in figure 7.4, for any value of the unemployment benefit corresponds a level of public consumption under which involuntary unemployment prevails.

What are the features of such an equilibrium? Its main characteristic is that it involves involuntary unemployment according to the definition given at the beginning of section 3, and this can easily be proved. Indeed, if a type-a jobless individual is hired and does not shirk, he will perceive an additional satisfaction equal to $(w - \bar{w})/\gamma(m_0) - a$. Therefore, involuntary unemployment corresponds to type-a individuals such that $\hat{a} < a < \text{Min}\{a_1, (w - \bar{w})/\gamma(m_0)\}$ and according to (7.22) this set is not empty.

We can also observe that the equilibrium is completely independent from the variations in the unemployment benefit $\bar{w}$, while a transitory rise in g leads to a rise in the employment level. Indeed, in this case the curve C_1 shifts as shown by the arrow in figure 7.3, there is a decrease in w and therefore a rise in the employment level. A definite increase in public consumption would alter expectations of future prices and it would not be possible to consider function ψ as given. We will reconsider this question in section 4 dealing with the perfect foresight case.

Is voluntary unemployment reduced when g increases? The answer is not obvious. Indeed, involuntary unemployment (in per cent of the total population) is equal to

$$G\left[\frac{w - \bar{w}}{\gamma(m_0)}\right] - G(\hat{a}) \qquad (7.29)$$

If $a_1 < (w - \bar{w})/\gamma(m_0)$, there are only involuntary jobless people and a rise in g automatically reduces their number. While, if $a_1 > (w - \bar{w})/\gamma(m_0)$ a rise in public expenditure may lead to a greater number of people willing to work by providing effort, if $(w - \bar{w})/\gamma(m_0)$ also increases, and the total effect on the involuntary unemployment rate is uncertain.

It is worth noting that the rise in public consumption causes the equilibrium price to increase and the relative price p^e/p to decrease, since the elasticity of the expected future price with respect to the current price is less than 1. The decrease of p^e/p generates an intertemporal substitution of consumption that enables production real wages w to decrease and to meet the incentive constraint for a greater number of individuals.

Let us now contemplate the consequences of a transitory variation in public consumption from a normative point of view. An economic policy measure is said to improve social welfare if it leads to a high enough rise in the young individuals' utility levels to compensate the older generation for the rise in current prices that might result, or in other words if it leads to a Pareto improvement through adequate transfer payments. Using utility functions as a criterion of individual welfare is questionable if households' satisfaction depends on their expectations which can be rather arbitrary. In order to ensure an objective character to that criterion, we will confine ourselves here to the situation where the expected price does not depend on the current price (this will hold in the next section dealing with perfect foresight). The growth rate of the money supply being given, the expected price is thus given.

Let $W(g,g_0)$ be the sum of the welfare levels of the young when public consumption is equal to g and the young generation compensates the old for the rise in prices that might result from the rise in public consumption from g_0 to g. Therefore, we have

$$W = \frac{R}{I(p,p^e)} - N \int_{a_0}^{\hat{a}} a \, dG(a) + NU_2(g)$$

and now with

$$R = \pi M_0 + p(Jy - g) - (p - p_0)M_0/p_0 \tag{7.30}$$

where p_0 stands for the equilibrium price in the initial situation where public consumption is equal to g_0. Therefore, a rise in public consumption is desirable if

$$\frac{\partial W}{\partial g}(g,g_0) > 0 \qquad \text{if } g = g_0$$

Let us first describe the change in equilibrium due to the compensated change in public consumption. From (7.30), the goods market equilibrium condition can be written as

$$Jy_s^*(w) = K(\psi(1,(1+\pi)m_0))\left[(1+\pi)m_0 + Jy_s^*(w) - g - \frac{M_0}{p_0}\right]$$
$$+ \frac{M_0}{p_0} + g \tag{7.31}$$

Assume that at the equilibrium the net excess demand for goods is locally a decreasing function of the price, taking into account the compensating transfer payments from the younger to the older generation. We thus assume that the function

$$p \to K\left(\psi\left(1,(1+\pi)\frac{M_0}{p}\right)\right)\left[(1+\pi)\frac{M_0}{p} + Jy_s^*(w) - g - \frac{M_0}{p_0}\right]$$

is locally decreasing in the neighbourhood of $p = p_0$.

In figure 7.5, the curve C_1 corresponds to the equation (7.23) when $g = g_0$ and the curve C_2 to (7.24). The curves C_0 and C_0' correspond to the equation (7.31) when $g = g_0$ and $g > g_0$ respectively. The compensated increase in public consumption makes the equilibrium shift from X_0 to X_1 and therefore causes a decrease in the real wage rate and a rise in the employment level as when the older generation is not compensated.

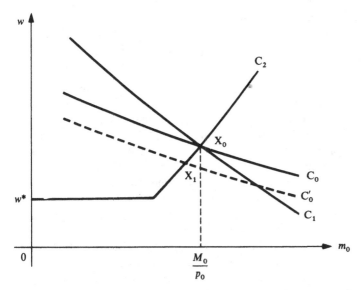

Figure 7.5   Effects of a compensated increase in public consumption

Consider R, $â$ and p as functions of g. By applying Roy's relation, and writing the young generation's current consumption as $Y - g - \dfrac{M_0}{p_0}$, we have

$$\frac{\partial W}{\partial g} = \frac{1}{I(p,p^e)}\left[\frac{dR}{dg} - \left(Y - g - \frac{M_0}{p_0}\right)\frac{dp}{dg}\right]$$
$$- N â \frac{dG(â)}{dg} + N U'_2(g) \qquad (7.32)$$

where $Y \equiv Jy$ stands for aggregate production. From (7.30), we have

$$\frac{dR}{dg} = \left(Y - g - \frac{M_0}{p_0}\right)\frac{dp}{dg} + p\left(\frac{dY}{dg} - 1\right)$$
$$= \left(Y - g - \frac{M_0}{p_0}\right)\frac{dp}{dg} + p\left(w\frac{dL}{dg} - 1\right)$$

where L stands for the employment level, with $Jf(L/J) = Y$ and $dL/dg = N\, dG(â)/dg > 0$. This implies

$$\frac{\partial W}{\partial g} = \frac{1}{I}\left[N I U'_2 - p + (pw - âI)\frac{dL}{dg}\right] \qquad (7.33)$$

And using $\bar{w} = \bar{s}/p$ we finally obtain

$$\frac{\partial W}{\partial g} = \frac{1}{I}\left[NIU_2' - \left(p - \bar{s}\frac{dL}{dg}\right) + p\left(\frac{\theta_2 w}{\theta_1} - \bar{w}\right)\frac{dL}{dg}\right]$$

Let us consider a small increase in public consumption dg. Then $NIU_2'\,dg$ corresponds to young individuals' willingness to pay for it; $(p - \bar{s}\,dL/dg)dg$ corresponds to the net money cost of these additional expenditures for the government budget. Therefore, the difference $[NIU_2' - (p - \bar{s}\,dL/dg)]\,dg$ represents the project's cost–benefit balance, as it would result from a traditional second-best analysis, in an economy where competition prevails, but where a tax on the labour market generates misallocations of resources (see Diamond and Mirrlees, 1971).[8] In what follows, when this difference is positive, we simply say that the welfare economics criterion is met. As $\theta_2 w > \theta_1 \bar{w}$ in the involuntary unemployment regime, a rise in g may be beneficial even though the welfare economics criterion shows the contrary, which is summarized in the following proposition:

> *Proposition 7.4* When involuntary unemployment prevails, any transitory increase in public consumption satisfying the welfare economics criterion is desirable, while the opposite is not true.

3.2 *Voluntary unemployment*

At a voluntary unemployment equilibrium, we have

$$\hat{a} = \frac{w - \bar{w}}{\gamma(m_0)} < \text{Min}\left\{ a_1, \frac{(\theta_1 - \theta_2)w}{\theta_1 \gamma(m_0)}\right\} \tag{7.34}$$

and (m_0, w) is given by (7.23) and

$$Jl_a^*(w) = NG\left[\frac{w - \bar{w}}{\gamma(m_0)}\right] \tag{7.35}$$

(7.35) defines a curve C_3 and the equilibrium is achieved at the intersection point between C_1 and C_3. In the case $\bar{w} \le w^*$ drawn in figure 7.6, $\tilde{m}_0(\bar{w})$ is given by

$$\gamma(\tilde{m}_0) = \frac{w^* - \bar{w}}{a_1}$$

Note that a unique intersection point exists if

$$g \le \text{Min}\{Jf(N/J), Jy_s^*(\bar{w})\} \tag{7.36}$$

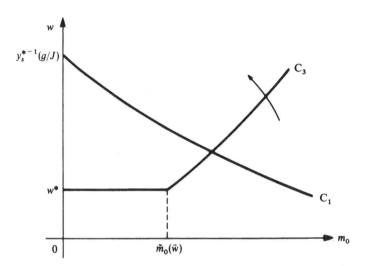

Figure 7.6   Voluntary unemployment equilibrium. Case $\bar{w} \leqslant w^{*}$

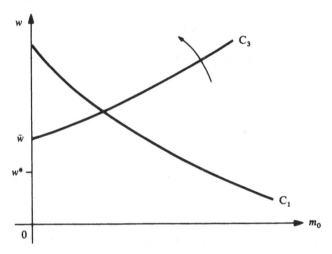

Figure 7.7   Voluntary unemployment equilibrium. Case $\bar{w} > w^{*}$

Let us now analyse condition (7.34). The inequality $\hat{a} < a_1$ is equivalent to $w > w^{*}$, that is to say:

$$\begin{cases} Jf(N/J) > K(\psi(1,(1+\pi)\tilde{m}_0(\bar{w})))[\pi\tilde{m}_0(\bar{w}) + Jf(N/J) - g] + \tilde{m}_0(\bar{w}) + g \\ \text{if } \bar{w} \leq w^{*} \end{cases} \quad (7.37)$$

As regards the condition $\hat{a} < (\theta_1 - \theta_2)w/\theta_1\gamma(m_0)$, it is equivalent to

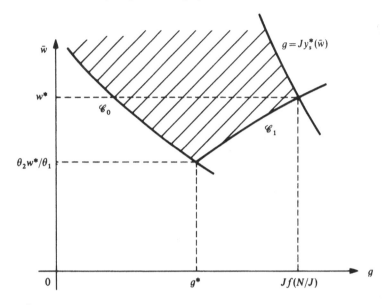

Figure 7.8   The voluntary unemployment regime

$w < \theta_1 \bar{w}/\theta_2$ which holds at the intersection point between C_1 and C_3 if and only if

$$
\begin{aligned}
\text{either} \quad & \theta_1 \bar{w}/\theta_2 > y_s^{*-1}(g/J) \\
\text{or} \quad & w^* < \theta_1 \bar{w}/\theta_2 \le y_s^*(g/J) \text{ and} \\
& J l_d^*(\theta_1 \bar{w}/\theta_2) < NG\left[\frac{(\theta_1 - \theta_2)\bar{w}}{\theta_2 \gamma(\hat{m}_0(\theta_1 \bar{w}/\theta_2, g))} \right]
\end{aligned}
\tag{7.38}
$$

which results in:

> *Proposition 7.5*   A voluntary unemployment equilibrium exists if
> and only if (7.36), (7.37) and (7.38) hold, in which case the
> equilibrium is unique.

If $\bar{w} \le w^*$, (7.37) defines a region on the $(g, \bar{w})$ plane delimited by the increasing curve $\mathscr{C}^1$. Condition (7.38) leads us to select that part of the plane $(g, \bar{w})$ above $\mathscr{C}^0$. Using (7.36), we obtain figure 7.8 where the shaded area corresponds to the voluntary unemployment equilibria.

When voluntary unemployment prevails, any change in unemployment benefit alters the equilibrium. If $\bar{w}$ increases, curve C_3 shifts in the direction of the arrow in figures 7.5 and 7.6, while curve C_1 does not move. Consequently, at the equilibrium, w increases and m_0 decreases. Therefore, there is a simultaneous rise in the equilibrium price and a decrease in the employment level.

If we assume that the expected price does not depend on the current price, we can check that a transitory increase in the employment benefit is not Pareto improving. Let $W(\bar{w},\bar{w}_0)$ be the total welfare of the young when unemployment benefit is equal to $\bar{w}$ and the old receive a compensatory transfer payment, calculated on the basis of an initial situation where the benefit is equal to $\bar{w}_0$. Indeed, if we consider L as a function of $\bar{w}$ (with $dL/d\bar{w} < 0$), we obtain

$$\frac{\partial W}{\partial \bar{w}} = \frac{\bar{w}}{I(p,p^e)} \frac{dL}{d\bar{w}} < 0$$

This result is not surprising: under voluntary unemployment, the inefficiency is due to the distortion caused by the unemployment benefit, which is equivalent to a tax on the labour supply. Increasing $\bar{w}$ worsens this distortion.

In case of a transitory increase in public consumption, C_1 shifts downward, while curve C_3 does not move. As in the involuntary unemployment situation, a rise in public consumption causes the equilibrium price to increase, the real wage rate to decrease and therefore the employment level to increase. However, normative analysis of public expenditure differs from involuntary unemployment analysis. Indeed, here we obtain

$$\frac{\partial W}{\partial g} = \frac{1}{I}\left[NIU_2' - \left(p - \bar{s}\frac{dL}{dg}\right)\right]$$

so that a transitory rise in public consumption is socially desirable if and only if it meets the welfare economics criterion. Hence:

> *Proposition 7.6* In a voluntary unemployment regime, in the absence of the redistribution objective, any transitory rise in unemployment benefits reduces social welfare, and a transitory increase in public consumption is desirable if and only if it meets the welfare economics criterion.

3.3 Full employment

At the full employment equilibrium, we have

$$\hat{a} = a_1 < \text{Min}\left\{\frac{(\theta_1 - \theta_2)w}{\theta_1 \gamma(m_0)}, \frac{w - \bar{w}}{\gamma(m_0)}\right\} \tag{7.39}$$

$$w = w^* \tag{7.40}$$

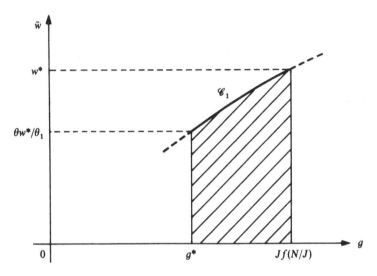

Figure 7.9 The full-employment regime

$$Jf(N/J) = K(\psi(1,(1+\pi)m_0))[\pi m_0 + Jf(N/J) - g] + m_0 + g \quad (7.41)$$

(7.41) defines m_0 provided (7.25) holds. Moreover, (7.39) implies

$$a_1 < \frac{(\theta_1 - \theta_2)w^*}{\theta_1 \gamma(m_0)}$$

that is to say $m_0 < \tilde{m}_0$, which will be obtained at the equilibrium if and only if

$$g > g^* \tag{7.42}$$

(7.39) also gives

$$a_1 < \frac{w^* - \bar{w}}{\gamma(m_0)} \tag{7.43}$$

which implies $\bar{w} < w^*$. Then, (7.43) is equivalent to $m_0 \leq \tilde{m}_0(\bar{w})$, that is

$$Jf(N/J) < K(\psi(1,(1+\pi)\tilde{m}_0(\bar{w}))[\pi \tilde{m}_0(\bar{w}) \\ + Jf(N/J) - g] + \tilde{m}_0(\bar{w}) + g \tag{7.44}$$

Thus, we have:

> *Proposition 7.7* A full-employment equilibrium exists and is unique if and only if (7.25), (7.42) and (7.44) hold.

Curve $\mathscr{C}^1$ in figure 7.9 determines the region where (7.44) holds and the full-employment regime corresponds to the shaded area.

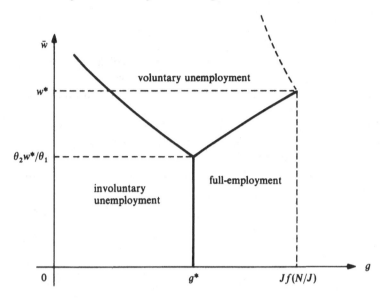

Figure 7.10   The three regimes

In the full-employment regime, the value of the unemployment benefit is of course neutral since nobody receives it. Furthermore, a rise in public consumption causes a crowding-out effect on private consumption, owing to a rise in prices. Therefore it is socially desirable only if the marginal willingness to pay exceeds the price.

The condition

$$g \le \text{Min}\{Jf(N/J), Jy_s^*(\bar{w})\}$$

is not really restrictive since it only means that public demand does neither exceed full-employment production nor the total supply when the real wage rate is equal to the unemployment benefit. Under this hypothesis, the immediate consequence of propositions 7.3, 7.5 and 7.7 is the existence of a unique equilibrium.

In the following pages, for the sake of simplicity, we will assume that $\bar{w} = 0$: there is no unemployment benefit and the only possible equilibria are the involuntary unemployment and full-employment regimes.

4   Equilibrium with perfect foresight[9]

In order to analyse the consequences of perfect expectations as simply as possible, we will postulate here, a particular form of function U_1. Assume that

$$U_1(x,z/p^e) = \alpha^{-\alpha}(1-\alpha)^{\alpha-1}x^\alpha(z/p^e)^{(1-\alpha)} \quad 0 < \alpha < 1 \tag{7.45}$$

which implies $I(p,p^e) = p^\alpha(p^e)^{(1-\alpha)}$ and $K(p^e/p) = \alpha$.

Periods will be designated by $t = 1,2,3, \ldots$, with $t = 0$ for the current period. Let g_t be the public consumption at period t, with $g \equiv g_0$.

Let us first note that there exists a unique stationary equilibrium where prices increase at the constant rate π and where expectations are fulfilled, when public consumption is fixed at a constant level $g_t = \hat{g}$ for all t and the government leads a monetary policy π in all periods. Let p_t be the equilibrium price in period t and p_{t+1}^e the price in $t+1$, expected in period t. Therefore, we have $p_{t+1}^e = p_{t+1} = (1+\pi)p_t$, at the stationary equilibrium, which is characterized by

$$(1-\alpha)[Jy_s^*(w) - \hat{g}] = (1+\alpha\pi)m \tag{7.46}$$

$$Jl_d^*(w) = NG\left[\text{Min}\left\{ a_1, \frac{(\theta_1 - \theta_2)w}{(1+\pi)^{(1-\alpha)}\theta_1} \right\} \right] \tag{7.47}$$

Let $w = \hat{w}$ and $m = \hat{m}$ be that stationary equilibrium: (7.47) defines $\hat{w}$ and we have

$$\hat{m} = (1-\alpha)(\hat{Y} - \hat{g})/(1+\alpha\pi) \tag{7.48}$$

with $\hat{Y} = Jy_s^*(\hat{w})$. We either have $\hat{w} > w^*$, or $\hat{w} = w^*$. In the first case, the stationary equilibrium corresponds to an involuntary unemployment regime and in the second case, it is a full-employment equilibrium. It is worth noting that the output level $\hat{Y}$ associated with the stationary equilibrium does not depend on public consumption $\hat{g}$ (since $\hat{w}$ does not depend on $\hat{g}$) but on the growth rate of the money supply π which is also the equilibrium inflation rate. To this stationary equilibrium is associated a sequence of prices

$$p_t = (1+\pi)^t M_0/\hat{m} \tag{7.49}$$

We may also note that there exists a highest growth rate of the money supply compatible with full employment at the stationary equilibrium. This rate, written π^*, is defined by

$$a_1 = \frac{(\theta_1 - \theta_2)w^*}{(1+\pi^*)^{(1-\alpha)}\theta_1}$$

that is

$$\pi^* = \left[\frac{(\theta_1 - \theta_2)w^*}{\theta_1 a_1} \right]^{1/(1-\alpha)} - 1$$

If $\pi > \pi^*$, unemployment prevails at the stationary equilibrium. It is for instance the case when π^* is negative and when the government leads a policy of stable money $\pi = 0$.

Now let us assume that in the current period the government commits itself to stabilizing public consumption at a level $\hat{g}$ in the future periods (i.e. $g_t = \hat{g}$ for $t \geq 1$) and making the money stock increase at a rate π. Let us also assume that agents expect a stationary equilibrium for the periods to come. In view of (7.48) and (7.49), we have

$$p^e = p_1 = k(\hat{g})M_1 \tag{7.50}$$

with

$$k(\hat{g}) = \frac{1 + \alpha\pi}{(1 - \alpha)(\hat{Y} - \hat{g})} \tag{7.51}$$

If $\hat{g}$ is independent from g, that is, if the current variations in public consumption are purely transitory, (7.50) is a particular case of (7.6) and, therefore, all the results obtained in the previous section apply here. On the other hand, the consequences of a permanent increase in public consumption can be obtained by writing $\hat{g} = g$ and, therefore, $p^e = k(g)M_1$. In the involuntary unemployment regime the equations (7.23) and (7.24) can be rewritten as

$$(1 - \alpha)(Jy_s^*(w) - g) = (1 + \alpha\pi)m_0 \tag{7.52}$$

$$Jl_d^*(w) = NG\left[\frac{(\theta_1 - \theta_2)w}{\theta_1(k(g)(1 + \pi)m_0)^{(1 - \alpha)}}\right] \tag{7.53}$$

The system (7.52)–(7.53) admits $w = \hat{w}$, $m_0 = 1/k(g)$ as its unique solution. Thus, the real wage rate and the employment level in the current period are independent from public consumption g. A permanent rise in this consumption has no effect on involuntary unemployment: it only leads to a rise in the current price.

These are logical results. As we saw in the previous section, in a situation of involuntary unemployment, the effect of a rise in public consumption on unemployment goes through an intertemporal substitution of consumption which corresponds to a change in the relative price p^e/p. If the rise in public consumption is permanent and if agents perfectly expect future prices, this intertemporal substitution effect cannot take place.

These results also suggest that the optimal stationary level of public expenditures is not time-consistent insofar as at any period the government may decide on a transitory increase in public spending, so as to gain from a positive externality in employment. More precisely, at the optimal stationary equilibrium, one can improve the welfare of both generations living during a given period through a transitory increase in public spending and a compensating transfer to the old generation. This result is clearly in line with proposition 7.4 and can be checked as follows. To simplify matters, let us confine ourselves to the case where the government follows a policy of stable money, i.e., $\pi = 0$. Then, prices are constant at the stationary equilibrium and the welfare of any generation is given by

$$W = Y - g - N \int_{a_0}^{\hat{a}} a \, dG(a) + N U_2(g)$$

At a stationary equilibrium, $\hat{a}$ does not depend on g and W is maximized at $g = g^*$ with

$$N U_2'(g^*) = 1$$

From (7.33), starting from $g = g^*$, a *transitory* increase in public consumption is Pareto improving since

$$\left. \frac{\partial W}{\partial g} \right|_{g=g^*} = (\hat{w} - \hat{a}) \left. \frac{dL}{dg} \right|_{g=g^*} > 0$$

The time consistent public consumption g^{**} (i.e., the public consumption level from which one cannot deviate through a Pareto-improving decision) is given by

$$N U_2'(g^{**}) = 1 - (\hat{w} - \hat{a}) \left. \frac{dL}{dg} \right|_{g=g^{**}}$$

and when $U_2'' < 0$, this implies

$$g^{**} > g^*$$

5   Adverse selection

We now assume that firms cannot observe the types of applicants so that they are confronted with problems of moral hazard and adverse selection simultaneously. Within this framework, a wage policy δ can be defined as a set of contracts $(s_1(u), s_2(u))$ specifying the wage paid according to the signal observed: $s_1(u)$ if the signal is good and $s_2(u)$ if it is bad, with u standing for the contract belonging to a set of possible contracts $X(\delta)$

$$\delta = \{(s_1(u), s_2(u)) \in R_+^2, \ u \in X(\delta)\}$$

A worker should choose one between the contracts that are proposed to him.

Moreover, it goes without saying that only two types of contracts are likely to be picked by workers: those which maximize the non-shirkers' expected wages and those which maximize the shirkers' expected wages. The two average wages are respectively written $c^1(\delta)$ and $c^2(\delta)$, with

$$c^1(\delta)=\text{Max}\{\theta_1 s_1(u)+(1-\theta_1)s_2(u)\mid u\in X(\delta)\}$$
$$c^2(\delta)=\text{Max}\{\theta_2 s_1(u)+(1-\theta_2)s_2(u)\mid u\in X(\delta)\}$$

With a wage policy δ, a worker of type a will choose not to shirk if and only if $a\leq\bar{a}$, with

$$c^1(\delta)-c^2(\delta)=\bar{a}\ I(p,p^e)$$

The labour cost per unit of efficient labour $C(\delta)$ is given by

$$C(\delta)=c^1(\delta)+\frac{1-G(a^*(\delta))}{G(a^*(\delta))}c^2(\delta)$$

with

$$a^*(\delta)=\text{Min}\left\{a_1,\text{Max}\left\{a_0,\frac{c^1(\delta)-c^2(\delta)}{I(p,p^e)}\right\}\right\}$$

The firms would choose the wage policy δ which minimizes $C(\delta)$. The following proposition shows that it is optimal to have only one contract providing for a maximum penalty should the signal be bad.

Proposition 7.8 For any wage policy δ, there exists $\hat{\delta}=\{(\hat{s}_1,0)\}$ such that $C(\hat{\delta})\leq C(\delta)$.

Proof:
Let $\hat{s}^1=c^1(\delta)/\theta_1$. We have $c^1(\hat{\delta})=c^1(\delta)$ and $c^2(\hat{\delta})=\theta_2 c^1(\delta)/\theta_1\leq c^2(\delta)$ and we deduce: $a^*(\hat{\delta})\leq a^*(\delta)$, therefore $C(\hat{\delta})\sqsubset C(\delta)$.

Thus when the disutility of effort is not observable, it is not restrictive to confine ourselves to a unique contract $\delta=\{(s_1,0)\}$ and, in case of an interior solution, we have

$$a^*(\delta)=\frac{(\theta_1-\theta_2)s_1}{I(p,p^e)}=\frac{(\theta_1-\theta_2)w_1}{\gamma(m_0)} \tag{7.54}$$

$$w=C(\delta)/p=\theta_1 w_1+\frac{1-G(a^*(\delta))}{G(a^*(\delta))}\theta_2 w_1 \tag{7.55}$$

with $w_1=s_1/p$. Here the production real wage rate w is defined as the average price of efficient labour and set at its optimal level, that is to say

$$w=\text{Min}\{C(\delta)\mid s_1\geq 0\}/p \tag{7.56}$$

In view of (7.54), (7.55) and (7.56), we have

$$w=\omega\ \gamma(m_0) \tag{7.57}$$

where ω depends on the parameters θ_1,θ_2 and on the distribution $G(.)$.

In a nutshell, firms now offer only one contract and workers with a high disutility of effort choose to shirk. (7.54) shows that a rise in the real wage w_1, which is paid when the signal is good, urges a larger number of workers not to shirk. However, it leads to a rise in payments per worker. According to (7.56), the chosen contract is an optimal compromise between both consequences.

Now, an equilibrium corresponds to a pair (w, m_0) which satisfies (7.23) and (7.57). The public expenditure analysis that could be carried out in this framework, would lead to results qualitatively similar to those obtained in sections 3 and 4.

8 Labour market dualism, efficiency wages and optimal taxation

This chapter aims at analysing the optimal taxation policy, in an economy where inefficient underemployment results from real wage rigidity. Labour subsidizing is then a helpful policy instrument, since it allows the reduction of inefficiency due to production costs being too high, by disconnecting consumption and production wages. Unfortunately, the redistributive effects of such a policy usually involve additional distortions that may prevent the first-best optimum being reached. Consider for instance the Shapiro–Stiglitz efficiency wage model. The no-shirking constraint itself entails that there exists a difference between the (net of effort) incomes of employed and unemployed individuals and this may conceivably be considered as inefficient by an egalitarian social planner. Assume that no pure profit can be taxed away. Subsidizing employment and reducing simultaneously the unemployment benefit to balance the government budget constraint would allow the reaching of the perfect information employment level, but this policy obviously involves redistributive consequences. Individuals who get a job because of this tax policy are certainly better off, but unemployed workers are in a worse situation. It is this relation between equity and efficiency in labour taxation policy that we wish to examine in this chapter.

The real wage rigidity will be formalized by drawing from the theories of labour market dualism. The economy includes a number of individuals with differentiated abilities who may be employed either in the primary or the secondary labour market. For identical ability, those who are employed in the primary labour market (or primary sector) enjoy a higher wage rate than the other workers. Involuntary underemployment results from this wage discrimination. The remaining part of the model follows Diamond–Mirrlees' (1971) and Guesnerie's (1975) approach to second-best Pareto-optimality analysis. In particular, the government is able to disconnect production and consumption prices for goods and labour services. Our objective is to characterize the structure of prices and wages which would result from an optimal taxation policy in such a context. The issue of the desirability of aggregate productive efficiency will also be examined in this context.

Besides commodity taxation, the government will have two instruments at its disposal to achieve productive efficiency and redistributive objectives: inducing the creation of primary jobs through adequate tax incentives and increasing the minimum consumption wage rate paid for secondary jobs. However, lump sum transfers being unfeasible, the policy to be chosen has only one degree of freedom: subsidizing primary jobs implies higher uniform income taxes to balance the government budget constraint and this leads to lower consumption wages paid for secondary jobs. As we shall see, because of this redistributive effect, in some cases only is it optimal to stimulate primary employment through tax incentives.

The first section will introduce the notations and the government objective. In section 2, we will address optimal taxation rules and section 3 will further develop the basic results in the framework of a model where real wage discrimination results from an efficiency wage mechanism.

1   A model of optimal resource allocation with wage rigidity

Let us consider an economy with n goods, labelled $i = 1, \ldots, n$, and labour of r different types, labelled $k = 1, \ldots, r$. The economy includes a number of consumer-workers who are classified according to the type of labour they are able to provide: a worker of type $k \in \{1, \ldots, r\}$ is able to provide one unit of labour services of type k without suffering any disutility. In what follows, k is to be considered as a labour quality index. We assume that there are N_k workers of type k. Workers are labelled $h = 1, \ldots, N$, with $N = \sum_{k=1}^{r} N_k$. Let $S_k \subset \{1, \ldots, N\}$ be the set of type-k workers. A worker, whatever his type, will be employed either in the primary or secondary sector.

The economy includes m private firms (labelled $j = 1, \ldots, m$). Returns to scale are assumed to be constant and goods markets are competitive, so that private firms make no profit at equilibrium. Finally consumers' incomes only consist of their wages, and consumption and labour services may be taxed or subsidized. We will thus distinguish between consumption and production prices and between consumption and production wages. Let us now introduce the main notations and assumptions used:

1.1   *The production sector*

Let

$y_j = (y_{ji}) \in R^n$: be the net output vector of firm j; outputs bear a positive sign and inputs a negative sign: y_{ji} stands for the net output of commodity i.

$l_j^1 = (l_{jk}^1) \in R_+^r$: labour inputs of firm j in the primary labour market; l_{jk}^1 stands for type-k labour.

$l_j^2 = (l_{jk}^2) \in R_+^r$: labour inputs of firm j in the secondary labour market; l_{jk}^2 stands for type-k labour.

$Y_j \subset R^n \times R_+^r \times R_+^r$: the production set of firm j. We assume that Y_j is convex and defined by

$$Y_j = \{(y_j, l_j^1, l_j^2) | f_j(y_j, l_j^1, l_j^2) \leq 0\}$$

where the production function $f_j(.)$ is homogenous of degree one and twice continuously differentiable, with

$$\partial f_j / \partial y_j \geq 0, \partial f_j / \partial l_j^1 \leq 0, \partial f_j / \partial l_j^2 \leq 0.$$

$s^1 = (s_k^1) \in R_+^r$: the production wages vector in the primary labour market.

$s^2 = (s_k^2) \in R_+^r$: the production wages vector in the secondary labour market.

$p = (p_i) \in R_+^n$: the production prices vector; we normalize production prices by setting $p_1 = 1$.

1.2 Consumers

Let

$x_h = (x_{hi}) \in R^n$: be the consumption vector of consumer h where x_{hi} stands for the quantity of commodity i. If consumer h has some initial endowment in commodity i, x_{hi} stands for his net demand.

$w^1 = (w_k^1) \in R_+^r$: the vector of consumption wages in the primary labour market.

$w^2 = (w_k^2) \in R_+^r$: the vector of consumption wages in the secondary labour market; $t_s^1 = s^1 - w^1$ and $t_s^2 = s^2 - w^2$ are wage tax vectors.

$q = (q_i) \in R_+^n$: the vector of consumption prices; $t_q = q - p$ is a commodity tax vector. We normalize consumption prices by setting $q_1 = 1$.

L_h^1 and L_h^2 : the quantity of labour services sold by consumer h respectively in the primary and secondary labour markets. This is labour of type k if $h \in S_k$. Labour supply is inelastic and equal to one for each consumer. In what follows, all individuals will be full-time workers. We thus have $L_h^1 + L_h^2 = 1$.

R_h : consumer h income.

$U_h(x_h)$: consumer h utility function; $U_h(.)$ is supposed to be twice continuously differentiable and strictly quasi-concave.

$V_h(q, R_h) \equiv U_h(x_h(q, R_n))$: consumer h indirect utility function.

1.3 Real wage rigidity

We assume that consumption wages are rigid in the primary sector and perfectly flexible in the secondary sector. Since there is no job rationing in the secondary sector and no labour disutility, the acceptance wage is w_k^2 for a type-k worker. We will assume that primary sector jobs yield a premium ω_k over this acceptance wage, that is

$$w_k^1 = \omega_k + w_k^2 \tag{8.1}$$

and we suppose that ω_k depends on consumption prices and, possibly, on the corresponding employment level; we will write

$$\omega_k = \omega_k(q, E_k) \tag{8.2}$$

where $E_k \equiv \sum_j l_{jk}^1$; $\omega_k(.)$ is supposed to be homogeneous of degree one with respect to q (the premium is thus defined in real terms) and non-decreasing with respect to E_k. A possible interpretation is in terms of efficiency wages, in an economy where unemployment is a discipline device to prevent shirking, as in the Shapiro–Stiglitz model (1984). The lower the unemployment rate, the higher the premium that should be paid to workers to encourage them to make a sufficient effort. An alternative formalization is developed in section 3. As in chapter 7, the (publicly observed) disutility to effort is supposed to differ among individuals. As in the Shapiro–Stiglitz model, workers' efforts cannot be observed by firms but here contingent wage payments are feasible. When the employment level increases, the real premium must be higher for labour contracts of newly employed workers in the primary sector to be incentive compatible. Finally, another interpretation consists in considering (8.2) as the result of bargaining between firms and trade unions in the primary sector allowing workers to enjoy a rent, while the secondary labour market would be perfectly competitive.

1.4 *Job rationing*

In this economy, every individual should be able to find a job in the secondary sector, though one would be more willing to work in the primary sector. In that sense, workers may be involuntarily unemployed. We have to be explicit about the way primary sector jobs are rationed among applicants. In section 2 this will result from rationing schemes. A *rationing scheme* for market k is characterized by functions $\Phi_h: [0, N_k] \to [0,1]$ defined for all h in S_k. Here $\Phi_h(E_k)$ stands for the employment level of individual h in the primary sector, as a function of the total number of type-k jobs in the primary sector. Thus we have $L_h^1 = \Phi_h(E_k)$ and $L_h^2 = 1 - \Phi_h(E_k)$. We assume that functions $\Phi_h(.)$ are non-decreasing and continuously differentiable. We also have the following coherency condition

$$\sum_{h \in S_k} \Phi_h(E_k) = E_k \tag{8.3}$$

1.5   *Feasibility conditions*

For the time being, we consider firms' decisions as policy instruments: production prices and production wages will be introduced later. Feasible allocations are defined by the following conditions, where $\sum_h$ and $\sum_j$ stand respectively for $\sum_{h=1}^{N}$ and $\sum_{j=1}^{m}$

$$\sum_h x_h(q,R_h) - \sum_j y_j \leq 0 \tag{8.4}$$

$$R_h = \omega_k(q, \sum_j l_{jk}^1) \Phi_h(\sum_j l_{jk}^1) + w_k^2 \text{ if } h \in S_k \tag{8.5}$$
$$\text{for all } k = 1, \ldots, r$$

$$\sum_j (l_{jk}^1 + l_{jk}^2) \leq N_k \qquad \text{for all } k = 1, \ldots, r \tag{8.6}$$

$$f_j(y_j, l_j^1, l_j^2) \leq 0 \qquad \text{for all } j = 1, \ldots, m \tag{8.7}$$

2   Welfare maximization through optimal taxes

An optimal allocation of resources will be obtained by maximizing a utilitarian social welfare function $W = W(U_1, \ldots, U_N)$ with $W_h' \equiv \partial W / \partial U_h > 0$.

From previous equilibrium conditions, the government chooses $q_2, \ldots, q_n, w_1^2, \ldots, w_r^2, R_1, \ldots, R_N, l_1^1, \ldots, l_m^1, l_1^2, \ldots, l_m^2$ and $y_1, \ldots, y_m$ in order to maximize

$$W(V_1(q,R_1), \ldots, V_N(q,R_N))$$

subject to (8.4)–(8.7). We write $\sigma_h = W_h' \partial V_h / \partial R_h$. Let $\lambda = (\lambda_i)$, $\gamma = (\gamma_h)$, $\beta = (\beta_k)$ and $\mu = (\mu_j)$ be the Kuhn–Tucker multipliers associated respectively with constraints (8.4) to (8.7). Let $\mathcal{L}$ be the Lagrangean of this problem. The first-order optimality conditions can be written as follows

$$\frac{\partial \mathcal{L}}{\partial y_{ji}} = \lambda_i - \mu_j \frac{\partial f_j}{\partial y_{ji}} = 0 \qquad \begin{matrix} i = 1, \ldots, n \\ j = 1, \ldots, m \end{matrix} \tag{8.8}$$

$$\frac{\partial \mathcal{L}}{\partial l_{jk}^1} = \frac{\partial \omega_k}{\partial E_k} \sum_{h \in S_k} \gamma_h L_h^1 + \omega_k \sum_{h \in S_k} \gamma_h \frac{\partial \Phi_h}{\partial E_k}$$

$$- \beta_k - \mu_j \frac{\partial f_j}{\partial l_{jk}^1} = 0 \qquad \begin{matrix} k = 1, \ldots, r \\ j = 1, \ldots, m \end{matrix} \tag{8.9}$$

$$\frac{\partial \mathscr{L}}{\partial l_{jk}^2} = -\beta_k - \mu_j \frac{\partial f_j}{\partial l_{jk}^1} = 0 \qquad \begin{matrix} k=1,\ldots,r \\ j=,\ldots,m \end{matrix} \tag{8.10}$$

$$\frac{\partial \mathscr{L}}{\partial w_k^2} = \sum_{h \in S_k} \gamma_h = 0 \qquad k=1,\ldots,r \tag{8.11}$$

$$\frac{\partial \mathscr{L}}{\partial q_i} = -\sum_h \sigma_h x_{hi} - \lambda \sum_h \frac{\partial x_h}{\partial q_i}$$

$$+ \sum_{k=1}^r \sum_{h \in S_k} \gamma_h L_h^1 \frac{\partial \omega_k}{\partial q_i} = 0 \qquad i=2,\ldots,n \tag{8.12}$$

$$\frac{\partial \mathscr{L}}{\partial R_h} = \sigma_h - \lambda \frac{\partial x_h}{\partial R_h} - \gamma_h = 0 \qquad h=1,\ldots,N \tag{8.13}$$

From (8.8), (8.9) and (8.10) we deduce that there exists an optimal production price vector (the same for all firms), which can be written as

$$p_i = \tau \lambda_i \qquad i=1,\ldots,n \tag{8.14}$$

$$s_k^1 = \tau \left[\beta_k - \sum_{h \in S_k} \gamma_h \frac{\partial(\omega_k \Phi_h)}{\partial E_k} \right] \qquad k=1,\ldots,r \tag{8.15}$$

$$s_k^2 = \tau \beta_k \qquad k=1,\ldots,r \tag{8.16}$$

with a positive proportionality coefficient $\tau = 1/\lambda_1$. Thus we have:

> *Proposition 8.1*   At the optimum, all firms should face the same price vector.

More particularly, if this economy included a public sector, its projects would be socially desirable if and only if they were profitable after an evaluation based on production prices. This is reminiscent of second-best optimal taxation models where markets are competitive (Diamond and Mirrlees, 1971; Guesnerie, 1975). Therefore, this result remains true here, although consumption real wages are rigid and there is job rationing.

Let $\hat{\gamma}_h = \tau \gamma_h$ and $\hat{\sigma}_h = \tau \sigma_h$. We deduce from the usual interpretation of Kuhn–Tucker multipliers that γ_h is the incremental social welfare that would result from an additional unit of income paid exclusively to consumer h by means of an individualized lump sum transfer: $\hat{\gamma}_h$ is the valuation of this additional social welfare in terms of goods at production prices; $\hat{\gamma}_h$ will be called *the marginal efficiency of an individualized transfer to consumer h*. Furthermore, $\hat{\sigma}_h$ is the marginal social utility of consumer h's income, in terms of goods at production prices. From (8.13) and (8.14), we have

$$\hat{\gamma}_h = \hat{\sigma}_h - p\frac{\partial x_h}{\partial R_h} \tag{8.17}$$

The marginal efficiency of an individualized transfer to consumer h is thus equal to the difference between the marginal social utility of this consumer's income and the value of induced additional consumption at production prices. Since $\hat{\gamma}_h$ has zero mean (from 8.11), we intuitively understand that $\hat{\gamma}_h$ is positive for consumers the government would like to see better off and $\hat{\gamma}_h$ is negative for the others.

We deduce from (8.15) and (8.16)

$$s_k^2 - s_k^1 = \frac{1}{N_k}\sum_{h\in S_k}\hat{\gamma}_h\frac{\partial(\omega_k\Phi_h)}{\partial(E_k/N_k)} \quad \text{for all } k=1,\ldots,r \tag{8.18}$$

According to the definition of $\hat{\gamma}_h$, the right-hand side of (8.18) can be interpreted as the social welfare cost induced by additional wage payments that would result from a unit increase in labour demand in the primary market k. These additional wages result from the increase in the number of primary sector jobs E_k and also from the variation of the premium ω_k. Using (8.11), the right-hand side of (8.18) is also equal to the covariance of $\hat{\gamma}_h$ and $\partial(\omega_k\Phi_h)/\partial(E_k/N_k)$. Thus we have:

> *Proposition 8.2*   At the optimum, the difference between production wages in the primary and secondary type-k labour markets is equal to the covariance in S_k of the marginal efficiency of individualized transfers and additional wage payments that would result from a unit increase in the primary sector employment rate E_k/N_k, that is:
>
> $$s_k^2 - s_k^1 = \operatorname*{cov}_{h\in S_k}\left(\hat{\gamma}_k, \frac{\partial(\omega_k\Phi_h)}{\partial(E_k/N_k)}\right) \tag{8.19}$$

At a competitive equilibrium, equal wages would be paid to all individuals of a given type since working in the primary sector does not entail any additional disutility (a different case is developed in section 3). Proposition 8.2 shows that, for redistributive reasons, it is usually underoptimal to use taxation to totally cancel the distortions involved in consumption wage rigidity. On the contrary, considering the competitive equilibrium case as a benchmark, proposition 8.2 intuitively means that hiring new workers in the primary sector should be encouraged (discouraged) through labour taxation if additional wages were mostly paid to workers for which the marginal efficiency of an individualized transfer is positive (negative).

This entails a simple consequence when the social planner has egalitarian preferences. Assume that $\hat{\gamma}_{h_0} > \hat{\gamma}_{h_1}$, when $R_{h_0} < R_{h_1}$, for h_0, h_1 in S_k. Then, proposition 8.2 obviously implies that labour in the primary sector should be undertaxed (i.e., $s_k^1 < s_k^2$) if a rise in the employment rate mainly induces the creation of new primary jobs (rather than an increase in worked hours for individuals already employed in the primary sector). As we shall see in section 3, this result does not hold any more when work sharing is impossible, that is when individuals cannot be partially employed in each sector which corresponds here to some kind of intermediate professional position.

We now turn to the analysis of optimal consumption prices. Consider a given commodity i. Multiply each equality in (8.13) by the corresponding x_{hi} and add the obtained relations. We have

$$\sum_h \sigma_h x_{hi} - \lambda \sum_h x_{hi} \frac{\partial x_h}{\partial R_h} - \sum_h \gamma_h x_{hi} = 0 \tag{8.20}$$

where λ and x_h are respectively row and column vectors. (8.12) and (8.20) then yield

$$\sum_{j=1}^n \lambda_j K_{ji} = - \sum_{k=1}^r \sum_{h \in S_k} \gamma_h \left(x_{hi} - L_h^1 \frac{\partial \omega_k}{\partial q_i} \right)$$

where K_{ji} stands for the derivative of the total compensated demand for commodity j with respect to q_i (Slutsky coefficient). By using $p_i = \tau \lambda_i$ and $\sum_{j=1}^n q_j K_{ji} \equiv 0$, we deduce

$$\sum_{j=1}^n (q_j - p_j) K_{ji} = \sum_{k=1}^r \sum_{h \in S_k} \hat{\gamma}_h \left(x_{hi} - L_h^1 \frac{\partial \omega_k}{\partial q_i} \right) \tag{8.21}$$

Let $x_i = \sum_h x_{hi}$, $\bar{x}_i = x_i/N$ and

$$\eta_{hi} = \left(x_{hi} - L_h^1 \frac{\partial \omega_k}{\partial q_i} \right) / \bar{x}_i \text{ for all } h \text{ in } S_k$$

By using the symmetry of Slutsky terms, (8.21) can then be rewritten as follows

$$\frac{\sum_{j=1}^n (q_j - p_j) K_{ij}}{x_i} = \frac{1}{N} \sum_h \hat{\gamma}_h \eta_{hi} \text{ for all } i \tag{8.22}$$

Equation (8.22) provides a characterization of optimal consumption prices. The left-hand side gives the relative variation of the total demand for commodity i that results from an increase in taxation (i.e., from an increase in consumption prices proportional to taxes), assuming that consumers receive compensatory transfers. It will be called the *discouragement index* of commodity *i*. Furthermore, η_{hi} is a valuation of the welfare loss for consumer *h* due to an increase in the price of commodity *i*, evaluated as a percentage of the additional cost of the mean demand for this commodity: $\eta_{h_0 i} > \eta_{h_1 i}$ means that consumer h_0 suffers more intensively from an increase in the price of commodity *i* than consumer h_1 (in terms of equivalent income variation). η_{hi} will be called the *price dependence index* of consumer *h* with respect to commodity *i*. (8.11) gives $\sum_h \hat{y}_h = 0$ and consequently, the right-hand side of (8.22) is the covariance of the social efficiency of individualized transfers and of the dependence index for commodity *i*. The result obtained generalizes the well-known many-person Ramsey tax rule (Diamond, 1975) in an economy where some factor prices are indexed on consumption prices. This gives:

> *Proposition 8.3* At the optimum, for each commodity *i* the discouragement index D_i is equal to the covariance of the marginal efficiency of individualized transfers and price dependence indexes
>
> $$D_i = {}_{h=1} \text{COV}_{,N}(\hat{y}_h, \eta_{hi})$$

As usual in the theory of second-best Pareto optimality, optimal taxes have to be characterized exclusively through their consequences on consumers and firms' behaviours, since the numerical value of taxes depend on an arbitrary normalization hypothesis. To interpret proposition 8.3 in this way, let us say that a consumer *h* is 'poor' if $\hat{y}_h > 0$ and 'rich' if $\hat{y}_h < 0$. An individual is thus said to be poor (rich) if increasing (decreasing) his income through an individualized lump sum transfer is socially desirable. From (8.11), each group *k* includes both poor and rich consumers. Then proposition 8.3 implies that a compensated increase in taxation reduces (stimulates) the consumption of commodities for which the dependence index is low (high) for poor consumers and high (low) for rich ones.

3 An efficiency wage model with optimal taxation

The general principles developed in the previous sections will now be further developed through a model where wage rigidity results from an efficiency wage mechanism and where job positions are indivisible.[1]

3.1 *Labour market equilibrium*

We will assume that all individuals are able to supply one unit of the same type of labour (i.e., $r = 1$). They may be employed either in the primary or secondary sector but not in both. Primary sector jobs require an exogenously given level of effort. The choice of effort is restricted to either no effort ($e = 0$) or full effort ($e = 1$). Workers do not bear any disutility ($e = 0$) when employed in the secondary market. In the primary sector, the level of effort cannot be observed by the firm. Only a signal indicating this effort can be perceived. This signal can be 'good' or 'bad'. It is good with probability θ_1 when $e = 1$ and with probability θ_2 when $e = 0$. We assume: $0 < \theta_2 < \theta_1 \leq 1$

All individuals have identical preferences over consumption bundles; they only differ by their disutility to effort. The utility function of a typical worker-consumer writes: $U(x) - ea$ where $x = (x_1, \ldots, x_n)$ and a is a positive disutility parameter. $U(x)$ is supposed to be quasi-concave, twice continuously differentiable, such that $U' \gg 0$. We also assume that the indirect utility $V(q,R)$ is linear with respect to income, which yields linear Engel curves (see Gorman, 1953). Thus we assume that

$$V(q,R) = \frac{R}{I(q)} + J(q)$$

where $I(q)$ and $J(q)$ are continuously differentiable and $I(q)$ is strictly positive. Then we have

$$x_i(q,R) = A_i(q)R + B_i(q)$$

with

$$A_i(q) \equiv \frac{\partial I/\partial q_i}{I(q)}$$

$$B_i(q) = -I(q)\partial J/\partial q_i$$

To make the model more tractable, we describe the set of individuals as a continuum of mass N, with a cumulative distribution function $G(a)$ defined on the interval $[a_0, a_1] \subset R_+$.

The parameter a is supposed to be publicly observable. Firms are thus able to discriminate among individuals and they offer contracts depending on a and contingent on the perceived signal. A labour contract for type-a workers in the primary sector is thus a consumption wage schedule $\{w_1^1(a), w_2^1(a)\}$ where $w_1^1(a)$ ($w_2^1(a)$) is the wage received if the signal is good (bad).

A contract is incentive compatible if it induces effort. This will be realized for type-a workers if

$$\frac{\theta_1 w_1^1(a) + (1 - \theta_1)w_2^1(a)}{I(q)}$$

$$+ J(q) - a \geq \frac{\theta_2 w_1^1(a) + (1 - \theta_2) w_2^1(a)}{I(q)} + J(q) \tag{8.23}$$

that is

$$\frac{(\theta_1 - \theta_2)(w_1^1(a) - w_2^1(a))}{I(q)} \geq a \tag{8.24}$$

Let w^2 be the wage rate in the secondary market. The secondary market is supposed to be perfectly competitive. The reservation utility of any worker is thus $w^2/I(q) + J(q)$ and the individual rationality constraint for a type-a worker to accept a primary job can be written as

$$\frac{\theta_1 w_1^1(a) + (1 - \theta_1) w_2^1(a)}{I(q)} - a \geq \frac{w^2}{I(q)} \tag{8.25}$$

Finally, we assume that primary jobs cannot be underpaid, that is

$$w_1^1(a) \geq w^2 \tag{8.26}$$

$$w_2^1(a) \geq w^2 \tag{8.27}$$

A possible interpretation is that the terms of the labour contracts cannot be verified by a third party: in such a case, if wages lower than w^2 had to be paid, workers could claim that they have been hired for a secondary job and they would demand to be paid w^2. We may also assume that wages greater than w^2 would be paid by the firm on a question of reputation for instance.

Under these assumptions, the labour market equilibrium can be analysed as in chapter 7. Here we only give a simplified presentation of this analysis. Primary and secondary labour markets are supposed to be perfectly competitive but primary wage contracts have to meet the incentive compatibility requirement. Furthermore, firms consider wage taxes as given. Under these assumptions, the labour market equilibrium can be characterized as follows:[2]

1 The firms always offer contracts such that $w_2^1(a) = w^2$ for all a. Indeed assume (8.24) holds and $w_2^1(a) > w^2$. Then (8.25) holds and is not tight. By reducing $w_2^1(a)$, with $w_1^1(a)$ unchanged, firms would offer contracts which would be more profitable for themselves, incentive compatible and still acceptable to type-a individuals.

2 All the firms offer the same wage $w_1^1(a)$ for each type a (since we have in fact a continuum of competitive labour markets, one for each type).

3 All the workers employed in the primary sector receive the same wage whatever their types (otherwise the firms would slightly bid up wages of low-payed workers and would replace high-payed workers by low-payed workers). We thus have $w_1^1(a) = w^1$ if type-a workers are employed in the primary sector.

4 If type-a individuals are employed in the primary sector, all workers of type $a' < a$ must also be employed in the primary sector. If not, then firms could offer an incentive compatible contract $w_1(a') < w^1, w_2(a') = w^2$ and find individuals of type a' willing to work on these terms.

5 Let $E = NG(\hat{a})$ be the employment level in the primary sector. According to the incentive compatibility condition, we have

$$(\theta_1 - \theta_2)(w^1 - w^2) \geq \hat{a}I(q) \tag{8.28}$$

and (8.28) is necessarily binding if $G(\hat{a}) < 1$. Otherwise, firms could hire workers who are employed in the secondary sector at an incentive compatible wage $(\bar{w}^1, w^2)$, with $\bar{w}^1 < w^1$.

The labour market equilibrium is thus characterized by wages w^1, w^2, a desired employment level E (which results from firms' profit maximization) and a disutility parameter $\hat{a}$ such that

$$\begin{aligned}(\theta_1 - \theta_2)(w^1 - w^2) &= \hat{a}\ I(q) \qquad \text{if } G(\hat{a}) < 1 \\ &\geq \hat{a}\ I(q) \qquad \text{otherwise} \\ E &= NG(\hat{a}) \end{aligned}$$

A type-a individual is employed either in the primary sector if $a \leq \hat{a}$ or in the secondary sector if $a > \hat{a}$.

In what follows, we always have $E < N$ (since a number of workers have to be employed in the secondary market) and thus

$$w^1 = w^2 + \omega(q, E) \tag{8.29}$$

where

$$\omega(q, E) = G^{-1}(E/N)I(q)/(\theta_1 - \theta_2) \tag{8.30}$$

This defines the premium that is paid to workers in the primary sector.

3.2   Optimal taxation rules

The social welfare function W will be written as

$$W = \int_{a_0}^{a_1} S(v(a))\, dG(a)$$

where $S(.)$ is a concave continuously differentiable function and $v(a)$ stands for the expected utility of a type-a individual. This may be interpreted as the expected utility of a risk-averse individual, evaluated before he knows his being a type-a. From previous developments, we have

$$v(a) = \frac{w^2 + \omega(E, q)}{I(q)} + J(q) - a \qquad \text{if } a \leq \hat{a}$$

$$v(a) = \frac{w^2}{I(q)} + J(q) \qquad\qquad \text{if } a > \hat{a}$$

Thus we have

$$W = \int_{a_0}^{\hat{a}} S\left[\frac{w^2 + \omega(E,q)}{I(q)} + J(q) - a\right] dG(a)$$

$$+ S\left[\frac{w^2}{I(q)} + J(q)\right][1 - G(\hat{a})]$$

with $\hat{a} = G^{-1}(E/N)$.

The production sector is described exactly as in previous sections (but now l_j^1 and l_j^2 are scalars) and the feasibility conditions can be written as

$$A(q)[\omega(q,E)E + w^2 N] + NB(q) - \sum_j y_j \leq 0 \qquad (8.31)$$

$$f_j(y_j, l_j^1, l_j^2) \leq 0 \qquad j = 1, \ldots, m \qquad (8.32)$$

$$\sum_j (l_j^1 + l_j^2) \leq N \qquad (8.33)$$

where $E \equiv \sum_j l_j^1$, $A(q) = (A_1(q), \ldots, A_n(q))^t$ and $B(q) = (B_1(q), \ldots, B_n(q))^t$. We still have $y_j = (y_{ji})$.

Let $\lambda = (\lambda_i)$, $\mu = (\mu_j)$ and β be Kuhn–Tucker multipliers, associated respectively with (8.31), (8.32) and (8.33).[3] $\mathscr{L}$ denoting the Lagrangean, the first-order optimality conditions are

$$\frac{\partial \mathscr{L}}{\partial y_{ji}} = \lambda_i - \mu_j \frac{\partial f_j}{\partial y_{ji}} = 0 \qquad i = 1, \ldots, n; j = 1, \ldots, m \qquad (8.34)$$

$$\frac{\partial \mathscr{L}}{\partial l_j^1} = \frac{1}{N}[S(1,\hat{a}) - S(2)]$$

$$+ \frac{\partial \omega}{\partial E}\left[\frac{1}{I(q)} \int_{a_0}^{\hat{a}} S'(1,a)\,dG(a) - E\lambda A(q)\right]$$

$$- \omega\lambda A(q) - \beta - \mu_j \frac{\partial f_j}{\partial l_j^1} = 0 \qquad j = 1, \ldots, m \qquad (8.35)$$

$$\frac{\partial \mathscr{L}}{\partial l_j^2} = -\beta - \mu_j \frac{\partial f_j}{\partial l_j^2} = 0 \qquad j = 1, \ldots, m \qquad (8.36)$$

$$\frac{\partial \mathscr{L}}{\partial w^2} = \frac{\bar{S}'}{I(q)} - N\lambda A(q) = 0 \qquad (8.37)$$

$$\frac{\partial \mathcal{L}}{\partial q_i} = \bar{S}' \left[\frac{\partial J}{\partial q_i} - \frac{\partial I/\partial q_i}{I(q)^2} w^2 \right]$$

$$- \lambda \left[\frac{\partial A}{\partial q_i} R + E \frac{\partial \omega}{\partial q_i} A(q) + N \frac{\partial B}{\partial q_i} \right] = 0 \qquad i = 2, \ldots, n \qquad (8.38)$$

where

$$S(1,a) \equiv S \left[\frac{w^2 + \omega(E,q)}{I(q)} + J(q) - a \right]$$

$$S(2) \equiv S \left[\frac{w^2}{I(q)} + J(q) \right]$$

$$S'(1,a) \equiv S' \left[\frac{w^2 + \omega(E,q)}{I(q)} + J(q) - a \right]$$

$$S'(2) \equiv S' \left[\frac{w^2}{I(q)} + J(q) \right]$$

$$\bar{S}' \equiv \int_{a_0}^{\hat{a}} S'(1,a) \, dG(a) + [1 - G(\hat{a})] S'(2)$$

$$R \equiv \omega(q,E) E + w^2 N$$

Using (8.35) and (8.37) gives

$$\frac{1}{N} [S(1,\hat{a}) - S(2)]$$

$$+ \frac{\partial \omega/\partial E}{I(q)} (1 - G(\hat{a})) \left[\int_{a_0}^{\hat{a}} S'(1,a) \, dG(a) - S'(2) G(\hat{a}) \right]$$

$$- \frac{\omega \bar{S}'}{N I(q)} - \beta - \mu_j \frac{\partial f_j}{\partial l_j^1} = 0 \qquad j = 1, \ldots, m \qquad (8.39)$$

From (8.34), (8.36) and (8.39), optimal production prices $(p_1, \ldots, p_n, s^1, s^2)$ are

$$p_i = \tau \lambda_i \qquad i = 1, \ldots, n \qquad (8.40)$$

$$s^1 = \tau \left(\beta + \frac{\hat{a} \bar{S}'}{N} + H \right) \qquad (8.41)$$

$$s^2 = \tau \beta \qquad (8.42)$$

with $\tau > 0$ and

$$H \equiv \frac{1}{N} \left[\bar{S}' \frac{\omega - \hat{a} I(q)}{I(q)} - S(1,\hat{a}) + S(2) \right]$$

$$-\frac{\partial\omega/\partial E}{I(q)}(1-G(\hat{a}))\left(\int_{a_0}^{\hat{a}}S'(1,a)\,dG(a)-S'(2)G(\hat{a})\right)\Bigg]$$

In (8.41), $\tau\hat{a}\bar{S}'/N$ stands for the social value of effort (in terms of goods at production prices) that would result from an additional primary job. At the first-best perfect information optimum, we would have $s^1 = s^2 + \tau\hat{a}\bar{S}'/N$; s^1 would then be equal to the social opportunity cost of an additional primary job which is the sum of the secondary wage rate and the social value of marginal effort (see the appendix for an analysis of the perfect information case). Let $\Delta R^c = \hat{a}I(q)$ be the transfer that compensates the marginal individual for working in the primary sector. Using (8.37) and (8.40), we have $\tau\hat{a}\bar{S}'/N = pA(q)\Delta R^c$. Thus the social value of marginal effort is equal to additional consumption at production prices induced by this compensatory transfer and the first-best rule may be rewritten as $s_1 - s_2 = pA(q)\Delta R^c$. However, the real differential premium ω exceeds the compensatory transfer ΔR^c so that subsidizing the creation of new jobs in the primary sector involves an involuntary redistributive effect. Because of this redistributive effect, the social planner may prefer to increase or to decrease the wage differential $s_1 - s_2$ above or below $pA(q)\Delta R^c$. More precisely, the second-best production wage differential differs from first-best optimality rules if $H \neq 0$. Optimal taxation stimulates primary employment (by comparison with the first best wage differential) when $H < 0$ and it reduces primary employment when $H > 0$.

To interpret the sign of H, assume first that $\partial\omega/\partial E = 0$. This will be the case if the disutility to effort is constant among the population.[4] We then have $H < 0$ if

$$\bar{S}' < \frac{S(1,\hat{a})-S(2)}{(\omega/I(q)-\hat{a})} \tag{8.43}$$

In (8.43), the left-hand side is equal to the incremental social welfare that results from a uniform unit increase in the workers' utility level. This uniform variation may be obtained through an increase in w_2. As for the right-hand side, it is equal to the ratio of the incremental social welfare over the incremental utility of the marginal worker, when an additional primary job is offered. Intuitively, (8.43) means that, from a redistributive standpoint, increasing households' incomes uniformly through a rise in the minimum wage rate w^2 is socially less efficient than offering an additional primary job. In that case, hiring in the primary labour market should be encouraged. When (8.43) does not hold, increasing w_2 is a more efficient device to redistribute private wealth and primary jobs should be discouraged. This shows that, for redistributive reasons, it may be optimal for an egalitarian social planner to overtax primary jobs (that is to choose $s_1 - s_2 > pA(q)\Delta R^c$) because of an indivisibility phenomenon.

Assume now that $\partial\omega/\partial E > 0$. From $S'(1,a) < S'(1,\hat{a}) < S'(2)$ if $a < \hat{a}$, we deduce

$$H > \frac{1}{N}\left[\frac{\omega - \hat{a}I(q)}{I(q)}\bar{S}' - S(1,\hat{a}) + S(2)\right]$$

In that case, H may be positive (that is hiring in the primary labour market should be discouraged by comparison with the first-best rule) even if (8.43) is not satisfied, meaning even if offering additional primary jobs at a constant real premium were socially a more efficient instrument for redistributing private wealth than increasing households' income uniformly. This is due to the fact that a rise in the real premium which results from an increase in the number of primary jobs, has unfavourable redistributive consequences, since this premium is paid to high utility workers (those who are already employed).

When function $S(.)$ is linear, we have $H = 0$ and consequently the first-best optimality rule holds. In other words, when one incremental dollar paid to an individual a is socially equivalent to one dollar paid to any other individual a', reaching the first-best is thus possible through labour taxation. But, as soon as the government cares about the redistributive consequences of its decisions, labour taxation is insufficient to implement a first-best optimum and the redistributive consequences of firms' decisions should be taken into account when designing second-best taxation rules.

Finally, let us consider optimal commodity taxation. Using (8.37), (8.38), and after some computations, we obtain

$$\sum_j \lambda_j K_{ji} = 0 \tag{8.44}$$

where

$$K_{ji} \equiv \left[a_j A_i + \frac{\partial A_j}{\partial q_i}\right]R + N\frac{\partial B_j}{\partial q_i} + NA_j B_i = 0$$

We can easily check that K_{ji} is actually the (aggregate) Slutsky term for commodities i and j, so that (8.40) and (8.44) imply that q, λ and p are proportional. If prices are normalized by $p_1 = q_1 = 1$, we have $p = q$. Commodity taxation is thus useless. This result is in fact nothing but a consequence of proposition 8.3, since in this model all consumers have identical price dependence indexes, but it would not hold anymore in a more general setting with non-linear Engel curves.

Appendix   The perfect information case

In the model developed in section 3, the first-best optimum is defined as the solution of the following problem where the unknown variables are consumption prices q_i, $i = 2, \ldots, n$, individual income $R(a)$, $a_0 \le a \le a_1$ and production vectors (y_j, l_j^1, l_j^2), $j = 1, \ldots, m$:

$$\text{Max } W = \int_{a_0}^{\hat{a}} S\left[\frac{R(a)}{I(q)} + J(q) - a\right] dG(a)$$

$$+ \int_{\hat{a}}^{a_1} S\left[\frac{R(a)}{I(q)} + J(q)\right] dG(a) \tag{8.45}$$

under the constraints

$$N\left[A(q) \int_{a_0}^{a_1} R(a) \, dG(a) + B(q)\right] - \sum_j y_j \le 0 \tag{8.46}$$

$$f_j(y_j, l_j^1, l_j^2) \le 0 \qquad j = 1, \ldots, m \tag{8.47}$$

$$\sum_j (l_j^1 + l_j^2) \le N \tag{8.48}$$

where

$$\hat{a} = G^{-1}\left(\sum_j l_j^1 / N\right)$$

At the optimum, owing to the concavity of $S(.)$, all individuals reach the same utility level. Thus, there exists $M > 0$ such that

$$\begin{array}{ll} R(a) = M + aI(q) & \text{if } a \le \hat{a} \\ R(a) = M & \text{if } a > \hat{a} \end{array}$$

and we have

$$W = S\left[\frac{M}{I(q)} + J(q)\right] \tag{8.49}$$

The commodity market equilibrium condition is

$$NA(q)\left[M + I(q) \int_{a_0}^{\hat{a}} a \, dG(a)\right] + NB(q) - \sum_j y_j \le 0 \tag{8.50}$$

We maximize W given in (8.49) subject to (8.47), (8.48) and (8.50) with respect to $M, q_i, y_j, l_j^1, l_j^2$. We introduce Kuhn and Tucker multipliers $\mu = (\mu_j)$ and $\lambda = (\lambda_i)$, and the first-order optimality conditions can be written as

$$\frac{\partial \mathcal{L}}{\partial y_{ji}} = \lambda_i - \mu_j \frac{\partial f_j}{\partial y_{ji}} = 0 \qquad i = 1, \ldots, n; j = 1, \ldots, m \tag{8.51}$$

$$\frac{\partial \mathcal{L}}{\partial l_j^1} = -\beta - \hat{a}I(q) \sum_i \lambda_i A_i(q) - \mu_j \frac{\partial f_j}{\partial l_j^1} = 0 \qquad j = 1, \ldots, m \tag{8.52}$$

$$\frac{\partial \mathscr{L}}{\partial l_j^2} = -\beta - \mu_j \frac{\partial f_j}{\partial l_j^2} = 0 \qquad j = 1, \ldots, m \tag{8.53}$$

$$\frac{\partial \mathscr{L}}{\partial M} = \frac{S'}{I(q)} - N \sum_i \lambda_i A_i(q) = 0 \tag{8.54}$$

$$\frac{\partial \mathscr{L}}{\partial q_i} = \left[\frac{\partial J}{\partial q_i} - \frac{M(\partial I / \partial q_i)}{I(q)^2} \right] S' - \sum_j \lambda_j \left[\frac{\partial A_j}{\partial q_i} R + N \frac{\partial B_j}{\partial q_i} \right]$$

$$+ N \frac{\partial I}{\partial q_i} A_j(q) \int_{a_0}^{\hat{a}} a \, dG(a) \bigg] = 0 \qquad i = 2, \ldots, n \tag{8.55}$$

where

$$R \equiv N \left[M + I(q) \int_{a_0}^{\hat{a}} a \, dG(a) \right]$$

(8.52) and (8.54) yield

$$\mu_j \frac{\partial f_j}{\partial l_j^1} + \beta + \frac{S'}{N} \hat{a} = 0 \tag{8.56}$$

From (8.51), (8.53) and (8.56), the optimum production price vector is given by

$$p_i = \tau \lambda_i \qquad\qquad i = 1, \ldots, n$$

$$s^1 = \tau \left[\beta + \frac{S' \hat{a}}{N} \right]$$

$$s^2 = \tau \beta$$

The difference between primary and secondary production wages $\tau S' \hat{a}/N$ is thus equal to the social value of the effort disutility required from the marginal worker employed in the primary sector.

Using (8.54) and (8.55), we also deduce

$$\sum_j \lambda_j K_{ji} = 0$$

where K_{ji} is the (aggregate) Slutsky term for commodities i and j. This implies that λ and q are proportional. Production prices and consumption prices are thus proportional at the optimum.

Notes

1 Price rigidities and temporary equilibrium

1 See O'Donnel (1989, pp. 229–30).

2 See Grandmont (1977) for a broad survey on temporary general equilibrium theory.

3 See Blanchard and Fischer (1989, chapter 10) on macroeconomic models with anticipatory wage setting. Green and Laffont (1981) develop a disequilibrium model in which the wage–price vector is set at the expected Walrasian equilibrium.

4 See, for example, Blanchard and Kiyotaki (1987).

5 The Walrasian temporary equilibrium is thus defined by the equality of demand and supply on the goods markets. Walras' law implies that the equality of supply and demand for money is then necessarily achieved.

6 This example is drawn from Grandmont (1983).

7 The idea of this proof is drawn from Bénassy (1977b). Note that *strict* quasi-concavity of V_i is needed in the proof.

8 Proofs are given by d'Autume (1985) and Silvestre (1982).

9 Silvestre (1982) gave a counter example demonstrating that a K-equilibrium is not necessarily a Drèze equilibrium when the differentiability requirement is not met.

10 However, the K-equilibrium concept is compatible with non-frictionless markets (if C_4 does not hold), which is not the case for the Drèze equilibrium.

11 Conditions that guarantee the uniqueness of fix-price equilibria are established by Laroque (1978, 1981), Laroque and Polemarchakis (1978) and Schulz (1983).

12 Here we use $z_i^*(\theta)$ rather than $\bar{z}_i(\theta), \underline{z}_i(\theta)$ in the right-hand side of the quantity constraints because $z_i^*(\theta)$ is continuous while $\bar{z}_i(\theta)$ and $\underline{z}_i(\theta)$ are discontinuous at $\theta = 0$ if the fixed price equilibrium corresponds to Drèze's definition.

2 Wage rigidity and short-run macroeconomic equilibrium

1 The representative agent assumption is restrictive, since the aggregation of individual behaviours is not alluded to. K. and W. Hildenbrand (1978) emphasized this point in their study of Keynesian unemployment equilibria.

They show, for instance, that the effect of a change in the wage rate on the unemployment level depends on how money holdings are distributed among consumers.

2 This formulation is more restrictive than the one given in chapter 1. The main simplification lies in that the quantity constraints perceived in the current period do not appear as arguments in function U, because for instance the short-term constraints are perceived as consequences of transitory shifts from a Walrasian equilibrium or because households review their expectations of the rationing constraints slowly enough so that the expected constraints can be considered as independent from the current constraints. It is worth noting Neary and Stiglitz's work (1983), where the emphasis is on the relationship between the expectation-making process and the fix-price equilibrium. Furthermore, the household's utility depends on $m = M/p$ which implies that price expectations are unit elastic with respect to p. Section 3.4 of this chapter presents a more general formulation.

3 This is related to the concept of 'rational K-equilibrium' introduced by d'Autume (1985). Other perception schemes are possible. Indeed we could, for instance, assume that an agent perceives a constraint on a market, only if he is actually rationed, i.e., if the transaction he makes is different from his trade offer (effective demand or supply). Under this hypothesis, only agents located on the 'long side' of the market, are likely to perceive quantity constraints. This is the 'strong K-equilibria' approach introduced by d'Autume (1985). Such a formulation would not alter the basic characteristics of our model. More precisely, the direction of the disequilibrium prevailing on a market (excess supply or demand) would not be altered, but the extent of the disequilibrium, in terms of net effective excess demand, could change.

4 This is not a basic hypothesis but it makes studying the consequences of a change in public expenditures simpler.

5 The variables m_0, w and l intervene independently as arguments of the function $\tilde{x}$ and not through the global variable $(wl + m_0)$, which represents the household's total resources. This is due to the fact that the employment level may also influence the demand for consumption by modifying consumption's and money holdings' marginal utilities. Such a mechanism will not work if function U is separable between the vector (x,m) on the one hand and leisure time $(l_0 - l)$ on the other. Only in this case, can the demand for consumption $\tilde{x}$ be considered as a function of total resources $wl + m_0$. See Neary and Roberts (1980) for a general study of consumer's behaviour within a rationing context.

6 φ is a unimodal function if

$$\varphi(\lambda l + (1 - \lambda) l_s^*) \geq \varphi(l) \text{ if } 0 \leq \lambda \leq 1 \text{ and } 0 \leq l \leq l_0$$

Note that the vector $[\lambda \tilde{x}(l) + (1 - \lambda) x_d^*, \lambda \tilde{m}(l) + (1 - \lambda) m^*]$ is a feasible solution of the problem $P_2[\lambda l + (1 - \lambda) l_s^*]$. Consequently, according to the definition of the function φ and the quasi-concavity of U,

$$\varphi(\lambda l + (1 - \lambda) l_s^*) \geq$$
$$U[\lambda \tilde{x}(l) + (1 - \lambda) x_d^*, l_0 - \lambda l - (1 - \lambda) l_s^*, \lambda \tilde{m}(l) + (1 - \lambda) m^*] \geq$$
$$\text{Min}\{U(\tilde{x}(l), l_0 - l, \tilde{m}(l)), U(x_d^*, l_0 - l_s^*, m^*)\}$$

that is to say:

$$\varphi(\lambda l + (1 - \lambda)l_s^*) \geq \text{Min}\{\varphi(l), \varphi(l_s^*)\} = \varphi(l)$$

which establishes the wanted result.

7 This can be easily shown as for function φ.

8 This can be related to Patinkin's analysis (1956, chapter 13) of the behaviour of a firm that lowers its labour demand due to a sales constraint.

9 This results from the hypothesis of a frictionless market and from the priority given to public demand on the goods market.

10 Such hypotheses are made by Böhm (1978). See Schulz (1983) for the conditions of a unique global fix-price equilibrium in the general n-goods models.

11 The cross derivatives of compensated (notional) demands are positive. We can also easily check that assumption A is satisfied if we have $\partial \tilde{x}/\partial l > 0$ and $\partial \tilde{l}/\partial x > 0$ (as we assumed) but also $\partial \tilde{m}/\partial l > 0$ and $\partial \tilde{m}/\partial x < 0$. According to these two inequalities, the consumer rationed on the labour market increases his savings when the employment level increases; similarly, when he is rationed on the goods market, the consumer reduces his savings if he is able to consume more.

12 A general analysis of fix-price equilibria located in the neighbourhood of the Walrasian equilibrium was carried out by Laroque (1978, 1981) and Laroque and Polemarchakis (1978). Besides, Laroque (1978) presents assumption A as one of his general results. Note d'Autume's study (1980), showing the possibility of a multiplicity of fix-price equilibria, if we are not restricted to the equilibria located in the neighbourhood of the Walrasian equilibrium.

13 The model presented in this chapter was subject to many extensions presenting the firms' behaviour within an intertemporal context where the firms may possess stocks or money holdings. Such a model has been studied by Muellbauer and Portes (1978), and, in the framework of a dynamic analysis, by Green and Laffont (1981) and Honkapohja and Ito (1980). In these models, the fourth regime characterized by $l_s < l_d$ and $y_d < y_s$, actually appears.

14 Note that equations (2.15) and (2.16) give $y = f(l)$ at the equilibrium.

15 Under classical unemployment, there is an excess demand for goods and households' consumption is rationed. This situation seems rather unrealistic, at least if we consider that it describes the general state of the economy. Actually, in market economies, demand rationing generally prevails in specific sectors, where prices are controlled, or during limited periods of time, owing to a temporary shortage in stocks. This characteristic of the classical unemployment case mainly stems from our highly rudimentary formalization. More realistically, we could assume that the firms keep stocks to make up for an insufficient output. Then, the consumer would be rationed only if demand exceeds available stocks. Moreover, in an open economy, imports generally offset the insufficient domestic supply so that the consumers' demand is not rationed (see chapter 4).

16 This supply multiplier has been studied by Barro and Grossman (1974).

17 This hypothesis has been advanced by Howard (1976), while Portes and Winter (1980) reached different conclusions; see also Charemza and Quandt (1982) and Portes (1981).

18 We have assumed that public expenditures are financed by money creation. Fluctuations in public consumption thus induce variations in the money supply. However, one can easily check that nothing fundamental has changed if additional public expenditures were financed by levying taxes so as to obtain purely real demand shocks.

19 If s were less than s^*, the line OD would cross the curve C_3. We would then obtain a full-employment equilibrium with an employment level inferior to the employment level of the Walrasian equilibrium X, however.

20 Considering an economy with involuntary unemployment implies that the employment level is equal to the firm's demand for labour if shocks are not too large. The equality between employment and labour demand is also postulated in Gray's and Fischer's models although they assume that initial wages (fixed one period in advance and possibly conditional on the price level) coincide with expected Walrasian wages. In that case, unexpected shocks may lead to an excess demand for labour as well as to an excess supply, which is at variance with the postulate that employment is equal to the demand for labour (at least if the voluntary exchange rule is assumed). Involuntary unemployment models do not present this inconsistency.

21 For instance, if agents' expectations follow an autoregressive log-linear process:

$$\text{Log } X_{t+1} = a \text{ Log } X_t + b + \varepsilon \qquad 0 \le a \le 1$$

where ε is a random disturbance with zero mean, we have

$$\psi(p, M_1) = k p^a M_1^{1-a} \text{ with } k = E_\varepsilon[\exp(b + \varepsilon)](1 + \pi^e)$$

22 Note that movements in the rate of growth of the money stock would not be neutral in a more complete setting, including for instance several generations living during the current period, as in the Allais–Samuelson overlapping generation model (see chapter 7 for such a model with rigidity of intertemporal real wages).

3 Real wages and the inflation–unemployment dilemma

1 This model follows Picard (1983).

2 In this section, we implicitly assume that the real wage rate is less than the productivity of labour; this assumption will be realized at the steady state of the dynamic model.

3 For the sake of simplicity, we assume that firms and government are never rationed on the goods market; only households may be rationed on this market. Realized investment is then equal to investment demand I, and actual government expenditures are equal to government demand G.

4 Technically, this is a differential equation system with regime-switching; see Honkapohja and Ito (1983).

5 We assume that $\bar{w}$ exists.

6 We assume that the stationary point is not located on a borderline between two regions. This guarantees the differentiability of functions R, S and T at this point.

4 External constraint, oil shock and economic policy

1 For a survey on disequilibrium open economy models see Neary (1990).
2 See Bruno and Sachs (1981), Hénin (1983), Picard (1985) and Van Wijnbergen (1985) for the analysis of an oil shock in fix-price models.
3 This proposition was defended by Bruno and Sachs (1985).

5 Implicit contracts and unions

1 To simplify matters, variations in profitability are exclusively due to the technological parameter θ. This allows us to consider the model as a two-commodity general equilibrium model (labour and a consumption good).
2 We assume $f'(0) = +\infty$ and $U'(0) = +\infty$ which implies $l_i > 0$, $\bar{w}_i > 0$ and $w_i - k > 0$ for all i.
3 According to the condition $\partial\phi/\partial N = 0$ and $U^{-1}(u_0) > 0$, we have $\sum_{i=1}^{n} \pi_i(\theta_i f'(l_i^*) - k) > 0$ and thus $\partial^2\phi/\partial N^2 < 0$ when $N = N^d$.
4 This case was addressed by Azariadis (1975).
5 When the firm is risk-neutral, the condition for underemployment to hold in state i writes as

$$\theta_i f'(N) - w + \frac{U(w-k) - U(\bar{w})}{U'(w-k)} < 0$$

6 We could describe the equilibrium prevailing on the contract market as we did previously.
7 Note that $\tilde{j}(.)$ may be a correspondence. For simplicity, we consider $\tilde{j}(.)$ as a function.
8 This follows Azariadis (1983); see Hart (1983) for more general results.
9 This result can be obtained when leisure is not an inferior good; see Chari (1983), Stiglitz (1986). This can be proved by the same argument as in section 2.2.
10 One could also assume that a union and a firm bargain over the wage rate, with the firm choosing employment *ex post*. This corresponds to the 'right to manage model' developed by Nickell and Andrews (1983).
11 This can be rigorously proved as in section 1.3.
12 See Lindbeck and Snower (1986, 1987) on insiders–outsiders models and Grossman (1983), Blair and Crawford (1984) and Oswald (1985) on models with seniority.
13 $\psi(x)$ may also be interpreted as the probability for the median voter to be employed under lay-offs by seniority.
14 On unemployment persistence in the context of insiders–outsiders models see Blanchard and Summers (1986), Gottfries and Horn (1987), Lindbeck and Snower (1987).
15 The following developments follow Rosen (1985).

6   Introduction to efficiency wage models

1 This section follows Weiss (1980). Other efficiency wage models with adverse selection have been developed in particular by Malcomson (1981) and Stiglitz (1976).

2 We assume that each firm hires a great number of individuals so that we can identify the average endowment in efficient labour and the expected efficient labour endowment of a worker hired.

3 An equilibrium with a wage rate w less than w^* cannot exist, otherwise the firms would find it more profitable to attract the labour force by increasing the wage rate up to w^* since they would then bear a lower unit cost of efficient labour.

4 w_2^* is negative if $\pi_2 k > (\pi_1 - \pi_2)u(\bar{w})$. This condition will hold if the unemployment benefit is not too large.

5 See Carmichaël (1985, 1987).

6 See Stiglitz and Weiss (1981).

7 We assume that $L < N/(b+1)$ so that $\pi < 1$. This condition holds at the equilibrium if b is small enough, e.g., if the period is short enough.

8 Bulow and Summers (1986) adapt the Shapiro–Stiglitz model to a dual labour market, by assuming that monitoring the effort is costly in the primary sector but easy in the secondary sector, which leads to a wage differential and job rationing in the primary sector. The Bulow–Summers model is compatible with a wait in unemployment if being unemployed is a necessary condition to finding another job in the primary sector. Unemployment will be involuntary in the sense that the jobless would accept work in the primary sector for a lesser wage. At the equilibrium, secondary sector workers are indifferent to becoming unemployed and the jobless are indifferent to accepting secondary sector jobs. This situation is similar to the kind of situation encountered in models of developing economies where the primary sector corresponds to the urban sector and the secondary sector corresponds to the rural sector and where unemployment results from the fact that workers cannot simultaneously search for a job in the cities while working in rural areas (see Stiglitz, 1991).

9 A steeper profile is also an incentive for the employer to break the contract. In Lazear's model, the optimum contract imposes a double constraint: it must provide an incentive for the employee to make effort and also an incentive for the firm not to default.

10 This model is inspired by Carmichaël (1987).

11 We assume that workers may accept one job at the most in the primary sector in that period. At the end of the period, the firms replace the whole labour force.

12 The example is drawn from Akerlof (1982).

13 The hypothesis $a > b(1 - \gamma)$ implies that $w > w_r$ at the optimum.

7   Efficiency wages, employment fluctuations and fiscal policy

1 See appendix 2 in chapter 1.

2 The fact that the stability of expected prices may explain a certain disconnection between money wages and current prices is not new. This idea was notably introduced by Hicks (1946), who found an explanation for the rigidity of money

wages in the short run. As he writes: 'It cannot be maintained that wage-rates are fixed at a particular level in money terms because wage-earners want so much money for its own sake; the reason why money wages are rigid must be because these people who fix wages have some degree of confidence in the stable value of money that is to say, because they have fairly inelastic price-expectation. So long as they retain the view that a certain level of prices is "normal", it is perfectly rational for them to fix wage-rates in money terms at a level which seems to them "fair" in relation to this "normal" price-level.'

3 See Altonji (1982) and Mankiw, Rotemberg and Summers (1985), using American data; Bénabou (1985) using French data. However, if wages provide for an insurance component, real wages may differ from the marginal productivity of labour and, to some extent, this may enhance the validity of the explanation of employment fluctuations through intertemporal substitution in the labour supply (see the appendix of chapter 5).

4 The Kahn–Mookherjee model (1988) is somehow similar to the model analysed here, in the sense that the efficiency of an economic policy also goes through distortions of relative prices. Their model is purely static but it includes two sectors, industrial and domestic productions with efficiency wages and job rationing in the industrial sector. Kahn and Mookherjee show that a taxation policy aiming at stimulating demand for industrial goods is Pareto-improving.

5 This is similar to section 2.1 in chapter 6.

6 Thus, contracts requiring workers to pay to be employed and allowing for a reimbursement of the initial payment only if the signal is good are not allowed. This assumption was discussed in chapter 6.

7 These results can be more realistic if we include an elastic supply of labour. Suffice it to assume that individuals endure a more or less high disutility of labour, in addition to the disutility of effort. The previous results would not be modified since the labour supply curve observed on microeconomic data would depend on parameters different from those of the quasi-supply curve: it could be set arbitrarily close to a perfectly inelastic supply.

8 Since we do not consider redistributive issues, the employment benefit is strictly equivalent to a tax on the labour supply.

9 The perfect foresight case is analysed in detail by Jullien and Picard (1989).

8   Labour market dualism, efficiency wages and optimal taxation

1 The efficiency wage model is very similar to the one developed in chapter 7.

2 We follow here Jullien and Picard (1989).

3 β is now a scalar.

4 $G(.)$ should then be interpreted as a Dirac measure at $a = \hat{a}$.

References

Akerlof, G.A., 1982, 'Labor contracts as partial gift exchange', *Quarterly Journal of Economics*, 97, 543–69.

Akerlof, G.A. and L.F. Katz, 1989, 'Workers' trust funds and the logic of wage profiles', *Quarterly Journal of Economics*, 104, 525–36.

Akerlof, G.A. and Y.L. Yellen, 1985, 'A near-rational model of the business cycle with wage and price inertia', *Quarterly Journal of Economics*, 100, supplement, 823–38.

Altonji, J., 1982, 'The intertemporal substitution model of labor market fluctuations: an empirical analysis', *Review of Economic Studies*, 47, 783–824.

Arrow, K.J. and G. Debreu, 1954, 'Existence of an equilibrium for a competitive economy', *Econometrica*, 22, 265–90.

d'Autume, A., 1980, 'L'influence des effets de répartition sur l'unicité et la stabilité de configurations de déséquilibres' in *Etudes sur l'Economie en Déséquilibre*, ed. by P.Y. Hénin, Economica, Paris.

1985, *Monnaie, Croissance et Déséquilibre*, Economica, Paris.

Azariadis, C., 1975, 'Implicit contracts and underemployment equilibria', *Journal of Political Economy*, 83, 1183–202.

1983, 'Employment with asymmetric information', *Quarterly Journal of Economics*, 98, supplement, 157–72.

Baily, M., 1974, 'Wages and employment under uncertain demand', *Review of Economic Studies*, 41, 37–50.

Barro, R.J., 1976, 'Rational expectations and the role of monetary policy', *Journal of Monetary Economics*, 2, 1–32.

Barro, R.J. and H.I. Grossman, 1971, 'A general disequilibrium model of income and employment', *American Economic Review*, 61, 82–93.

1974, 'Suppressed inflation and the supply multiplier', *Review of Economic Studies*, 41, 87–104.

1976, *Money, Employment and Inflation*, Cambridge University Press, Cambridge.

Bénabou, R., 1985, 'Le modèle d'optimisation dynamique de la consommation et de l'offre de travail: un test sur données françaises', *Annales de l'INSEE*, 57, 75–97.

Bénassy, J.P., 1973, 'Disequilibrium theory', unpublished Ph.D. Dissertation, University of California, Berkeley.

1975, 'Neo-Keynesian disequilibrium in a monetary economy', *Review of Economic Studies*, *42*, 503–23.

1976a, 'The disequilibrium approach to monopolistic price-setting and general monopolistic equilibrium', *Review of Economic Studies*, *43*, 69–81.

1976b, 'Théorie néokeynésienne du déséquilibre dans une économie monétaire', *Cahiers du séminaire d'Econométrie*, *17*, 81–113.

1977a, 'A neo-Keynesian model of price and quantity determination in disequilibrium', *Equilibrium and Disequilibrium in Economic Theory*, Reidel Publishing Company, Boston.

1977b, 'On quantity signals and the foundations of effective demand theory', *The Scandinavian Journal of Economics*, *79*, 147–68.

1982, *The Economics of Market Disequilibrium*, Academic Press, New York.

Blair, D.H. and D.L. Crawford, 1984, 'Labor union objective and collective bargaining', *Quarterly Journal of Economics*, *99*, 547–66.

Blanchard, O.J. and S. Fischer, 1989, *Lectures on Macroeconomics*, MIT Press, Cambridge, MA.

Blanchard, O.J. and N. Kiyotaki, 1987, 'Monopolistic competition and the effects of aggregate demand', *American Economic Review*, *77*, 647–66.

Blanchard, O.J. and L. Summers, 1986, 'Hysteresis and the European unemployment problem', *NBER Macroeconomics Annual*, 15–77.

Böhm, V., 1978, 'Disequilibrium dynamics in a simple macroeconomic model', *Journal of Economic Theory*, *17*, 179–99.

Bruno, M. and J. Sachs, 1981, 'Supply versus demand approaches to the problem of stagflation', in *Macroeconomic Policies for Growth and Stability. An European Perspective*, Symposium 1979, ed. by H. Giersch, Institut für Weltwirtschaft an der Universität Kiel, Mohr, Tübingen.

1985, *Economics of Worldwide Stagflation*, Harvard University Press, Cambridge, MA.

Bulow, J. and L. Summers, 1986, 'A theory of dual labor markets with application to industrial policy, discrimination and Keynesian unemployment', *Journal of Labor Economics*, *4*, 376–414.

Carmichaël, L., 1985, 'Can unemployment be involuntary?: comment', *American Economic Review*, *75*, 1213–14.

1987, 'Efficiency wage models of unemployment: a survey', mimeo, Queen's University.

Charemza, W. and R.E. Quandt, 1982, 'Model and estimation of disequilibrium in centrally planned economies', *Review of Economic Studies*, *49*, 109–16.

Chari, V.V., 1983, 'Involuntary unemployment and implicit contracts', *Quarterly Journal of Economics*, *98*, supplement, 107–21.

Clower, R.W., 1965, 'The Keynesian counterrevolution: a theoretical appraisal', in *The Theory of Interest Rates*, ed. by F.H. Hahn and F.R.P. Brechling, Macmillan, London.

Debreu, G., 1959, *Theory of Value. An Axiomatic Analysis of Economic Equilibrium*, Cowles Foundation monograph 17, Wiley, New York.

Diamond, P., 1975, 'A many-person Ramsey tax rule', *Journal of Public Economics*, *4*, 335–42.

Diamond, P.A. and J.A. Mirrlees, 1971, 'Optimal taxation and public production; I–II', *American Economic Review*, *61*, 8–27; 261–78.

Doeringer, P.B. and M.J. Piore, 1971, *Internal Labor Markets and Manpower Analysis*, D.C. Heath & Co., Lexington.

Drèze, J., 1975, 'Existence of an equilibrium under price rigidity and quantity rationing', *International Economic Review*, *16*, 301–20.

Fischer, S., 1977a, 'Long-term contracts, rational expectations and the optimal money supply rule', *Journal of Political Economy*, *85*, 191–205.

1977b, 'Wage indexation and macroeconomic stability', *Journal of Monetary Economics*, *5*, supplement, 107–47.

Friedman, M., 1968, 'The role of monetary policy', *American Economic Review*, *58*, 1–17.

Gordon, D., 1974, 'A neoclassical theory of Keynesian unemployment', *Economic Inquiry*, *12*, 431–59.

Gorman, W.M., 1953, 'Community preference fields', *Econometrica*, *21*, 63–80.

Gottfries, N. and H. Horn, 1987, 'Wage formation and the persistence of unemployment', *Economic Journal*, *97*, 877–86.

Grandmont, J.M., 1977, 'Temporary general equilibrium theory', *Econometrica*, *45*, 535–72.

1983, *Money and Value, A Reconsideration of Classical and Neoclassical Monetary Theories*, Econometric Society Monographs in Pure Theory, Cambridge University Press, Cambridge and Editions de la Maison des Sciences de l'Homme, Paris.

Grandmont, J.M. and G. Laroque, 1976, 'Temporary Keynesian Equilibria', *Review of Economic Studies*, *43*, 53–67.

Gray, J.-A., 1976, 'Wage indexation: a macroeconomic approach', *Journal of Monetary Economics*, *2*, 221–35.

Green, J.R. and J.J. Laffont, 1981, 'Disequilibrium dynamics with inventories and anticipatory price-setting', *European Economic Review*, *16*, 199–221.

Grossman, G., 1983, 'Unions wages, seniority and unemployment', *American Economic Review*, *78*, 277–90.

Grossman, H.I., 1971, 'Money, interest and prices in market disequilibrium', *Journal of Political Economy*, *79*, 943–61.

Guesnerie, R., 1975, 'Public production and taxation in a simple second-best model', *Journal of Economic Theory*, *10*, 127–56.

Hahn, F., 1978, 'On non-Walrasian equilibria', *Review of Economic Studies*, *45*, 1–17.

Hansen, B., 1951, *A Study in the Theory of Inflation*, Allen and Unwin.

Hart, O., 1983, 'Optimal labour contracts under asymmetric information: an introduction', *Review of Economic Studies*, *50*, 3–35.

Hénin, P.Y., 1983, 'L'impact macroéconomique d'un choc pétrolier', *Revue Economique*, *34*, 865–96.

Hicks, J.R., 1946, *Value and Capital*, 2nd edn, Oxford University Press, London.

Hildenbrand, K. and W. Hildenbrand, 1978, 'On Keynesian equilibria with unemployment and quantity rationing', *Journal of Economic Theory*, *18*, 255–77.

Honkapohja, S. and T. Ito, 1980, 'Inventory dynamics in a simple disequilibrium model', *Scandinavian Journal of Economics*, *82*, 184–98.

1983, 'Stability with regime switching', *Journal of Economic Theory*, *29*, 22–48.

Howard, D.H., 1976, 'The disequilibrium model in a controlled economy: an empirical test of the Barro–Grossman model', *American Economic Review*, *6*, 871–9.

Jullien, B. and P. Picard, 1989, 'Efficiency wage and macroeconomic policy', mimeo CEPREMAP, No. 8918.

Kahn, C. and D. Mookherjee, 1988, 'A competitive efficiency wage model with Keynesian features', *Quarterly Journal of Economics*, *103*, 609–45.

Keynes, J.M., 1936, *The General Theory of Employment, Interest and Money*, Harcourt Brace, New York, reprinted 1964.

Laroque, G., 1978, 'The fixed price equilibria: some results in local comparative statics', *Econometrica*, *46*, 1127–54.

1981, 'On the local uniqueness of the fixed price equilibria', *Review of Economic Studies*, *48*, 113–29.

Laroque, G. and H. Polemarchakis, 1978, 'On the structure of the set of fixed price equilibria', *Journal of Mathematical Economics*, *5*, 53–70.

Lazear, E., 1979, 'Why is there mandatory retirement?', *Journal of Political Economy*, *87*, 1261–84.

1981, 'Agency, earnings profiles, productivity and hours restrictions', *American Economic Review*, *71*, 606–20.

Leibenstein, H., 1963, 'The theory of underemployment in densely populated backward areas', *Economic Backwardness and Economic Growth*, Wiley, New York, chapter 6.

Leijonhufvud, A., 1968, *On Keynesian Economics and the Economics of Keynes*, Oxford University Press, Oxford.

Leontieff, W., 1946, 'The pure theory of guaranteed annual wage contract', *Journal of Political Economy*, *54*, 76–9.

Lindbeck, A. and D. Snower, 1986, 'Wage setting, unemployment and insider outsider relations', *American Economic Review*, *76*, 235–9.

1987, 'Union activity, unemployment persistence and wage-employment ratchets', *European Economic Review*, *31*, 157–67.

Lipsey, R., 1960, 'The relation between unemployment and the rate of change of money wage rates in the United Kingdom, 1862–1957: a further analysis', *Economica*, *27*, 1–31.

Lucas, R.E., 1972, 'Expectations and the neutrality of money', *Journal of Economic Theory*, *4*, 103–24.

1975, 'An equilibrium model of the business cycle', *Journal of Political Economy*, *83*, 1113–44.

Lucas, R.E. and L. Rapping, 1969, 'Real wages, employment and inflation', *Journal of Political Economy*, *77*, 721–54.

Malcomson, J., 1981, 'Unemployment and the efficiency wage hypothesis', *Economic Journal*, *91*, 848–66.

Malinvaud, E., 1977, *The Theory of Unemployment Reconsidered*, Basil Blackwell, Oxford.

1980, *Profitability and Unemployment*, Cambridge University Press, Cambridge, and Editions de la Maison des Sciences de l'Homme, Paris.

Mankiw, G., 1985, 'Small menu costs and large business cycles: a macroeconomic model of monopoly', *Quarterly Journal of Economics*, 100, 529–39.

Mankiw, G., J. Rotemberg and L. Summers, 1985, 'Intertemporal substitution in macroeconomics', *Quarterly Journal of Economics*, 100, 225–53.

McDonald, I. and R. Solow, 1981, 'Wage bargaining and employment', *American Economic Review*, 71, 896–908.

Muellbauer, J. and R. Portes, 1978, 'Macroeconomic models with quantity rationing', *Economic Journal*, 88, 788–821.

Neary, J.P., 1990, 'Neo-Keynesian macroeconomics in an open economy', in *Advanced Lectures in Quantitative Economics*, edited by F. van der Ploeg, Academic Press, London.

Neary, J.P. and K.W.S. Roberts, 1980, 'The theory of household behavior under rationing', *European Economic Review*, 13, 25–42.

Neary, J.P. and J.E. Stiglitz, 1983, 'Towards a reconstruction of Keynesian economics: expectations and constrained equilibria', *Quarterly Journal of Economics*, 98, supplement, 199–228.

Nickell, S., 1982, 'A bargaining model of the Phillips curve', Discussion Paper 105, London School of Economics, Centre for Labour Economics.

Nickell, S. and M. Andrews, 1983, 'Unions, real wages and employment in Britain, 1951–79', *Oxford Economic Paper*, 35, supplement, 183–206.

O'Donnel, R.M., 1989, *Keynes: Philosophy, Economics and Politics. The Philosophical Foundations of Keynes's Thought and their Influence on his Economics and Politics*, Macmillan, London.

Oswald, A., 1985, 'The economic theory of trade unions: an introductory survey', *Scandinavian Journal of Economics*, 87, 160–93.

Patinkin, D., 1956, *Money, Interest and Prices*, 2nd edn (1965), Harper and Row, New York.

Phelps, E.S., 1968, 'Money-wage dynamics and labor-market equilibrium', *Journal of Political Economy*, 76, 678–711.

Phillips, A.W., 1958, 'The relation between unemployment and the rate of change of money wage rates in the United Kingdom, 1861–1957', *Economica*, 25, 283–99.

Picard, P., 1983, 'Inflation and growth in a disequilibrium macroeconomic model', *Journal of Economic Theory*, 30, 266–95.

1985, 'Choc Pétrolier et politique économique: une analyse de déséquilibre', in *Déséquilibres en économie ouverte*, ed. by P.-Y. Hénin, W. Marois and P. Michel, Economica, Paris.

Pigou, A.C., 1943, 'The classical stationary state', *Economic Journal*, 653, 343–51.

Portes, R., 1981, 'Macroeconomic equilibrium and disequilibrium in centrally planned economies', *Economic Inquiry*, 19, 559–78.

Portes, R. and D. Winter, 1980, 'Disequilibrium estimates for consumption goods markets in centrally planned economies', *Review of Economic Studies*, 47, 137–59.

Rosen, S., 1985, 'Implicit contracts: a survey', *Journal of Economic Literature*, 23, 1144–75.

Salop, S.C., 1979, 'A model of the natural rate of unemployment', *American Economic Review, 69*, 117–25.

Samuelson, P. and R. Solow, 1960, 'Analytical aspects of anti-inflation policy', *American Economic Review, Papers and Proceedings, 50*, 177–94.

Sargent, T. and N. Wallace, 1975, 'Rational expectations, the optimal monetary instrument and the optimal money supply rule', *Journal of Political Economy, 83*, 241–54.

Schulz, N., 1983, 'On the global uniqueness of fix-price equilibria', *Econometrica, 51*, 47–68.

Shapiro, C. and J.E. Stiglitz, 1984, 'Equilibrium unemployment as a worker discipline device', *American Economic Review, 74*, 433–44.

Silvestre, J., 1982, 'Fix-price analysis in exchange economies', *Journal of Economic Theory, 26*, 28–58.

Solow, R.M., 1979, 'Another possible source of wage stickiness', *Journal of Macroeconomics, 1*, 79–82.

Stiglitz, J.E., 1974, 'Wage determination and unemployment in L.D.C.s: the labor turnover model', *Quarterly Journal of Economics, 88*, 194–227.

1976, 'Prices and queues as screening devices in competitive markets', IMSSS Technical Report No. 212, Stanford University.

1986, 'Theories of wage rigidities' in *Keynes Economic Legacy: Contemporary Economic Theories*, edited by J.L. Butkiewicz *et al.*, Praeger, New York.

1991, 'Economic organization, information and development', in *Handbook of Development Economics*, edited by H. Chenery and T.N. Srinivasan, North Holland, Amsterdam.

Stiglitz, J.E. and A. Weiss, 1981, 'Credit rationing in markets with imperfect information', *American Economic Review, 71*, 393–410.

Taylor, J.B., 1979, 'Staggered wage setting in a macro model', *American Economic Review, 69*, 108–13.

Tobin, J., 1980, *Asset Accumulation and Economic Activity*, Yrjö Jahnsson Lectures, Basil Blackwell, Oxford.

Van Wijnbergen, S., 1985, 'Oil price shocks, investment and the current account: an intertemporal disequilibrium analysis', *Review of Economic Studies, 52*, 627–45.

Weiss, A., 1980, 'Job queues and layoffs in labor markets with flexible wages', *Journal of Political Economy, 88*, 526–38.

Author index

Subject index